To

Ingrid

Third, revised, expanded Edition, March 1994
First Printing, February 1982
Second Printing, January 1985

Library of Congress Catalog Card Number: 62-90110
ISBN 0 9 608798 03

Published by
A. A. P. R.
3910 Wesley Chapel Road NE
Marietta, GA 30062   USA

A DOG WILL READILY, AND HAPPILY, COMPLY
WITH ANY REASONABLE REQUEST, HE USUALLY
KNOWS ALREADY HOW TO DO IT.

THE TRAINER, HOWEVER, MUST FORMULATE THE
REQUEST IN A MANNER THAT IS UNDERSTOOD BY
THE DOG.

ACKNOWLEDGEMENTS

A vast number of people have, knowingly or unknowingly, helped in gathering the information presented in this book. While it is impossible to list all names, their contributions are acknowledged with gratitude.

I am indebted to the many authorities on canine matters, here and abroad, who have shared their knowledge with me; to the numerous dog trainers who have worked with me on various projects; to the large number of people and groups who have given me a chance to help them with their training and to learn from their problems; and to all the correspondents, clients and friends who have consulted with me and who have encouraged me to write this book.

A special "thank you", however, goes to the ones who started it all: my dogs

Anka von Berg, SchH II, CDX

Asta (Waldeslust's Jetta)

Brika von Berg, SchH III, CDX

Catja von Berg, SchH II, CD.

Dina von Berg

PREFACE TO THE THIRD EDITION

Tahiti is one of the nicest places in this world, if you want to get away from it all. It is here where most of the editing for the third edition of TOP WORKING DOGS took place.
(Haiti was the location for the first edition, by the way.)

Significant changes have been made, much new information has been added, and training instructions have been further expanded, clarified and streamlined, as needed.

Since the first edition was published in 1982, several new books by others have appeared. Yet throughout the world, **TOP WORKING DOGS** is still the only complete manual for the training of working dogs, police dogs, and Schutzhund dogs in tracking, obedience and protection work.

With a very large number of copies sold, only one copy was ever returned. Readers and reviewers rave about the book and the results obtained with it's help. They tell us that TOP WORKING DOGS gives them the most complete, the most comprehensive, the most detailed, the most useful and the most easily to follow instructions. They say that TOP WORKING DOGS describes many valuable training techniques which can not be found anywhere else. And they like TOP WORKING DOGS's extensive coverage of problem recognition and resolution.

We appreciate such information and, once again, we encourage our readers to bring to our attention suggestions for changes so that the next edition can further be improved.

Dietmar Schellenberg
March 1994

PREFACE TO THE SECOND EDITION

"TOP WORKING DOGS" seems to have filled a void - judging by the demand for it, and by the positive feedback we have received. Press reviews and reader comments were complimentary, without exception.

From front to back cover, the book has been revised, updated and significantly expanded. New techniques have been added, current descriptions have been simplified, amplified and clarified where needed, and additional information on various new topics has been included. Reader response played an important role in this process, and we continue to invite your comments.

Dietmar Schellenberg
December 1984

PREFACE TO THE FIRST EDITION

"Start today"
is my advice when asked at what age working dog training should begin.

Many tasks that a young puppy playfully learns in a few days will require weeks, or even months of intense training when introduced to an adult dog. The habits formed, and the skills acquired by the young who are much more flexible, adaptable, willing and able to learn than adults, will be difficult to change at a later time. In addition, an early start eliminates time pressure, allowing to build a more solid foundation. A multi-faced working dog program such as Schutzhund will benefit greatly from such an approach.

Successful Schutzhund trainers are typically reluctant to share their secrets. As a result, the majority of the few books available on the subject concentrate on explaining trial routines and on the instruction of adult dogs via force training.

" TOP WORKING DOGS " the manual for the training of working dogs in tracking, obedience and protection work, is novel and unique in several ways:

- it aids the trainer in using psychological
principles, by giving descriptions and explanations,
- it presents in detail the methods used by experts
not usually revealed,
- it offers a multitude of approaches for the individual
routines,
- it lists, for each task, the problems most often
encountered, and it suggests a variety of remedies,
- it concentrates on the general components of working
dog training which the handler can readily apply to
specific situations,
- it stresses and explains playful instruction of the
young dog.

The ultimate goal of this book is to make the man/dog relationship more meaningful, and more enjoyable, for both partners.

D. Schellenberg
February 1982

CONTENTS

III. THE STRATEGIES

I. THE OBJECTIVE

A. WORK FOR WORKING DOGS

Since the early days of domestication many thousand years ago, dogs had to earn their keep. To be useful, they had to be taught, and dog training, therefore, can be considered one of the oldest skills of mankind.

Methods and approaches have changed over the years, usually in tune with advances in the field of psychology. Many of the ancient training procedures, however, still have some application in our modern way of thinking.

Working Dogs were bred to work.

Yet the work is in short supply these days. Many tasks that dogs have handled with excellence in the past have gradually been taken over by modern technology.

While there are still specific areas where canines outperform even the most sophisticated equipment, such as nose work, guarding, or protecting, "job openings" are extremely rare compared to the number of applicants. The "unemployed" live on "welfare" since the provider usually forgets that in addition to food and care, engagement in a meaningful activity is necessary to maintain physical and mental health.

It has become fashionable these days to own a working dog.

To meet the ever-growing demand, some breeders have specialized in impostors: they intentionally outbreed the characteristic temperament traits of a working dog, cranking out "lap dogs in Doberman suits" as one supporter calls it. Yet mother nature can't be fooled: the docile Rottweiler still carries the genes of his ancestors.

Many of the behavior problems we are facing today, especially in the working breeds, are the direct result of this irresponsible breed manipulation.

There is no such thing as a "pet Shepherd" who will not bark, growl or bite when provoked.

If people like the looks of a working dog but not the working temperament, then they should buy a statue.

Anyone who wants to own a working dog must realize that this involves a commitment, a moral obligation to provide some meaningful activity for the canine.

The owner may not want to join the Police Force, and he may not be prepared to start a herd of sheep either. Training for competition, or for enjoyment, however, are available as viable alternatives.

The type of training the owner prefers, and the organization he wants to affiliate with, are certainly his choice. There is, however, one faction of working dog training which incorporates elements of all the other possibilities. It can be called a universal training program; as a matter of fact, many special working dog programs require that the dog has proven his competence in this particular field first. Sled dogs, water dogs, hunting dogs, Search and Rescue dogs, herding dogs, military dogs, police dogs, etc., all of them will be ahead of competitors in their special fields if they first have been exposed to it, or to portions of it. This book will rely heavily on this universal training program which is known worldwide by the name of Schutzhund ("protection dog"; German).

Schutzhund training combines tracking, obedience and protection work. For the responsible working dog owner this sport has proven to be an ideal program. Training is versatile, challenging, enjoyable, it provides physical and mental exercise for both handler and dog, and it can be done in very small groups of participants, if necessary. Training locations are generally available, time requirements are reasonable, and benefits even for the average owner are obvious. Knowing how a dog behaves in critical situations, for instance, is reassuring and provides better control over the animal.

B. SCHUTZHUND VS. ATTACK DOG

Unfortunately, but understandably, many dog owners are unaware of the fact that Schutzhund and Guard/Attack Dog do not mean the same thing. There are some superficial similarities, such as type of dogs involved, display of hostility in specific situations, and outrageous claims of some of their owners/trainers. There are, however, many more important and meaningful dissimilarities, culminating in the fact that only after difficult, extensive, and rarely successful retraining one type of dog could be used for the duties of the other.

Although dogs have been domesticated for thousands of years, they still resemble their wild ancestors in many ways. By nature they would, for instance, rather avoid than fight a large enemy like a human. The attack dog trainer uses the survival instinct, while the Schutzhund trainer utilizes the prey and the pack instinct. This is the most crucial difference between these two types of service dogs.

To fulfill the duties of an attack/guard dog, the animal must regard ALL humans (except his master) as enemies. In training, he is being prevented from escaping and then, in the absence of his master, threatened, scared, beaten, abused until he sees no way to survive but to bite whoever and whatever gets close enough to him. The dog comes to realize that he has no friend but his master who cares for and feeds him. After "graduation", frequent refresher courses are needed. No friendly contacts with anyone but his master are permissible.
    The dog has come to hate mankind.

What a contrast to the Schutzhund dog. He is trained with love, not hatred. He works together with his master as a team. He does not regard a human as enemy until this human becomes hostile to him, or to his master.
The Schutzhund dog takes his cues to be protective from the hostile BEHAVIOR, not the mere PRESENCE of a man or woman or child. In a Schutzhund trial, for instance, the dog is sent about 100 yards after a fleeing "criminal". He will never attempt to bite the judge who stands near the "bad guy", nor will he bother one of the close-by spectators. Yet he loves the moments of fighting, as one can see by his wagging tail.
The Schutzhund can be left all by himself with a group of children, or with a group of adults, without anybody being threatened or bothered. Yet afterwards, on the training field, the same dog will be a top performer in tracking, obedience and in protection work as well!

Man work is a controversial issue, and the opposition almost always comes from dog owners unfamiliar with Schutzhund training. They often ask the question: "What happens when the dog misreads a gesture from a harmless person, a child for instance, as a sign to attack?"

People usually give our four-legged friends much less credit than they deserve. Even the authors of another book on Schutzhund claim - wrongfully - that "dogs, well trained or not, simply do not possess the capacity to safely and reliably judge when and whom they should bite, and when not". Such a statement is irresponsible as well as ignorant of every bit of evidence available on the subject. Documented incidents of aggression against humans always indicate either mentally or physically ill animals, or dogs that were provoked, abused or improperly trained. At fault were the dog's owners/keepers, not the ability of sensibly trained canines to make the right decision.
Any normal dog, cared for and trained in a reasonable way, will use his judgement in situations we are concerned about here. They can very well decide if the cue was real or accidental. Although the very first step in the chain of reactions might be spontaneous, there is a natural barrier, or inhibition, before the dog takes step #2.

For example:
In Schutzhund training, the dog is asked to bite the bad guy who runs toward him, threatening him with a raised stick. This is the so-called courage test.

The same dog is going for a stroll with his master when he sees
a child in the distance, running toward him with a raised stick. If the handler does not interfere, the dog may very well run toward the youngster. Dogs respond to moving things; they do, however, have problems recognizing details in the distance.
If he is a normal, healthy dog who was not tormented by children
at an earlier time, and if the child is not hostile toward the dog now, one of the following five things will happen:
1. the dog recognizes the harmless youngster from a distance and returns to his handler.
2. the dog recognizes the harmless youngster from a distance, approaches him and wants to play with him or with the stick - he may of may not bark for the stick to be thrown.
3. the dog recognizes the harmless youngster from a few feet away - he may or may not bark, sniff, circle him.
4. the dog recognizes the harmless youngster too late for a stop and bumps into him - his behavior after contact indicates apology, maybe even embarrassment.
5. the dog recognizes the harmless youngster too late and opens his mouth for a bite - the bite is inhibited and the child will not be injured although it may rip the clothing. Again, his behavior after contact will indicate apology or embarrassment.
So far we have assumed that the dog owner does not interfere. If he does, the situation is under much better control.
Both dog and handler have been in similar (training) situations before, both know how the other reacts. The dedicated Schutzhund trainer has practiced the "no" and "out" with his dog, and the dog has learned not only to obey commands, but also to rely on his masters judgements.

In addition, the trained Schutzhund dog is not pressed to take advantage of a random situation in order to relieve frustrations that may possibly have accumulated.

It was already pointed out that the dog is not quite sure of
the situation, he really reserves the final decision to bite or not to bite for the last moment. In addition to this uncertainty the dog becomes less aggressive the farther away he is from his master. One command will change the course of events and bring the dog back to his handlers without any harm done to the child.
An untrained dog, on the other hand, is much less predictable and much less controllable. It is most likely that neither the dog nor the owner have experienced a similar situation before, and that either one may misread the intentions of the other, and those of the child. Furthermore, the untrained dog has not learned to reliably obey his masters commands, nor has he learned to recognize genuine provocation and to respond properly to it, using his own judgement.
A trained Schutzhund dog, therefore, poses a much lower risk in the above described situation than the untrained dog.
Area protection dogs, or canines trained by irresponsible people who use the dog to cover up their own inferiority complex, do not respond in this fashion. They are, however, the exception and here we are not concerned with these types of animals (or trainers), anyway.

Schutzhund dogs are well behaved, happy, friendly yet alert,
controllable family dogs that become an asset,
and not a nuisance, or even a danger, to society.

At a fox hunt, one female hound is permitted to join the all-male pack. The dogs disappear in a hurry.

The confused hunters question a farmer standing on the roadside: "Did you see a pack of dogs running past here?"

"Sure did!"

"Where did they go?"

"Dunno, but that's the first time I ever saw a fox chasing hounds!"

II. THE PLAYERS

A. THE IDEAL HANDLER

Out of one hundred police officers volunteering for duty with a canine unit, on the average less than ten are accepted.

This is, admittedly, the result of very tough selection criteria but it still indicates that some people are considered better suited for working with dogs than others.

We are not concerned here with men and women who are ill-tempered, reckless, cruel, very impatient or drug and alcohol addicts. None of them should be given custody of a dog.

With these exceptions, anyone who is determined to train a dog can attain a certain proficiency. Taking an intelligent approach, spending enough effort, and soliciting the help of available experts may indeed lead to outstanding training results. Some people will have to work very hard to reach this goal, others do it effortlessly if they have that certain flair for working with animals, and for teaching.

Determining factors are the personality of the handler, and his motivations.

The following categories are applicable to people who are actively participating in training.

** The easiest person to deal with is the true **COMPETITOR**. As a sportsman he is genuinely interested in improving his performance, and in comparing it with others. He works systematically and diligently, and he remains objective. The dog is his partner and as such receives proper attention and care. Suggestions offered to him are scrutinized and implemented if meaningful. In the long run, only talented, gifted dog handlers will remain in this category.

** The **TROPHY HUNTER** differs from the former group in that his primary goal is not the training by itself but the reward, the trophy, the certificate or the recognition, for successful trial competition. He will accept advice only if it guarantees better trial performance.

The professional trainer may belong to this group.

** The **FITNESS TYPE** got into dog training because he considers it to be a meaningful alternative to jogging (etc) and he happened to have a suitable dog. He is easy-going and will casually follow up on suggestions. Competition is of lesser importance to him.

** The **DOG LOVER** has come to realize that his dog enjoys training. Anthropomorphism, or relating to the dog by human standards, is the big problem here and because of it the owner will reject many valuable training suggestions. A diplomatic and considerate trainer has the best chance to work with such a person. Trial performances, nevertheless, may be marginal.

** The **DOG KEEPER** supports the idea of the service dog, he may even work with such an agency. For him, dog training is a means to accomplish certain tasks with the help of the dog, and he will modify the concept so that it suits his training purpose.

** The **DOG BREEDER** wants to prove to the world that his bloodlines are top quality.
Because of an intimate knowledge of his animals, he often accomplishes tasks that others had considered impossible.
The breeder is usually open to suggestions and willing to experiment with training suggestions, if it suits his purpose.

** The **MILLIONAIRE** typically starts out as a novice, but with an expensive, fully trained and titled dog - usually imported from overseas.
He travels with his dog extensively and demands top honors everywhere. Objective judges and trainers are not always welcome, on occasion they are even met with hostility.

** The **WARRIOR** uses his dog as a weapon, often to compensate for his own personal insecurity.
Unless there is definite hope to remodel this person's thinking, he should tactfully be removed from training. Dogs owned by such persons are conditioned to attack on command, even when the situation does not warrant it. Since the hostility is directed toward unsuspecting people, the image of the dog sport is discredited.

Everything considered, one should be looking for these qualities in a top handler:
> open-mindedness
> tolerance
> willingness to learn and to share
> cooperation
> patience
> empathy
> adaptability
> common sense
> authority
> consistency
> persistence
> a well balanced mixture of gentleness and firmness.

You got 'em all? Terrific!

B. SELECTION OF A SUITABLE CANINE

1. HEREDITY and ENVIRONMENT

A dog's physical and mental characteristics are determined by heredity and environment. Heredity provides the raw block from which the owner/trainer shapes the final product by manipulating the environment.
Both factors must be considered when trying to find the most promising dog for Schutzhund training. It is unreasonable, even irresponsible, to dismiss a dog just because he does not bite well on the first try-out, as suggested by the authors of a popular Schutzhund book. To bite a human full-force is not an innate response of any normal dog but a skill that must be developed and refined, and the better trainer will end up with the better dog.
Of course, it is much easier to blame the breeder, junk the dog and get another one. But can we really justify such an approach? We too want to start out with the most promising candidate. But we also accept the challenge, and the responsibility, to develop our dog's capabilities to the fullest extend.

Here is some more food for thought:
Of all the young working dogs in the world, less than one percent would bite a human full force without training. YOUR chance of getting one of these dogs is remote, at least. If you believe the

"experts" (who will not tell you their training secrets), then you can never successfully compete against them and they will retain their preeminent position forever.

2. BREEDS

For training purposes, for service duty, and even for most competitions, working dogs do not have to be pedigreed. When buying a puppy, however, purebreds offer the advantage to predict fairly accurately the physical and mental characteristics of the adult dog, which in turn can be passed on to the offspring.

The official Seal of
WORKING DOGS OF AMERICA, INC. (WDA)

Starting with the top position, going clockwise and ending in the center, the eight major recognized working dog breeds are

Hovawart, Boxer, Bouvier des Flandres, Giant Schnauzer, Rottweiler, Doberman, Airedale, German Shepherd Dog.

GERMAN SHEPHERD DOG
(originally used for herding sheep - Max von Stephanitz is the founder of the breed)

Intelligence, alertness, courage, willingness, endurance, easy trainability and devotion to his master, as well as his all-weather coat and low demands on food and housing have made the German Shepherd Dog the #1 dog for private persons and for dog-employing agencies. It is said that the German Shepherd Dog is not best in anything, but second-best in everything.

BOXER
(the name makes reference to the head form)
This powerful, energetic and courageous dog has a somewhat difficult behavior pattern, and he is a slow learner. He compensates, however, with devotion and gentleness towards his master.

AIREDALE TERRIER
(the breed originated in the Aire Valley in England)
This dog is easily trainable but needs much exercise and grooming. He is inquisitive and full of temperament, dependable and unafraid.

GIANT SCHNAUZER
(German: Schnauze = snout, Schnauzer = beard)
He is eager to learn but needs much exercise and grooming. He is a sturdy, prudent, self-conscious working dog, full of temperament, sometimes even a daredevil.

DOBERMAN
(Karl Dobermann, a German, is the creator of the breed)
The Doberman is very devoted to his master, eager to learn and willing to work, alert and full of temperament. He needs much exercise and attention and does not adapt easily to inclement weather.

ROTTWEILER
(the breed originated in the town of Rottweil/Germany)
He is a sound working dog, originally used for herding cattle. Power, persistence, endurance, alertness and willingness give this breed its distinction.

HOVAWART
(Old-German for 'guardian of the farm')
This breed is rarely found outside of Germany. The dogs have a certain resemblance to a Golden Retriever, and they are alert, courageous, protective and easily trainable.

BOVIER DES FLANDRES
(the breed originated in Flandres/Belgium)
Bouviers were originally used to herd cattle. They are strong-willed and strong-muscled, lively, courageous and loyal working dogs.

OTHER BREEDS
Traditional working dog training is open to dogs of all breeds, and mixed breeds, if they can do the work. This was also true for Schutzhund competitions where the dog was required to be of sufficient size to clear the 40 inch hurdle, and to have enough power to do effective protection work.
These requirements excluded all small breeds from competition, yet very large breeds were discouraged also. A Great Dane, for instance, is too powerful a dog so that even the police have abandoned earlier attempts to use this and similar breeds. In Schutzhund training, such a dog can be dangerous to, or at least very demanding on the part of, the decoy.

Under pressure from breed clubs, some European countries now restrict participation in Schutzhund trials to dogs of 13 breeds. Before, there were eight officially recognized service dog breeds which up to this date still provide the majority of working dogs in training: German Shepherd Dogs,

Dobermans, Rottweilers, Boxers, Airedales, Giant Schnauzers, Hovawarts and Bouvier des Flandres. German Shepherd Dogs outnumber all others, though. This should not come as a surprise, since the Schutzhund sport originated with, and for, that breed.
To that list of eight, the following breeds have been added:

Bauceron, Lakenois, Tervuren, Malinois and Groenendael.

Besides the officially recognized service-dog breeds there are many others who also participate in Schutzhund training. To name just a few:

Briard
Bulldogs (var.)
Bullmastiffs (var.)
Collie
Dalmatian
Great Dane
Hounds (var.)
Husky
Komodor
Kuvasz
Malamute
Mastiffs (var.)
Newfoundland
Pointers (var.)
Poodle
Puli
Retrievers (var.)
Samoyed
Setters (var.)
Terriers (var.)
Viszla
Weimaraner

3. FUNCTIONAL COMPATIBILITY

While there are some notable exceptions, many of the breeds that are not officially recognized as service-dog breeds have difficulties meeting the requirements for advanced working dog training, like Schutzhund, UD and TDX. Bred to serve mankind in other capacities, their size, weight, agility, temperament, protective instinct, fighting drive etc. make them less successful.
If, however, the handler of such a dog is more interested in training than in official recognition, if he is willing to accept the additional workload required to train his particular dog, if he wants to play by rules that were developed for other breeds, and if he also realizes that if he were to compete, outstanding trial performances were more difficult to obtain, then he should not be discouraged. He and his dog will greatly benefit from participating in this training, and with a patient, knowledgeable, versatile and understanding instructor, such a person often becomes one of the most reliable and loyal club members.

Regardless of the breed, faulty temperament, structural faults such as overangulation, illnesses such as arthritis, hereditary problems like hip dysplasia and other physical deficiencies may require to withdraw a dog from training. Contrary to popular belief, mental illness is rare in dogs and it hardly needs to be mentioned.

4. PHYSICAL COMPATIBILITY

Since training is a team effort, the partners must be compatible.
A little girl handling a powerful male Rottweiler, for instance, might look cute. Rarely, however, will such a combination be a happy and successful one.

By the same token: A husky, bold-type construction worker will probably not do too well with a sensitive Airedale bitch.

The handlers age, sex, bodily strength, physical handicaps, illnesses etc. should all be considered when selecting a dog for the sport.

This is not to say that only perfect dog/handler combinations should be allowed to participate. The handler must understand, however, that anything but the ideal not only requires additional efforts but also stacks the odds against him for doing well in competitions.

The young girl, for instance, can be taught to manipulate expressions of her mood, to employ exaggerated voice control, to skillfully use her bodily strength or to refer to tools not normally recommended for training (the prong collar, the double leash etc.).
The roughneck, on the other hand, must learn to restrain himself, to be more responsive, more considerate and more gentle than ever before.

In instances like these it is generally necessary to seek the advice of an experienced trainer. Under his guidance, problems can be detected and addressed more easily, yet this is still no guarantee for spectacular trial performances afterwards.
Assistance, and tolerance, also help to span the time during which the serious handler discovers the shortcomings of his animal by himself. This will cause him to look for a more suitable dog in due time.

5. PSYCHOLOGICAL COMPATIBILITY

To make a well functioning dog/handler team, not only the bodies, but also the minds of the two partners must be compatible.
A phlegmatic person is bound to be very unhappy with a hyperactive Doberman, and so will be an agile, snappy handler with a lethargic Boxer.

Breeds of working dogs differ in their general temperamental make-up, and the breed standard can often be a valuable guide when selecting a team mate.

Nevertheless, even within one breed a wide variety of different personalities can be found. Many handlers with preference for a particular breed can be accommodated if enough effort is spent on finding a suitable animal. Fortunately, though, people seem to instinctively select the dog that suits their personalities. The keen observer will often find a striking resemblance in appearance and behavior of a dog and his master, provided a close relationship exists between the two partners.

6. TEMPERAMENT TESTING

" A sound mind in a sound body "
was one of the slogans of the Roman Empire. While it primarily addresses humans, it holds equal value for working dogs.
Von Stephanitz, the founder of the breed of German Shepherd Dogs, for instance, proclaimed "function is beauty", requiring both the right temperament and the right physical structure.

The American Heritage Dictionary defines temperament as "the manner of thinking, behaving and reacting, characteristic of a specific individual". As such, it is a combination of inherited character traits and learned behavior.

A **HANDLER** is concerned with this combination, as it is displayed by his dog. To him, a temperament test merely means taking inventory. Since he knows his dog intimately, formal procedures to determine temperament traits are not even needed.

A **BREEDER**, or a **BUYER** of a young puppy, however, needs to separate the learned behavior from the inherited character traits. The buyer wants to predict what the mature dog will be like, the

breeder needs to know what kind of offspring this dog or this bitch can produce.
This group of dog owners is very much interested in an objective procedure to classify their dog's inherent temperament characteristics.

Temperament testing has become quite fashionable, recently, and several American temperament testing organizations have been founded. They give passing (or failing) grades to pure-bred dogs of any breed, based on a (one) standardized testing routine.
The efforts are commendable, the conclusions drawn, however, are questionable, maybe even damaging, for several reasons:

a) Dogs serve different purposes, their temperament must match the job.
   For instance: Aggressiveness is desirable in a German Shepherd Dog on duty with a military installation while it would be disastrous for another GSD serving a blind person. Standardized tests make no provisions for those different purposes.
b) Each breed has different temperament requirements.
   Judging a dog according to a universal standard will necessarily do injustice to some.
c) A standardized test can not take into account superficial modifications to the temperament caused by a manipulation of the environment.
d) Standardized tests give the owner of a dog access to the test requirements and allow him to "train" his dog for a passing grade.
e) Standardized tests submit the dog and the owner to a certain amount of stress which will influence at least some of the results.

If the reader accepts the above reasoning then he probably will feel comfortable with the following conditions that should govern a temperament test:

a) Each dog should be judged on his own merits, giving .consideration to the requirements of his breed, his owner, his keeper. If, for instance, the owner wants a (docile) companion, then an aggressive dog would have "bad" temperament.
b) There should be no awarding of passing (or failing) grades. Instead, tests and responses should be stated in a factual manner. Comments, if given at all, should be restricted to a list of individual temperament traits and how pronounced they are for the particular dog, and to an assessment of the dog's potential to serve in certain capacities, for instance as a
   good breed specimen (for temperament)
   stud dog / brood bitch (for temperament)
   guide dog
   herding dog
   draft dog
   Schutzhund
   Search & Rescue dog
   police dog
   guard dog
   alarm dog
   companion dog
   pet
   etc.
c) Standardization has no place in temperament testing.
   Test situations should be varied or unique, and unpredictable in nature, to the owner and to the dog.
d) Moderation and consideration must govern all test situations.
   Precautions have to be taken to prevent physical or mental damage to the dog as the result of a temperament test.
e) Tests should be geared to the age group of the dog.
   Puppies, for instance, should be subjected only to those tests that they can handle well.
f) Tests should be scheduled outside of transitory critical developmental phases.
   There is evidence that one such phase where testing should not be conducted is the fourth week in a puppies life, and again the seventh and eight week.

g) Testing should be extended over several days, and maybe weeks, to eliminate chance results.

h) Testing should be done on familiar and on unfamiliar grounds, to assess the influence of territorial instincts.

i) Information on the behavior of the dog in the past, provided by the owner in good faith, or secured from other reliable sources, should be considered by the tester. A questionnaire   m a y serve this purpose.

EVALUATION

Evaluating the temperament of a dog is done by observing his response

> to novel and to familiar stimuli,
>
> to neutral, to pleasant and to unpleasant experiences,
>
> to subtle and to gross changes in the environment.

The dog can be tested

> in familiar and in unfamiliar surroundings,
>
> with and without his pack members,
>
> in the presence and in the absence of his owner.

Since conducting such tests is a delicate task, a repeat of the earlier comment that moderation and consideration must govern all test situations is in order.

This warning is especially meant for people in search of a new dog. In addition to the moral obligation they have toward the dog as God's creature, they also have an obligation toward the present owner of the dog who may not be able to place an animal that was ruined by the "tests" of a prospective earlier buyer.

An inexperienced person can do great damage to a dog that would have been an excellent choice for certain types of owners.

For instance: Firing a cannon next to an unsuspecting and unconditioned animal will make any dog but a deaf one gun shy.

Another example: If preliminary investigations have shown that the dog under test is shy and soft, then there are pitifully few justifications for conducting the "Henze Courage Test" where the dog is threatened and hit with a stick before he bites the sleeve.

Some of the temperament traits that will become apparent during testing are:

energy	loyalty
initiative	affection
persistence	discrimination
intelligence	curiosity
willingness	rapport
responsiveness	alertness
attentiveness	body sensitivity
tractability	ear sensitivity
trainability	nose ability
competitiveness	shyness
wildness / tameness	fear
submissiveness/dominance	sharpness
stability	aggressiveness
trust	fighting drive
confidence	protective instinct
self-confidence	courage
self-right (sovereignty)	hardness, etc.

The relative weight of each of these factors will vary, depending on the dog, the tester, the handler/owner, the test situation, and other incidentals.

The tester must make sure, thought, that the results of the individual tests are consistent. Apparent discrepancies should be cleared up through additional testing.

For example: A dog that is not at all impressed by the self-opening umbrella might show great fear of a flag flapping in the wind during a night exercise.

Additional testing will reveal that the dog was either familiar with the umbrella test in one form or another, or that the flag was associated with an earlier unpleasant incident in the dog's life which left a lasting impression.

Usually such past experiences, or earlier training, will modify and condition the responses of a dog so that an inexperienced tester may draw the wrong conclusions. The response to gun shots, for instance, will be completely different for a (police) dog trained to bite the weapon arm, for a hunting dog, for a pet belonging to the owner of a pistol range, and for a dog that has never experienced such loud noises before. Of course, only the last dog will display his true temperament. The other three will do whatever their owners have trained them to do (if they would not, the owner would not keep them), although the way HOW they do it provides a wealth of information for the experienced tester.

There are two practical ways to exclude learned behavior:
> a) to test only very young dogs, or those that have not
> received any training or conditioning
> b) to devise test situations that are novel and unfamiliar
> to dog and handler.

The first choice has limited but very valid applications and should be used with much discretion.

The second option requires a lot of imagination on the part of the tester. He must have an extremely large repertoire of tests to draw from, and he must constantly alternate and modify them to solicit "natural" responses.
While this approach is still no guarantee for a complete elimination of learned behavior, it comes close to the ideal and the knowledgeable tester can form a valid opinion.

The remainder of this chapter presents, in systematic order, a compilation of suggestions for test conditions. While the stimuli listed are common to, and representative of, the temperament tests described in the literature, there is no agreement between the different methods on classifying the information they generate. The inherent complexity, delicacy and dependence on difficult to control variables is held responsible for it.
Some recently published methods use a numerical approach for rating predetermined responses to specific test conditions, then they try to find prevailing grades. The assignment of numbers (1-10) is based on the movement or cooperation of the dog (forward, remaining, backward), on the way how he behaves (confident, hesitant, afraid), on body language (eyes, lips, teeth, ears, tail, head carriage, fur raised or flat, etc.) and on other incidental observations. Important is not only the first, initial response of a dog to a new stimulus, but also how, and how quickly, he recovers from any surprise effect.

As a more flexible variation of the above concept, the following scale is proposed for rating each one of the test conditions listed lateron:

insecure uncooperative (neg. response)		undecided indifferent (no response)		confident cooperative (pos. response)
- 2	- 1	0	+ 1	+ 2

EXPLANATION:

0   The dog acknowledges the stimulus but does not act on it. He is undecided and reserves judgment, waiting for further developments.

-2   The dog is overwhelmed by the new circumstances, in a negative sense. He is uneasy, insecure, suspicious, afraid, uncooperative, and he would give a million if he could avoid that situation. He may retreat, observe the challenge(r) out of the corner of his eyes, lower his head, lay the ears flat, tuck his tail between the legs, and in some situations he may also raise his fur, curl his lips, show his teeth, growl, snarl and bite, as a last resort.

+2   The dog accepts the new situation as another exciting part of life. He is content, confident, sure of himself, trustful, unafraid, uninhibited, inquisitive, cooperative, he advances to check out the stimulus or to face the challenge. He looks straight ahead, carries head and ears erect (depending on the breed), and his tail is wagging or up.

To describe the rating system in more detail, a litter of 9-10 week old puppies may serve as an example.

A stranger enters the kennel and drops a couple of empty tin cans on a hard surface. He then kneels.

-2   The puppy that runs away in terror, hiding in the pen or behind the bitch for a prolonged time would receive a -2 rating.

-1   If the puppy first runs away but then comes back again after a while, without approaching cans or stranger, then he receives a -1 rating.

0   A puppy that is surprised by the noise but neither runs away nor comes forward to investigate, receives a 0 rating.

+1   A +1 rating would be given to a dog that is startled initially by the disturbance but then comes forward right away to investigate the cans and/or the stranger.

+2   A puppy that alerts to the stranger and to the noise in a confident manner, approaching stranger and/or tin cans to investigate, ears up, tail wagging, receives the +2 mark.

Similar ranking principles apply to all the other test conditions described on the following pages.

It is suggested to compile a list of the various temperament traits, similar to the one introduced earlier in this chapter, and to enter the rating behind the applicable item(s) as testing progresses. The completed chart will then aid in determining the suitability of a given dog for a given home or working environment (see also under "RESULTS", below).

The +2 classification is not always the most desirable score. In confrontations with other dogs, for instance, the +2 rating identifies a potential for dog fights, a +2 rating for olfactory acuity disqualifies the dog from the Seeing Eye program, the +2 rating in the Henze Courage Test spells trouble for an insecure owner, a +2 rating for having the teeth checked by a stranger may identify low potential for Schutzhund training, and so on.

TESTS
Temperament tests should cover two areas: action and reaction.

ACTION
Common to this group of tests is that the DOG initiates the action while the tester remains a passive observer.

It is desirable to select a fair size, confined area, and to spread around a few novel objects, like
rubber and wooden toys
paper bag, cardboard box
a small ball, a large ball
a balloon
a broom
a wet sponge
a bucket
a large, flat box

a piece of cloth, plastic, aluminum foil
a knuckle bone (reserve this one for inactive dogs)
a mechanical toy
a chime (hanging low)
four or five empty tin cans stacked on end, with
a piece of meat hidden under the bottom can, etc.

Then the dog is, or several dogs are, admitted to the test area. They should be given ample time to adjust and to investigate. The tester remains passive and takes notes.
The test should be repeated at some other time, with other objects.

Some of the questions that should be answered, and character traits to which they relate, are listed below:

Does the dog do something ? (initiative)
What does he do ? (discrimination, shyness, fear)
How does he do it ? (intelligence)
How involved does he get ? (intensity)
How much effort does he spend in pursuing this activity ? (vigor, persistence)
Does he pursue in spite of obstacles ? (determination, stamina)
Does he pursue in spite of competitors ? (self-confidence, competitiveness, shyness, aggressiveness)
Is he startled easily ? (fear)
Does he recover quickly ? (self-confidence)

REACTION

This group of tests has in common that the dog is challenged, either by the tester, or through his efforts. Up to that point the dog was passive, now he is confronted with a challenge and he has to react to it.
Reactions are responses to stimuli that have been perceived by an organism via its five senses:

smell
taste
hearing
sight
touch.

These stimuli may be novel, or they may be familiar to the dog. The tester should provide a large variety of them, in many different ways and intensities. The same stimulus should generally not be used more than once with the same dog, for testing purposes that is.

Some conclusions on the intelligence of an animal, how discriminate, how confident, and how content it is, can be drawn from its reactions to taste and smell stimuli.
A much heavier emphasis, however, must be placed on responses to stimuli that relate to hearing, sight and touch. These responses show best how much the individual dog has adopted to domestication, how well he is suited to live in a human pack under often quite "unnatural" conditions, and how well he can serve mankind in the many different fields of employment.

Smell

Various objects can be placed in small, secure containers with vent holes, or in wire cages. The dog's reaction should be noted to the odor of, for instance:

ammonia
vinegar
laundry bleach
freshly cut garlic or onions
fresh or decaying fish
meat
a small live animal (mouse, rabbit, gerbil)
a piece of clothing worn (and thereby scented) by his owner
a piece of clothing worn (and thereby scented) by a stranger, etc.

Taste

Small samples can be placed conveniently within reach of the dog or offered to him. His reaction should be noted.

Examples are:
- a raw piece of meat
- a vegetable / fruit
- a block of salt
- carbonated (bubbling) water
- a straight alcoholic drink
- a small piece of a plastic meat wrapper
- a rubber tire with cooking grease splashed on it
- etc.

Hearing

a) familiar sounds
- handlers voice
- food bowl handling
- barking of another dog
- car / bus / train / airplane

b) unfamiliar sounds
- tape recorder with prerecorded noises
- gun shots
- fire crackers
- tin can clatter
- large metal sheet to imitate thunder
- siren
- bells
- whistle
- exotic car horns
- music box
- musical instruments (incl. drums)

Sight

a) familiar things
- his master
- food bowl
- leash
- toy
- cat

b) unfamiliar things
- mechanical toys
- remote-controlled toy animals
- self-opening umbrella
- self-inflating life vest
- strange dog
- strange person
- grotesquely dressed person
- a person acting like a drunk
- water sprinkler (erratically operated)
- camp fire
- during a night excursion, the surprise by
    - a bright light (flashlight, car headlights)
    - a "ghost" (scare crow) lowered from above into the path
    - a bed sheet, etc.

Touch

a) <u>familiar</u> (done by, or with, the owner)
        stroking
        praise
        correction
        heeling
        lifting / carrying the dog
        checking teeth
        clipping toenails
        administering medicine (small food pellets as a pill, water as liquid medicine)
b) <u>unfamiliar</u> (done by a stranger)
        as above

Combinations

There are some tests that overlap into several areas:
a) <u>Obstacles</u> (relates to the temperament traits listed for the testing of hearing, sight and touch)
        steep incline or decline in terrain
        mud / sand
        walking on various surfaces: gravel, wood, metal, plastic, water (very large, shallow puddle), ice (if available), deep mud, etc.
        water
        various jumps (easy, low heights or widths)
        stairs
        ladder
        plank walking (1 and 6 ft. above ground)
        log walking
        inclined plank
        seesaw
        small room (enter a tiny closet with the dog)
        elevator
        escalator
        revolving door
        wheelbarrow ride
        bus / streetcar ride
        recall through a group of 10 - 20 people
        stepping or jumping over another dog
        stepping or jumping over a person lying flat on the ground
b) <u>Friendly Challenges</u> (relates to temperament traits listed for testing of hearing, sight and touch)
        - one passive stranger, motionless
        - one passive stranger, moving around but not paying attention to the dog
        - several passive strangers, motionless
        - several passive strangers, moving around
        - a friendly stranger, playing with, praising, handling the dog (tug of war, ball, stick)
c) <u>Hostile Challenges</u> (relates to most of the temperament traits listed for the testing of hearing, sight and touch, with emphasis on the protective instinct). These tests should be reserved for mature dogs:
        - Guarding
        The dog is placed in a down position, next to an article belonging to his handler.
        An assistant in unobtrusive protective clothing approaches in a suspicious but frightened manner, with the obvious intention to steal the article. There is no threat to the dog, nor will the article actually be taken if the dog guards well.
        - Attack on the Handler
        The handler with his dog on leash is harassed and then attacked by a stranger in protective clothing. The attack is directed toward the handler, not the dog.

- Double Attack

At first, there is an attack on the handler like above. Then a second decoy attacks the handler. In contrast to the first assailant, he wears concealed (hidden) protective gear, or he is unprotected and the dog wears a muzzle.

- Courage Test

The handler is harassed by a decoy who then runs away. At a distance of about 50 feet he turns around, charging and threatening the dog which was sent after him. This attack is directed toward the dog.

CLASSIC TESTS

There are also a few classic temperament tests available which have been developed almost exclusively for working dogs:

Newborn Puppies

This is an old and forgotten German method, used by breeders of herding dogs.

The newborn puppies, having been licked dry by the bitch, are removed from the whelping box. They are kept in a dry, warm place for about 12 hours. Then the bitch is held and comforted in one corner of the whelping box, and all the puppies are placed in the opposite corner.

Those puppies that struggle, wiggle, roll and make it back to the mother are the best working dog prospects. They have demonstrated - although only in rudimentary form - intelligence (they can not see yet), physical fitness (they can not walk or crawl yet), stamina (it is a long way for a newborn), and above all a sound survival instinct (they need warmth and food).

Those puppies that give up after a while and just cry will have to be nursed through life.

Puppy's Choice

From 4 days to 3 1/2 weeks after birth, watch for the puppy that shows the most interest in you, always pays attention to your presence, follows you with his eyes constantly. This pup will - as an adult - always be interested in you.

Olfactory Acuity

A scent trail is laid, for instance with meat on a drag line. The dog must follow it in order to get the food reward at the end.

Manipulation Tests

- A piece of choice meat is hidden in a closed cardboard box. The dog must "unpack".
- A piece of meat is tied to a string. Only the string is within reach of the dog. The dog must scratch and claw the string in order to retrieve the meat.
- A piece of meat is suspended on a string. The dog must pull an available box under it, in order to jump from it and to reach the meat.
- A filled food bowl is slid into a shallow, low clearance compartment, with the front open. The dog must scratch or claw the bowl to get it out of the box, before he can eat.

Detour Tests

- Dog and owner are fairly close to each other but separated by a barrier (wall, fence). The dog has to move AWAY from the handler in order to get around the barrier, to his handler.
- The same arrangement is used as before but meat serves to attract the dog.

Maze Tests

T-Maze and regular Maze tests require the dog to find his way through a labyrinth to get to the reward at the exit.

Test for Gun Shyness

Unnoticed by dog and handler, an assistant fires a pistol at a distance of about 15 paces.

Basically, there are four possibilities:

a) The dog pays no attention at all to the shots.

While this is not the most desirable behavior, no points will be deducted if the test was part of a Schutzhund examination.

b) The dog acknowledges the shots, maybe even turns the head, but he remains in position.
This is the behavior the Schutzhund trainer would like to see.
c) The dog leaves his position and runs toward the shooter.
This reaction is the result of training.
In a Schutzhund trial, point deductions will occur yet this is NOT gun shyness.
d) The dog leaves his position, shows signs of fear and runs toward his handler or another familiar person or place (the car, for instance).
This behavior is called gun shyness and causes the dog to be excused from further examination in a Schutzhund trial.

Courage Test
The handler holds, encourages and then sends his dog while a decoy in the (not so far) distance advances with threatening gestures and sounds. The dog is expected to charge and to bite the decoy.

Henze Courage Test
The handler holds, encourages and then releases his dog while a decoy in the (not so far) distance advances with threatening gestures and sounds. The dog must charge and bite the decoy inspite of a hit with the stick which occurs just BEFORE the dog gets a hold on the sleeve.
This is a controversial test in our times. One must admit, though, that only courageous dogs will have the fighting drive to bite the bad guy AFTER having received a good whack.

Civil Agitation
A decoy in civilian clothes threatens and assaults the handler. The dog should prevent the attack by biting (the decoy wears hidden protective gear) or by attempting to bite (the dog wears a muzzle).

Re-directed Agitation
The dog should prevent a sudden attack on his handler by seizing the decoy's sleeve and biting hard. The decoy then surrenders the sleeve.
Now, another decoy in civilian clothes and with hidden protective gear attacks the handler again. The dog is expected to forget about the just captured sleeve and to defend his handler for the second time.

RESULTS
At the conclusion of the testing phase the evaluator will want to summarize his findings.
In reference to earlier stated requirements we suggest to describe the tests and the responses in a factual manner. If so desired, the tester can also express his opinion on how pronounced various temperament traits are in that particular dog, using the results from his score sheet.
Such a report will provide current and future owners of the dog with the information needed to utilize the dog's capabilities to the fullest extend.

Humphrey and Warner in their studies of guide dogs at FORTUNATE FIELDS gave an example of how this information can be used.
They concluded that a dog can serve man best in a particular capacity if certain temperament requirements are met.

For a POLICE DOG, they wanted a high degree of self-right, sharpness, fighting drive and protective drive, and a low degree of ear sensitivity, intelligence and willingness.

The TRAILING DOG was required to have a high degree of olfactory   acuity, intelligence and willingness, and a low degree of body sensitivity, confidence and fighting drive.

The best SEEING EYE DOG as selected by Humphrey had a high degree   of confidence, medium ear sensitivity and low olfactory acuity.

7. SCHUTZHUND TEMPERAMENT

If one would apply Humphrey's approach to the temperament requirements of a good Schutzhund dog, then the following list might evolve:

high degree (+2) of	energy	
	alertness	
	courage	
medium degree (+1) of	willingness	body sensitivity
	trainability	protective instinct
	nose ability	fighting drive
	ear sensitivity	sharpness.

As mentioned before, the tester must be able to distinguish between the natural potential of a (untrained) dog and the image he presents as a result of training. Learned behavior is a facade which will crumble if enough pressure is applied.

COURAGE is probably the single most important characteristic of a Schutzhund dog. Finding his strength in the pack instinct, the courageous dog will challenge an aggressor not only when his own life is in danger but also when his team mate, the handler, is threatened. Instead of running away or staying at a safe distance, he will attempt to stop the aggressor by biting, without hesitation and without a command. Facing possible injury or even death, he will intercept regardless of the severity of the threat or of the chance of victory.
To evaluate a puppy for his courage is somewhat difficult. The most promising Schutzhund candidate is probably the one who vigorously plays with his littermates, maybe even bosses them around - or the one who leads his siblings to the fence and barks at an approaching stranger.

Closely related to courage is PROTECTIVE INSTINCT.
A pronounced desire to protect his master in critical situations
is absolutely necessary for a Schutzhund dog. How effective this protection is depends to a great deal on the courage the dog possesses. A dog biting only softly and reluctantly in an attack on the handler shows little courage. On the other hand, there are quite a few hard biting dogs around that have little courage. Their strong protective instinct has its foundation in fear, the survival instinct, or a well developed pack instinct.
In a puppy, the protective instinct is rather difficult to assess.
Some information may be gained, though, from watching him guard a prized possession, a bone, for instance.

FIGHTING DRIVE is of lesser importance when compared to the protective instinct. Nevertheless, a certain level is expected from a Schutzhund candidate. Dogs with a well developed fighting drive always show a great amount of self-confidence, and they are always courageous. They enjoy the fight, they look forward to it - although not to the extent of initiating trouble themselves.
Puppies clue us in on their potential fighting drive while playing with their litter mates, or when mouthing our hands.

SHARPNESS is still another criterion. We define it as the ability to react instantaneously to subtle artificial changes in the environment. The reactions may be of a passive, a semi-active, or of an active nature, like recognizing the change, alerting his master to it, or biting the intruder. Suspicion, mistrust and sensibility (bordering sometimes on nervousness) are typical for a sharp dog. For all these reasons the Schutzhund trainer wants a dog with average sharpness.
The characteristics of a sharp dog can be recognized fairly easily in a puppy.

In order to make Schutzhund training for competition worthwhile, a dog must measure up to certain minimum standards of courage, protective instinct, fighting drive and a certain level of sharpness. In a trial, the judge is actually required to conduct an informal temperament test before the official proceedings begin. Here is a description of how one judge (the author) handles the situation:

"I make it a point to observe from a distance dog and handler while they are getting ready for tracking. Since people, and often other dogs, are close by, I can learn quite a bit from it.

I continue the observation when walking toward the tracking contestant. By doing so, we meet away from the starting flag and I have a chance to involve the handler in a casual conversation while we three - handler, dog and judge - advance to the start. During this walk the dog responds in some way to me being next to his handler, which I again record in memory.

Then follows the handler's report. I try to put him at ease by chatting some more or answering any of his questions. This occupies the handler's mind enough so that he does not consciously or subconsciously influence his dog. If there was no problem so far, I will at that time quite naturally lower my right hand, and I will happen to come maybe within an inch of the dog's head. I also might decide to step to the side and make gentle body contact with the dog - as if by accident. While continuing the conversation with the handler I will take note of the dog's reaction, out of the corner of my eye. All these movements are quite natural on my part, neither too slow (afraid), nor too fast (threatening). An observer, and even the handler, will probably not connect them in any way with the temperament test I am conducting.

All pieces and bits of information collected this way will then enable me to come up with a fairly accurate assessment of the dog's temperament."

8. WERTMESSZIFFER

In the former Communist countries in Eastern Europe, Schutzhund and working dogs were rated by the "Wertmessziffer " (German: "measured value number"). This system has been essentially abandoned by now even though it provided a uniform and fairly accurate description of an adult working dog's physical and mental constitution, benefitting especially breeders (and the breed) and buyers of working dogs.

The Wertmessziffer was entered in a dog's registration papers. It has six digits, each digit describing a particular feature.

A Doberman with a Wertmessziffer 8643/33, for instance, would be a heavy, large dog (8xxx/xx), showing good endurance (x6xx/xx) and good angulation (xx4x/xx), being suspicious and aggressive (xxx3/xx) and displaying sufficient sharpness (xxxx/3x), courage and hardness (xxxx/x3). These characteristics suggest that he is a good watch (alert) dog.

The ideal Schutzhund/working dog, on the other hand, would have a Wertmessziffer of 5555/55. Dogs rated between xxx3/33 and xxx7/33, however, are still useful for the demanding police and military duties.

9. WHICH AGE ?

Puppies are such a tremendous source of joy, and their personality is so easily influenced in a positive, or in a negative, way that the dedicated working dog owner will almost always acquire his dog at a very young age. Seven to ten week old puppies are the best prospects.

If the bloodlines have been researched sufficiently, if the parents have been evaluated personally, if earlier litters of the same pairing have been checked, if the puppy itself is healthy, active, vigorous, inquisitive and otherwise of sound temperament, and if the new owner is willing and able to provide the right environment for the development of the puppy, then few things can go wrong.

People with more money, less patience and less tolerance prefer to buy a grown dog. This is a choice of the lower risk since structure, temperament, as well as physical and mental capabilities of the dog are readily apparent. These people, however, must share any sense of accomplishment with the previous owner.

10. WHICH SEX ?

Time and experience have shown that both male and female dogs are capable of outstanding performance in the working dog world.

While the choice between a male and a female becomes mostly a matter of personal preference,

WERTMESSZIFFER SYSTEM

value	first digit body type with respect to breed standard	second digit constitution	third digit build (structure)	fourth digit temperament	fifth digit sharpness	sixth digit courage and hardness
0	little resemblance	delicate, weak, sensible	cryptorchid	nervous afraid, very shy		
1	poor representative	deficient (weak) sexual characteristics	poor angulation or poor chest	spooky, timid, noise-sensitive	none	none
2	too light	teeth or pigment faulty	faulty leg proportions	insecure, fearful at times possibly sharp	some	some
3	too high	coat faulty, weak foundation	average angulation	reserved, suspicious, or aggressive		
4	sufficient	maturing problems	good angulation	aggressive, sharp hard, dangerous	sufficient	sufficient
5	average	ideal	excellent	relaxed, friendly very hard when provoked	good	good
6	powerful	coarse, resilient	good build, good chest	relaxed, friendly, hard when provoked	very good	very good
7	too low	weak muscles, incl. ears	long body	relaxed, friendly, sensitive		
8	heavy	spongy	overangulation	relaxed, friendly, indifferent, little sharpness		
9	coarse	crippled	excess in all of the points 6-8 (above)	soft, indifferent depressed, no sharpness		

there are some factors which should not be ignored. **FEMALE** dogs (bitches) are often more tractable, they are less likely to roam, and their performance does not suffer as much in the presence of members of the opposite sex. They require, however, time off from work: when they are in heat, or because of a pregnancy.

MALE dogs are often bolder, tougher and more independent than bitches. Protection work, therefore, comes natural. For the same reasons, however, and for a more pronounced sex drive, for a greater tendency to roam, and for a somewhat greater chance to get involved in dog fights, it is more difficult for the handler to exercise control.

11. WHICH BLOODLINE ?

All purebred dogs have "papers".

Procedures regarding these registration documents differ significantly between various countries, various kennel clubs, and various breed organizations.

The German Shepherd Dog Club in Germany (SV), for instance, issues them with very detailed information, including a description of physical and temperament characteristics of both parents and of all four grandparents. This information is collected for all dogs registered with the club, and published annually in book form.

The same club supports and enforces its system with breed surveys, with limits for the number of litters and stud services per dog per year, with limits for the number of puppies left with the mother, with an elaborate network of breed wardens who will tattoo every puppy, with licensing of veterinarians (HD), and with a large clerical staff.

In the US, the American Kennel Club (AKC) provides the owner, upon application, with just a single registration card. It is an honor system, and it has been criticized heavily since it can be, and is being, abused.

Much valuable insight can be gained by studying a dog's "papers", and by following the leads they provide. Information given on the registration papers can, for instance, be used to compile a pedigree - if the breeder has not provided one in the first place.

The pedigree shows in an easily understood schematic all the names of a dog's ancestors, for several generations. This enables the owner to study the genetic background of his dog and to be alerted to certain strengths and weaknesses in a particular bloodline, provided sufficient effort is spent to secure this information.

When selecting a puppy or a dog, first hand information on both parents, hopefully on the grandparents, and especially on the offspring from an earlier litter of the same parentage, is invaluable (unfortunately, it is often unavailable).

Proper upbringing is necessary to fully develop a dog's potential, but even the best environment can not compensate for hereditary deficiencies.

12. HARD or SOFT DOG ?

For Schutzhund competition, and especially a novice trainer, we recommend to get a hard dog. There are soft and hard dogs, and there are many dogs in between as there are many shades of gray between pure black and pure white.

Hard dogs are defined as the strong-willed, bold types with an extrovert personality. In training, they respond best to a firm handler and a strong correction, combined of course with love, praise and rewards.

Soft dogs, on the other hand, are the very sensitive, easily impressed, sometimes even timid animals. They thrive on gentleness, carefully proportioned amounts of force, and empathy as well as skill supplied by the trainer.

Hard dogs don't get disturbed when handled wrongly, they forget it in an instant and retain their happy working spirit.

Soft dogs are different: Even a harsh word may cause them to be emotionally disturbed, and rough treatment leaves an ever-lasting impression with them. Training mistakes, handler errors, a snappy leash correction can easily spoil a soft dog for further training. Outstanding knowledge in canine matters, expert training abilities, and much patience are the only virtues that can temporarily improve the situation. A backlash, however, occurs as soon as the dog is confronted with too much pressure.

For example: On the retrieve over the hurdle a dog comes in too low, hits the barrier and knocks it over.

The hard dog soon forgets the mishap and further training poses no problem. The soft dog, however, remembers the pain and the noise of the tumbling boards for a long time. He will try to avoid the hurdle in the future, walk around it or remain on the other side. It requires a patient, understanding and skillful trainer to repair the damage.

For these reasons, novice handlers are always better off with a hard dog.

13. WHICH ONE ?

Comparative shopping is very important for the prospective buyer of a working dog. The last one in a litter, the mailorder puppy, the phone order dog, or the impulsive buy have rarely met the long-range expectations of the owner.

It is best to narrow down the choices systematically, and to spend enough time and effort on research at each individual step:

        breed of dog
        bloodline
        age, sex
        kennel/breeder
        individual dog (physical and mental health,
                and suitability for the need he fills).

C. SELECTING AN INSTRUCTOR

The first major project contemplated by the owner of a newly acquired dog is usually obedience training. Finding the right class and the right instructor usually determines if the owner enjoys the companionship of his dog over the years, or if he constantly worries about him.

Instructors do not have to be licensed, so almost anyone can (and seems to) get into the business. It is therefore well worth the effort to search for the best instructor available.

Recommendations by friends are often not sound. A collection of trophies and training titles does not necessarily make the owner an expert instructor. Diplomas and certificates issued by the various kennels and institutions merely attest that the owner has paid a fee and met certain minimum (often unrelated) requirements.

Even large amounts of money spent on advertising do not guarantee the qualification of a trainer, as a highly publicized series on national TV networks (originally broadcast by BBC) has amply demonstrated.

The best approach is to ask for permission to observe two or three sessions of a current class, and to take note of what is going on. If this is not possible, then the handler can enroll and decide at the end of the second session if he wants to continue.

(For simplicity we will refer to "him" as the instructor, although "she" might do just as well or better.)

DOES YOUR DOG APPROVE OF HIM ?

If the instructor has a natural way to gain the confidence and the respect of all the dogs in the class (maybe with one exception), and without faking friendliness, you can trust him too.

WHAT KIND OF RAPPORT EXISTS BETWEEN THE INSTRUCTOR AND HIS OWN (DEMONSTRATION) DOG ?

If there is mutual respect, and admiration, between the two members of this team, if the dog works happily, if the instructor is kind but firm, if his dog trusts him, you can trust him too.

DOES THE INSTRUCTOR TEACH THE DOGS, OR THE OWNERS ?

Even a mediocre instructor can make a dog perform for him - yet that is not the purpose for attending a dog training program. The owner, not the instructor, has to live with the dog. The instructor must tell and show the OWNER how to handle his dog.
Beware of instructors who show off with clients dogs.

CAN THE INSTRUCTOR INSTRUCT ?

Can he make his point, do the handlers understand?
Can he get people to do what he wants them to do?
Does he accomplish something, do all the handlers progress satisfactorily?
Does he motivate the class?
Beware of the instructor who just socializes.

DOES THE INSTRUCTOR EXPLAIN

why certain things should be done and others should not?
You need to know the reasons since in your particular situation and with your particular dog the approach may have to be modified.
Beware of the instructor who just says: Do it my way.

IS THE INSTRUCTOR RESPONSIVE, FLEXIBLE ?

Each dog, and each handler, is different. Each needs a somewhat different approach.
Beware of the instructor who says: Do it my way, and only my way.

IS THE INSTRUCTOR TOLERANT ?

Watch how he handles the situation when someone gets him into a tight spot.
Or test him yourself. You could, for instance, refuse to follow an explicit direction of the instructor, especially if your common sense tells you that he might be wrong.
Be prepared to intelligently argue your case. See how he responds.
Beware of the instructor who blows his stack.

IS THE INSTRUCTOR KNOWLEDGEABLE ?

Ask relevant questions, get his advise on pertinent problems you have, or those you can imagine.
Be prepared to enter into an intelligent discussion, read up on the subject.
Beware of the instructor who is uncooperative or who can not give -or not get - you an answer.

CAN THE INSTRUCTOR HANDLE A CRITICAL SITUATION ?

Tell him your dog bit the mailman, twice, and ask for his suggestions.
If he throws you out of class (quite a few will), or if he suggests the dog pound, leave. He just admitted to practicing a profession without the proper qualifications.

There is no such thing as a perfect instructor. Some are good, some are not so good.
Go and get the good ones.

"You play chess with your dog?
He must be very smart!"

Oh no, he isn't.
I beat him most of the time. "

III. THE STRATEGIES

A. TRAINING THEORY

Canis Familiarize, the common dog, is considered to be the oldest domesticated animal. He has been a loyal companion, guardian and servant to his master and to his masters family, generation after generation, over thousands of years. Two factors have helped the dog to become man's best friend:

> 1. Next to primates, dogs are probably the most common trainable animals, with regard to versatility, and to usefulness.
> 2. Dogs are pack animals, and they are used to taking orders from their leader.

1. PACK LEADERS / PACK MEMBERS

Like their wild ancestors, dogs are sociable creatures. They live in groups, structured according to a pecking order, with special duties and privileges assigned to each position.

The playful fight for dominance with littermates begins already during puppyhood, it leads to serious rivalry during adolescence and results in the establishment of a pecking order which all pack members will acknowledge and honor. Challenges and modifications, however, take place when the performance of any one pack member changes significantly. Especially the pack leader, or alpha animal, is in a vulnerable position. When he loses his strength or his superior instincts, he also loses respect, credibility and his dominance.

In dog training it is essential that the trainer assumes the role of the pack leader. He must earn and keep (!) his dog's acceptance, respect, trust and loyalty in order to be recognized as the leader.

Although most dogs will strive for dominance at one time or another, they are as happy to be a follower as they are to be a leader. If challenged, the handler must show them their place by responding intelligently and understandably (to the dog) with a firm, yet loving hand.

The domestication process has strengthened in dogs an innate desire to please their masters. This is a very precious asset available to a dog trainer and he should not jeopardize it. He must realize that a subordinate has rights too. Violating them will result in mutiny, and rightfully so. There is no justification for abusing a dog, reason or not. Likewise, punishment administered out of sequence with the undesirable deed will ruin the best dog/handler relationship.
Unreasonable, inconsiderate, impatient, ill-tempered or violent persons should not train a dog. Yet anthropomorphism (treating a dog like a human being) may cause just as much harm. Since the dog's brain operates at a different level, the trainer must lower himself to this level when he wants to relate to, or communicate with, his dog. There is a limit to this suggestion, however: barking back at a dog instead of giving a command, or exchanging saliva with him (as suggested by some "experts") is hardly justifiable.

Properly treated and guided, a dog will go out of his way to perform all sorts of difficult tasks within the limits of his capabilities, even though they might appear to him superfluous or ridiculous.
Problems in dog training usually lie not with the dog, but with his human partner.
Everyone can be a follower, but it takes a leader to lead.

2. VERBAL COMMUNICATIONS

We know that dogs have no comprehension of the human language. The inflections in a trainer's voice, the degree of loudness or harshness in his verbal communication, however, signal to the dog his mood, his commitment, his determination, his approval or disapproval. A dog can NOT understand words or sentences as we understand them. He does respond to certain sounds (words) in a specific way, but this is the result of conditioning, not understanding.

It does not matter which word the trainer chooses for a command, as long as it is short (to be practical) and unique in its sound characteristics (to avoid confusion with similar commands). You can command your dog to "sit", "knit", "mitt", "fit" etc. and he will most likely do the same thing, he will sit. If, however, you change the emphasis or the manner in which you pronounce "sit", if for instance in the excitement of a trial you shout "sit" in a very stern, commanding manner, your dog will get confused, and he probably will lay down. You have changed the input, "pushed the wrong button" so to speak, and therefore the dog will try to read your mind and come up with a (new) response that he thinks will please you.

While the commands can be given in any native tongue, it is believed that the more guttural languages (like Russian) have a slight advantage over the more melodic ones (like French).
Of greater importance, though, is consistency. Once a particular word has been selected for a command, it must be used for this exercise, exclusively and religiously.
Initially, during the conditioning stage, command and physical guidance go together. The dog, for instance, is smartly manipulated ("handled") into a sitting position while the word "sit" is spoken. Once the association has been formed in the dog's mind, the guidance is eliminated, and the dog will sit with a command only. The word "sit" has become a substitute for the physical manipulation into a sitting position - or in other words - the primary cue (force) has been replaced with a secondary cue (command).

3. SIGNAL COMMUNICATIONS

Dogs are keen observers. It is much more natural for them to interpret, and to cue in on, a gesture rather than to respond to a spoken word. If both stimuli are present, the choice is obvious. The serious trainer will, therefore, watch out for unnecessary body movements which he might subconsciously make while giving a verbal command (like moving a hand, repositioning his feet, bending forward, bending the knees in a recall etc.).

Intentional signal communications ("hand signals") have very limited practical use. It impresses novices tremendously when a dog lies down on signal, without a spoken command. But what do you do when the dog happens not to look in your direction, call for his attention first? And what do you do when it is dark, shine a flashlight on your arm?
A softly spoken command beats a signal every time.

4. BEHAVIOR COMPONENTS

Canine behavior is shaped - and determined - by two factors:
> heredity and
> environment.
The hereditary influence on working performance is, unfortunately, often ignored. Many people do not realize that even the best environment can not compensate for a lack of natural qualities. It always pays to select the top candidate, rather than trying to build up a deficient sale item.

Many people already own a dog when they get seriously interested in dog training. Since they can not change their pupils hereditary background, they must operate the second criterion, the environment.

Fortunately, canines belong to the group of high-ranking mammals, able to adapt readily to new situations. Dog training, therefore, concentrates on soliciting specific, desired actions, or RESPONSES (R) as a result of a change in the environment which is called STIMULUS (S). A stimulus might be a tug on the leash, teaching the dog to move with his handler.

Such a pattern is the basis for an adaptive system: the animal adjusts to changes in its environment. The changes must stand out, however, so that the student can notice and recognize them.

This requires two things:
    a) *constancy*: the environment, the overall system, must be constant to a certain degree, so that
        changes can stand out, and
    b) *consistency*: the changes, or cues, must be distinct, as well as consistent, in order to guarantee
        a patterned response.
If the cues vary, or if they are erratic, training results will be erratic too.

A constant environment means, for instance, one trainer instead of several family members; a relaxed, well coordinated handler who avoids body language; familiar, secluded training grounds and a regular daily schedules for feeding, exercise etc.; elimination of erratic interferences like nasty kids from the neighborhood teasing the dog, and the like.

The cues in such a "sterile" environment will then be easily recognizable by the student. A leash correction, for instance, interrupts the dog in whatever he was doing before. To adapt to the change and to restore the former state of no-conflict, the dog has two options:
    1) *assimilation*, e.g. trying to change the environment
        (trying to get the handler to quit the leash corrections by playing, growling, snapping,
        biting)
    2) *accommodation*, e.g. trying to change himself (heel properly).

A skillful trainer will, of course, discourage option 1) by making that choice even more unpleasant, and he will encourage option 2) by immediately rewarding the dog for desirable behavior.

Consistency, the second criterion, requires that the handler responds in a predictable way. Erratic responses of the handler confuse the dog and make learning nearly impossible.
Here is an example:
        During quartering in the protection work, the dog heads straight for the decoy instead of quartering the empty blinds first. The handler yells "here", and since this has no effect he tries "down", again to no avail. So the handler lets his dog proceed with barking, guarding, escape etc.
The problem lies with the handler and his inconsistency.
The dog is aware that the handler changes his mind very rapidly and unpredictably, so he just plays deaf.
After the dog ignores the first command, the handler should run to the dog, grab him by the collar or by the nape, and drag him back, firmly and quickly. He should then shove him in the direction he is supposed to go and praise him upon his return.

The smart trainer will stage situations where he is in absolute control and where he can correct (or reward) his dog at the proper time. A fenced-in training area, a long line, a sling shot, an assistant, an electronic collar or other means can be employed in that instance.

The example given above describes well what psychologists call operant conditioning.
The term is used for learning processes based on personal experiences which link an act and its consequences.
Most dogs will expect to be fed each day at the same place, and at the same time (going to the feeding area at a specific time will be rewarded with food, at other times it will not). By the same token, the dog that did not quarter will do so nicely now (to avoid the correction and to earn the praise).
The animals have been motivated to do something, or to refrain from doing something.

5. MOTIVATION

A dog will not normally volunteer to do his masters bidding since nearly all obedience training requirements are in conflict with natural behavior patterns. Motivation, therefore, is the single most important factor in dog training.
If the handler can motivate his dog wanting to do whatever HE wants him to do, then everything else will fall in place easily.

Motivation comes about for two reasons:
- a) the desire to get something (reward)
- b) the desire to avoid something (punishment/correction).

A fat paycheck is motivator enough for a human to work hard - to earn the reward.
A roaring hotel fire is motivator enough for a person to leave the building - to avoid something unpleasant. Dogs are not immune to similar reasoning.

REWARD

If a reward is supposed to motivate the dog then it must be something highly desirable. The stronger the desire, the more effective the reward.
There are basically three ways to increase the desire, and they can be used in combination:
- a) selecting the reward that is most attractive
  - use broiled liver instead of regular dog food
  - play ball with him if that is what he likes best.
- b) temporarily depriving the dog of the basic need to which the reward applies
  - withhold food for 24 hours (food)
  - temporarily confine the dog to isolation (play).
- c) reserving the reward for those times when the dog has earned it
  - if the dog gets treats all the time, why should he "work" for it.

The most common forms of reward are

a) **Praise**	- a kind word
	- a scratch on the head, chest
	- a belly rub
	- a pat on the shoulder
	- a hug
	- a dance of joy
b) **Play**	- ball / stick / frisbee
	- running, romping, swimming
	- chasing
	(all WITH the master)
c) **Food** highly effective:	- broiled liver
	- smoked sausage
	- bacon
	- meat in various other forms
	- fish
somewhat effective:	- cheese
	- flavored dog treats (grain products)
	- dog biscuits
less suitable:	- commercial dog food
	- cookies
	- sweets

There are two phases in dog training where rewards play an important role:
phase 1   establishing or "*shaping*" a desirable behavior (teaching the dog what   to do)
phase 2   "*maintaining*" a desirable behavior (refreshing the dog's memory about what he has learned).

In phase one, the ultimate goal can only be accomplished by taking many small, progressively more difficult steps, each one of which must be rewarded instantaneously.
A dog being taught to climb a ladder, for instance, will at first be rewarded for the slightest attempt he makes. From here on he will have to respond more and more distinctly to earn his reward.
The challenge for the trainer is to make the individual steps not too small to mislead or to bore the dog (waste time) nor too big to lose him in the process (extinguish the desirable response).
Since all efforts of the dog are rewarded, the term "constant reinforcement" can be applied.

By definition, the dog progresses to phase two once he understands what is asked of him and he can produce that particular response on request. A good trainer, then, will insure that the dog does not forget and that he responds reliably in the desired and learned way.

In practical experiments, psychologists have found that constant reinforcement during phase two leads to poor performance. Better results are obtained by slowly changing this ratio of 1:1 (one reinforcement per one desired response) to 1:2, 1:5, 1:10 and so on. These are "fixed ratios of intermittent reinforcement", meaning that for the 1:10 ratio only one out of ten good performances is rewarded.

Still better results can be obtained at this point by going to "variable ratio schedules of intermittent reinforcement". This is a completely irregular, haphazard pattern in which the dog might get rewarded two times in a row, then not at all for 5 times, then after 4, 1, 2 attempts and so on.
Since the student has no way of figuring out which one of his next responses will be rewarded, and since the occasional withholding may tell him that his performance was not quite good enough to earn the reward, he will - theoretically - do his best everytime from then on.

These reinforcement schedules must be tailored to the particular dog/handler team and to the exercise under consideration. It must also be understood that the dog needs feedback from his master about EACH performance, even though the handler may withhold the major reward, according to the intermittent reinforcement schedule.

CORRECTION - PUNISHMENT
Punishing a dog for having been bad is applying human standards to the training of animals, it is counterproductive since the dog has no moralistic values.
Nevertheless, the term has become part of the dog trainer's vocabulary, and we would like to have it understood in the sense of a correction, as an unpleasant experience triggered by an undesirable deed.
Corrections borrowed from the behavior repertoire of animals are most effective. The "nape grab" is a good example: Taking a hold of the loose fold of skin around the puppy's neck, lifting him up by it and shaking him is simulating a procedure that the mother dog would use to teach her offspring.
Some "authorities" recommend this for rebellious dogs of all ages; it does not work. Likewise, they tell you to literally sit on the dog in the "alpha posture" as they call it. Don't do it, it will worsen the situation - and you probably get bitten as well.

The scale of "punishments" is far reaching,
  it includes: threatening motions
                startling, loud noises
                reprimanding
                harsh scolding
                shaking (nape grab)
                slapping
                hitting
                choking (quick choke collar correction)
                pinching (quick pinch collar correction)
                shocking (electro shock),
  as well as: withholding the reward ("negative reinforcement")
                ignoring the dog

isolating the dog
restraining the dog's movement
confining the dog.

The corrections must be tailored to the occasion and to the temperament of the dog. A soft dog, for instance, is easily impressed by a harsh word from his trainer, while the hard dog often needs a physical correction before he responds.

A correction is a sequence of events, and it consists - ideally - of four parts:

1) a verbal command
   This "warning" is very important from a learning standpoint. It allows the dog to avoid the correction in the following step by reacting quickly in the desired (and previously learned) manner.
2) an unpleasant stimulus (correction)
   The stimulus must be forceful enough to make a lasting impression on the dog, but not so forceful as to cause psychological of physical damage. The stimulus must also be related to the objective of the exercise (don't pinch his EAR if you want him to open the MOUTH for the dumbbell)
3) a physical manipulation into the desired position or state (assistance)
   This is actually a shortcut in the learning process. Rather than letting the dog guess what the handler wants him to do, he is manipulated into the proper position (parts 2 and 3 are often tied together, for instance in the leash correction).
4) a reward for compliance
   While the HANDLER manipulates the dog into the desired position or state, the DOG gets the reward. As counterbalance for the preceding unpleasant experience, praise given here helps the dog to remember where his advantage lies. Praise also helps to maintain a happy working spirit in the dog.

All four parts must be in the proper order, and they have to follow one another very rapidly.

To find the right level of force required in step 2, it is suggested to start out gently and then, in increments, get tougher. The dog will not bother to respond to the correction until a certain level of force is reached. This level should be maintained during the initial training stage. Later on it can be lowered again.

The following example serves to demonstrate the principle:

OBJECTIVE: Teaching the dog to sit quickly and squarely.

SEQUENCE: Heel your dog at a brisk pace. Hold the leash very short. Make sure that the dog's shoulder is lined up with your left hip. Come to a halt.
               a) Give a short, factual instruction: "sit".
               b) About 1/4 of a second later simultaneously
               - tug the leash with your right hand, from the neck of the dog 45 degrees upward and slightly forward (backward) if your dog lags behind (forges ahead).
               - slap the dog on the rear. Contact is made for a very short moment between the FINGERS of the left hand and the croup of the dog.
               c) If the slap was hard enough, the dog wants to sit now.
               Guide him during this process (not after the dog sits already) into a straight, square sit, e.g. prevent him from sliding into an undesirable position. It does not mean that the dog is being PUSHED into a sitting position.
               d) Praise your dog.

The reward-correction concept is a rather important one in dog training, it is therefore justified to reemphasize the following points:

Rewards must be attractive.
Rewards must be earned, not given out of affection.
Corrections must be proceeded by a "warning".
Corrections must be forceful enough to get the dog's attention.
Corrections must be followed by praise.
Timing for both, reward and correction, must be accurate (see "memory", below).

B. LEARNING THEORY

1. MEMORY

Memory is "the faculty of retaining and recalling past experience, the ability to remember".

MEMORY PROCESSES
Compared to other animals, dogs have a relatively large brain; they can readily adapt to new and unusual situations. A highly sophisticated memory system enables them to relate new information to past experiences.
Three phases are involved in this process:
1) encoding information
2) storing information
3) retrieving information.

1) The encoding consists mainly of analyzing, processing and "digesting" new information which is then fitted into the "shelves" of the already existing memory storage facility, the brain.
2) Storing that information involves minute chemical changes in the brain cells of the student. Depending on how much he is impressed by the situation, these changes are more or less severe, resulting in long-term or short-term capabilities.
3) The retrieving, finally, occurs when new circumstances cause the brain to search for applicable stored information. Whatever is found is compared to the new situation and has a heavy influence on the decisions made by the student in response.

For example:
A young dog is taken to the clinic for his first shots. He happily greets the veterinarian, wagging his tail. Then comes the shot.

Never before had the puppy experienced that a friendly human being willfully caused him such pain. He analyzes the situation: veterinary clinic, the office and the equipment, strange sounds and smells, the other animal patients, the doctor's coat, the pain. All these pieces of information are combined, "processed" and then stored in the long-term memory since the impression on the dog was a lasting one.
The dog will have no problem to retrieve that information later on. Just pay another visit to your vet, or any vet.

MEMORY LEVELS
As stated above, the length of time during which information is being retained depends on how much the dog is impressed by the stimulating experience.
Psychologists have defined four such levels on which memory processes operate:

a) Very Short Term (or Ionic) Memory, VSTM
As "receptionist" for the brain, the VSTM discards or accepts, and processes and forwards all messages from the outside world. High stimulus intensity and stimulus duration help to increase the VSTM, while a high intensity of unrelated, surrounding stimuli tend to diminish the effect.
A gentle tug on the leash, for instance, has no effect on a dog that is straining to meet another fellow-canine. A sharp leash correction, on the other hand, lets him remember for a while that he is supposed to walk next to his master.

b) Short Term (or Working) Memory, STM
The STM is the "filing clerk" who picks up the information from the receptionist (VSTM), sorting and placing it in the respective filing cabinet. Knowledge is rearranged and put in the proper perspective.
While one sharp leash correction (VSTM) captures the dog's attention for a moment, several of them - properly timed and followed by praise - address the STM and convince the dog to behave properly for the rest of the lesson.

c) Intermediate Term Memory, ITM
The ITM retains knowledge temporarily, maybe for about a week. It is available for information that maintains its value - in the opinion of the owner - for a limited time only, like a drawer in which we keep tax return receipts. After a certain time the old material becomes unimportant and is replaced with new information.

A dog being taught tracking by the food method will remember up to about one week that he found his reward at the end of the trail. If the time between the first and the second tracking lesson, however, is much longer than a week, and if the dog was fed regularly in the meantime, evidence of prior learning will (normally) be missing.

d) Long Term Memory, LTM
The LTM is the place of permanent changes in memory.
After a long and elaborate screening process at lower memory levels, essential information finds its way into the LTM. Behavior or personality shaping has its origin here, attitudes, general approaches etc. are established within this region, and fundamental, far-reaching decisions are based on information retained in LTM.

If a dog has found through numerous experiences that he can please his master only by performing certain tasks - herding sheep for instance, then this knowledge becomes important to him, so important that he will acknowledge these tasks in his LTM as essential for his survival. He will become a herding dog, a working dog.

CONSOLIDATION

Transferring information from STM or ITM into LTM is called consolidation (or learning). The process takes time and the student should not be distracted, overly excited or otherwise disrupted.

When laboratory animals were given electro shocks right after a learning trial, they would not remember what they just had been taught.
However, if the same treatment was given some hours later, the learning process was unaffected and the animals would remember well.
These findings can be expressed in figure 1:

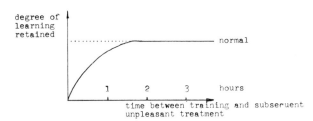

FIG. 1

TOP WORKING DOGS

Pleasant interferences, on the other hand, supported learned behavior.

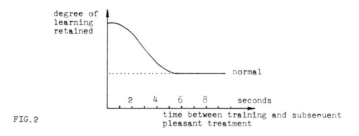

FIG. 2

Figure 2 shows that the pleasant experience (reward, e.g. praise, food, play, even chemical or electrical stimuli) must be given immediately after the learning trial. Otherwise the student will not see a connection between his action and a reward.

Example:
A trainer wants to teach his dog to clear the hurdle on the command "jump". He manages to get his dog over the barrier but since the student does not seem to pay attention - there are other dogs and other people around - he sends his dog over, and over, and over, and over, one time right after the other. The dog has no chance to digest the training procedure, he is too much distracted and he even gets to hate jumping because of the endless repetition which to him is a punishment.
Chances for success are much better when the trainer selects an area relatively free of distractions, for the first few training sessions. Rewarding the dog immediately after the jump, then giving him a chance to relax and not asking a repeat performance for the next few hours (maybe days, depending on dog and trainer) will further guarantee consolidation, meaning success.

ASSOCIATIVE MEMORY

To stack the LTM with useful information, the dog must be able to connect specific commands with specific (desired) responses.
Frequency, recency and arousal are important to make this association:

FREQUENCY means that the more often we practice a particular exercise - within a reasonable framework - the more reliable the dog's performance will become.

One of the authorities was asked how long it takes to teach a dog to track well consistently. "2000 tracks, at least" was his answer. Of course, it would not be such a good idea to do all 2000 tracks in one week.
Constant repetitions eventually cause the responses to be automatic, e.g. regulated by subconscious, rather than by conscious, efforts.

RECENCY is another important factor. Even we humans keep forgetting things when they are not fresh in our mind anymore, and forgetting becomes gradually worse as time goes by (physiological decay process).
The handler practicing heeling with his dog just before he enters the obedience ring has found a practical way to utilize the theorem that an association is the stronger the more recently it has been activated.

AROUSAL finally refers to various, not directly related stimuli present at the time of training or immediately thereafter. Here are two examples:

- An anxious or moderately excited dog (anticipating a reward like play, praise, food) is a better learner than his dull counterpart.
- Emotionally toned commands are better remembered and executed than neutral ones ("Your voice is the most elegant, the most effective, and the always present training tool", phrase by the author).

Depending on the exercise, however, different levels of excitement must be chosen for optimum results. Complex tasks like tracking require a lower level of arousal (don't use protection work as reward!) than simple jobs like heeling.
This becomes obvious when we consider that
- at a low level of arousal, irrelevant as well as relevant
  cues are processed
- at an optimal level of arousal, only relevant cues are
  processed
- at a high level of arousal, not all relevant cues are
  processed.

The smart trainer, therefore, will carefully select the proper level of arousal (stimulation), he will refresh his dog's memory as needed (recency), and he will make sure that his dog has performed the exercise often enough (frequency) so that he can do it like a dream.

LATENT LEARNING

"Latent learning" (latent = hidden) means that animals can accumulate knowledge and store that information for later use, without giving any indication of the learning process. Upon proper stimulation/motivation the latent information is retrieved, and this usually results in superior performances.

Let us take the "send out" as an example. The handler might have run with the dog, on leash, many times to the spot to which he wants his dog to advance. Off lead, and without the handler running along, the dog acts as if he did not get the message. Now we provide the proper motivation (encouragement, praise, a toy, food) and - everything else being right - the dog will perform the first time and thereafter like an expert.

CONTINGENCIES OF REINFORCEMENT

Training principles that were discussed so far have given not enough credit to the dog's initiative.

It is well known that success in teaching children, or in training dogs, is based on the students' curiosity, his personal experiences, and on opportunities to learn and to make mistakes.
These three parts have to be considered together, no single one would work satisfactorily all by itself. They are called the three contingencies of reinforcement.

Curiosity (learning by doing)
A curious dog (a puppy we might call mischievous) is more likely to accidentally discover the desired response than a dullhead. Accidental discovery is known to considerably enhance the learning process over manipulating (forcing) the dog through the exercise the first time.
On the obstacle course, for instance, the curious dog will learn to go through the tunnel without problems. A dog which must be pulled through the tunnel the first time will have considerably more difficulties, here and in repeats.

Personal Experience (learning by experience)
Curiosity alone, however, is not enough. To reliably respond to the command "crawl through the tunnel" the dog must be able to relate to earlier experiences. The sight of the large conduit, for instance, will bring back memories in the curious dog which stimulate him to go through it willingly. The situation, the circumstances, the environment must be such that the dog can relate to earlier occasions when it did something similar and got satisfaction in doing it.

Opportunities (learning by trial and error)

Performances will remain unpredictable as long as the dog was never given the chance to find out what the desirable AND (!) the undesirable responses are for a given situation.

Going halfway into the tunnel and then coming back would be undesirable. It is very risky for a trainer to never give his dog a chance to make a mistake (here: to turn around). The dog will probably do just that at the least opportune time. One should take care of that situation in training and then let the dog know he made the wrong decision.

This basic fact of dog training is ignored by many reputable trainers!

2. LEARNING THEORIES

Modern canine psychology refers to three general approaches for the theoretical understanding of behavior control, or learning and training. They are

>   a) Obedience Theory (dog trainers call it compulsive training)
>   b) Reinforcement Theory (trainers call it inducive training)
>   c) Cognitive Theory.

Each one of them has something to offer, yet the cognitive theory is the most effective approach, including elements of both the obedience and the reinforcement theory.

a) OBEDIENCE THEORY

This theory involves moral judgements, the dog is either
>   good or bad,
>   cooperative or uncooperative.

Training follows a pattern of increasing amounts of force or punishment, advancing to the next stage if the preceding one fails. This leads to an escalation of conflict and occasionally even to cruelty. Obedience theory has definite limitations and is, by itself, generally considered to be ineffective.

This can best be illustrated by using a dog-fight situation as an example (Fig.3). The handler who believes in obedience theory beats his dog, hoping that the dog will release the grip as a result of the punishment. (It rarely works).

The "forced retrieve" is another example of applied obedience theory.

b) REINFORCEMENT THEORY

This theory can be called neutral, or even a "spectators approach". It does not seriously consider the students goals, aims or even motivations. It operates under the assumption that a certain response (R) to a given stimulus (S) becomes more probable in time when it always had been rewarded or reinforced (F) in the past (S - R - F).

Reinforcement theory does reward desirable responses but it ignores undesirable ones, assuming that they will extinguish themselves in time. It fails to explain why many dogs continue to choose the undesired responses, even when plenty of reinforcement for the alternative is being offered. There are no provisions made for natural ("innate") responses which are strongly engraved in the dog's mind, and which can not be substituted by unnatural alternatives.

The "clicker" (rewarding the dog with a clicking sound followed by an actual reward) is an example of using this theory.

Referring to the dog fight situation, the dog's dignity, or his survival, depends on warding off the threatening attack. In the dog's view there is no alternative, reward or not, he has to take up the fight.

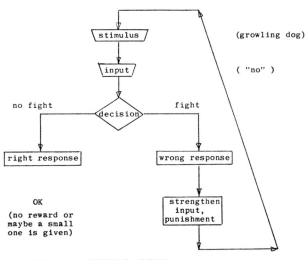

FIG.3   OBEDIENCE   THEORY

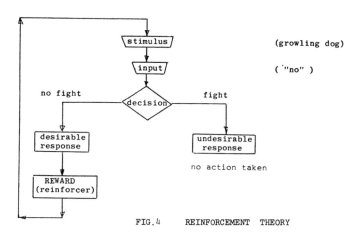

FIG.4   REINFORCEMENT   THEORY

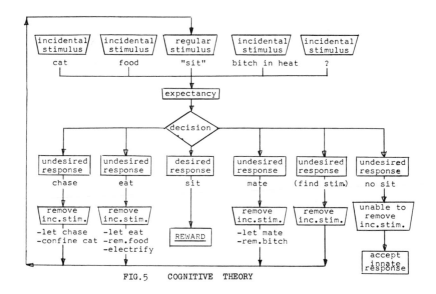

FIG.5   COGNITIVE   THEORY

c) COGNITIVE THEORY

This theory is similar to the reinforcement theory.

Instead of working with isolated S - R pairs, however, it acknowledges a chain of events as part of a more complex behavior flow system. Not single responses, but new expectancies must be formed and strengthened. This requires the "intellectual" involvement of the animal (as well as that of the trainer). To utilize the proper cues and motivational forces, a trainer must be interested in the reasons behind specific responses. He must also be interested in the pupil as an individual, in his students capacities and in the organization of his student's behavior. With that information he can devise modified behavior flow systems and incorporate training as an integral part of it.

Consider the following theoretical situation:

A trainer wants his dog to sit. He gives the command. There are four competing stimuli, forcing the dog to make a decision between several undesired and one desired response. In all probability the dog will not sit. Before giving the command again, the trainer will, according to the cognitive theory, eliminate the competing incidental stimuli, probably one at a time (cognitive theory also recognizes that not all incidental stimuli or responses can be eliminated, as it is the case with the innate responses).

This can be done by

a) satisfying the dog's needs (let him chase, eat, mate first)
b) removing the incidental stimulus (confine cat, remove food and bitch)
c) making the undesired response unpleasant (for instances connecting the food to an electric fence charger).

With all distractions removed, the chances are about fifty/fifty that the dog will perform as desired. To further increase the probability of the proper response, a reward is incorporated into the system, just like in the reinforcement theory. Here, however, the reward is also used as bait. The cognitive theory aims to create in the animal an anticipation, an expectation of the reward.

When the dog reaches the decision point he will, hopefully, realize two possibilities:
- undesired reactions mean being ignored by his handler, no attention, no fun, maybe even unpleasantness
- desired reaction means praise, reward, play, fun, food etc.

The dog remembers that he always was rewarded when he sat as requested. He probably will sit now.

Having accepted the reward as a motivator, cognitive theory goes one step further: By incorporating the desired response into a behavior chain, the dog has no choice but to do the desired task in order to be allowed to return to his regular activities. The daily routine for a dog might look like the outline shown in figure 6.

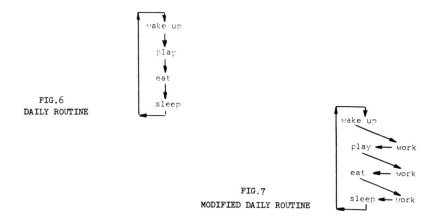

FIG.6
DAILY ROUTINE

FIG.7
MODIFIED DAILY ROUTINE

To demand work in competition with, of right after, a regular activity (sleep, food, play) is bound to cause serious problems. The cognitive theory, instead, requests work before AND AS A PREREQUISITE for such activity, as shown in figure 7.

That way the dog not only learns that food, play, sleep is a reward for work, he also learns that there is no way to get to these amenities but through work. Work becomes an integral part of the dog's complex behavior flow, and hopefully a pleasant one too.

3. A RECIPE

Now that we have discussed the theory of dog training in great detail we will want to apply it to specific problems. Let us try to put this in form of a recipe, realizing though, that each dog, each handler, each situation will require some modification.

   a) Goal: Teach a new exercise (shaping behavior patterns), and then
                      Insure that the dog reliably obeys the command once he understands what it means (maintaining behavior patterns).
   b) Ingredients: 1. a dog that does not know the command
                      2. a handler who has prepared himself for the task
                      3. proper tools (e.g. collar, leash, reward)
                      4. proper environment (e.g. quiet training area)
   c) Procedure:
      Part 1: Break down into simple parts any exercise that is complex and/or consists of multiple tasks. In the recall, for instance, teach the come, front sit, finish, independently of each other, in random order, and at random intervals.

Combine the three segments into a complete exercise only after the dog masters all separate parts.

Part 2: Introduce the command

- Guide your dog calmly, patiently, and in a very pleasant way. Show him what you want Manipulate him, "handle" him so that he ends up where you want him to be. (This is the primary stimulus).
- Introduce the command at the same time, say it over and over again. (This is the secondary stimulus).
- Praise him once he complies, e.g. "good boy, down"). (This is positive reinforcement).
- Repeat this over a period of days, or weeks, or months, until you are sure that the dog understands what the newly introduced command means. (This is consolidation).

Part 3: Secure reliable performance

Four rules apply here:

1. DON'T GIVE A COMMAND IF YOU ARE NOT IN A POSITION TO ENFORCE IT (except for emergencies).
   If your dog likes to chase cats then put him on a 30 foot leash and on a prong collar - then release the cat. If - during the training phase - you call him to you without this precaution, you only teach him disobedience (and you make a fool of yourself).

2. NEVER REPEAT A COMMAND MORE THAN ONCE,
   provided your dog is familiar with it. The first time the dog has a chance to do right. The second time you make him do right, manipulate him into the desired position. Make sure that you are in a position to enforce your command.

3. AFTER EACH CORRECTION, YOU MUST PRAISE YOUR DOG.
   The kind of praise varies, but there are no exceptions to this rule!

4. USE THE 1-2-3 RULE (see also the earlier chapter on "Correction - Punishment")
   Count "twenty one, twenty two, twenty three", to define a time frame for the following three steps:
   - give a command
   During the time it would take you to say "21", give the command.
   - observe your dog
   During the time it would take you to say "22", observe your dog. See if he obeys quickly, or if he does not.
   - correct or praise your dog
   During the time it would take you to say "23", either praise him for responding to your instruction, or correct him if he ignores your command, then give praise right away. As time goes on and your dog becomes more proficient, you can count faster and faster, thereby getting a quicker and quicker response from your dog.

"No, Henry,
DOGMA is not a mama dog!"

IV. THE TOOLS

A. SCHUTZHUND TRAINING EQUIPMENT

Without proper tools, the craftsman as well as the dog trainer can do only a mediocre job. Furthermore, improvising, using cheap and ineffective equipment, or using no protective gear at all can cause physical harm to the dog trainer.
Here are a few suggestions for recommended equipment:

1. TRACKING

FLAGS
Aluminum poles (3/8" pipe, pointed at one end) with a small piece of white or brightly colored cloth at the top are best.
Steel or aluminum ski poles (disc removed, flag attached), bicycle flags (fiberglass rods with metal tip) are useable too. Surveyor flags are too short, they tend to distract the dogs. Wooden poles and regular steel pipes are not recommended, the former ones break too easily, the latter ones are too heavy.

ARTICLES
Dark gloves, cut-off fingers from gloves, pieces of an old leather shoe or belt, a leather wallet are recommended.
The beginner should use leather articles since they hold human scent the longest. Advanced dogs can be taught to find metal, plastic, glass and wood articles as well. Color should be such that the dog does not hunt for it by sight.

HARNESS
Light-weight, non-restrictive, adjustable leather or web material harnesses are best.
For some years now the trend in Europe has been to do tracking without a harness. Attaching the leash just to the dead ring of the regular choke collar and guiding the leash under one front leg is "in". (This actually is a simplification of the "Boettcher harness" which cleverly guides the tracking leash along the rump, between the feet of the dog, and which forces the dog to put his head to the ground if he pulls.)

LEASH
The 30 ft. leash should be made of light-weight cord or web material. Leather tracking leashes, even the narrow-width ones, are often too heavy. Strength characteristics are important in very rare cases only, a tracking session is not a pulling contest.

MISCELLANEOUS
A clipboard, paper and pen are helpful to map out the track, to remember where it was laid, and to collect information on the dog's tracking performance.

A small FM or CB radio helps the tracklayer to stay in touch with the judge or the training director.

A carpenter's apron with its large pockets allows the handler to conveniently carry leash, articles, food rewards, a ball, a small water canteen and other items he might need on the track. It can also be used to store all tracking items in one place.

2. OBEDIENCE

LEASH
We suggest a leather leash, multi-adjustable, for its versatility.
A chain-link leash is out of the question. It is tough on the hands, and its weight signals to the dog unmistakenly when he is on or off the hook.

Nylon and cotton web leads are better than metal but they too are often tough on the hands of the handler.

A six foot leather leash, 1/2 or 3/4 inch wide, and with a medium-sized buckle, is a good choice. The multi-adjustable leather leash (not manufactured domestically) is slightly more expensive, yet it is useful for a variety of training purposes, such as exercising the dog, and in tracking (fully extended), in obedience (doubled) and in protection (partially extended and secured with the additional hooks).

SHORT LINE
A 15 inch long piece of cotton clothes line, or a nylon fishing line of the same length and with a handle on one end, is very useful during the transition from on to off lead.

LONG LINE
A 30 foot long cotton web lead, 1/2 inch wide, is light weight yet strong. It will not stretch, and it will not cut into your hands. Distance control is its major application.

COLLAR
Regular slip-chain collars are most effective, in rare instances pinch collars might be useful.

Small-link steel collars are preferred over "fur-savers" since they react more quickly. Nylon and leather collars (chokes) are less desirable.

Spike collars (sharpened nails inside a wide leather collar) are not training tools but torture instruments. They should not be confused with the pinch collars (also called prong or German training collars).

The pinch collar consists of individual steel links with two blunt prongs each. Momentarily tightening the collar presses the prongs against the dog's neck and causes some discomfort. If used sensibly on stubborn dogs, they can work wonders.

DUMBBELL
A set of 4 wooden dumbbells, standard weight (light-weight, 650 g, 1000 g, 2000 g), is recommended.

Ideally, the center bar should be two inches longer than the distance between the dog's eyes.

The all-wood 2000 g and 1000 g dumbbells are impressive looking but awkward to carry around, compared to the compact variety where metal weights are hidden inside the hardwood dumbbell body. Multi-adjustable dumbbells are bothersome to use, the frequent weight changes are annoying, the tightening screws get stuck, parts get lost.

THROW CHAIN
The conventional throw chain consists of two approximately eight inch long steel or brass link chains that are joined end to end by two metal rings to form a circle. A spare heavy-duty metal choke chain could serve the same purpose.

It is used to startle or to correct the dog while off lead. In most instances, a miss (on purpose) is as effective as a direct hit.

SLING SHOT
This very old but still very effective training tool is used for distance control, it is a long range substitute for a leash correction. The greatest benefits are obtained when the dog can not determine who fired the shot.

Dried peas or beans make suitable ammunition.

ELECTRONIC COLLAR
Radio-controlled shock treatment is used for distance control. The hand-held transmitter triggers an electric shock in the dog's specially equipped collar. Advanced models feature a warning sound before the electro-shock is activated so that the dog can avoid the punishment by quickly reacting in the expected fashion. Dummy collars of the same weight and size as the real thing are sometimes used during the second training phase.

Electronic collars take the fun out of dog training, anyone can steer a remote-controlled toy car. Besides, they have limited applications only, they can easily be abused or misused, and they can cause severe psychological damage. Inadvertent triggering by garage door openers or other radio-controlled equipment is a possibility and poses still another problem.
Only very experienced trainers should consider such equipment, and they must use it with much discretion.
German Working Dog Organizations have banned shock collars.

PISTOL
Blank pistols of .22 or .32 caliber should be used.
Regular revolvers can be fired with blanks but they might be ruined in time. Regular pistols are not recommended since even the automatic ones have to be reloaded manually for each shot.

3. PROTECTION

SACK
Burlap or jute sacks should be washed before use.
Sacks from a feed store, for instance, may contain insecticides etc. that can be harmful to dogs. In any case, the dust from an unwashed sack will annoy the animals.

BITE ROLL
A bite roll, or "sausage", serves purposes similar to the puppy sleeve. It can be made from a rolled jute or burlap sack, tied together with string. Some bite rolls are also stuffed with padding. They are fairly inexpensive.

PUPPY SLEEVE
Puppy sleeves are made from jute, with some padding, and not from leather. They have limited use for "soft" dogs, or for very young dogs. They can help to make the transition from sack to hard sleeve more palatable.

SLEEVE
Sleeves should be made from rigid leather with a flexible elbow joint, with or without bite bar. The handler should not be able to compress the sleeve structure by hand. The decoy should be able to twist his arm inside, without twisting the sleeve, or without rotating it (for teaching a firm hold).

Sleeves with bite bar are made for either right or left arm use. Those that can be worn on either arm are a compromise, they are not recommended for work with inexperienced dogs. Proper training exposes decoys and dogs to both a right and a left arm sleeve (one at a time, of course).
The bite bar may run the full length of the lower arm (easier on inexperienced dogs, more realistic training situation), or it may be an indentation in the middle of the lower arm only (tournament style training).

Some types of sleeves weigh less (thinner materials, modern manufacturing methods) yet have the same dimensions. They offer an additional degree of freedom for the decoy but they are not as durable as standard sleeves.

The bite bar should angle about 5 to 10 degrees downwards from the horizontal when the sleeve is worn properly and comfortably in front of the body (see Fig.8).

Sleeves made from ballistic nylon material lack the flexibility at the elbow, they are uncomfortable to wear (sweating), they are easily compressed and therefore they do not offer adequate protection for the decoy from a dog's hard bite, and some users have reported gum injuries to the dog.

bite bar

sleeve,
lower arm

5 degrees

FIG.8   SIDE VIEW OF BITE-BAR SLEEVE

Cover attachment:
To attach the sleeve covers, fasteners are provided on either the upper or the lower arm. Upper-arm attachment supposedly gives less cause to tooth injuries to the dog and offers a larger biting surface, but it limits the decoy's elbow flexibility and prohibits cover rotation (shorter cover life).

Lower-arm buckles are normally concealed by the upper edge of the sleeve cover. If they protrude, a double-layered shield cut from an old tire innertube should be slipped over them to avoid direct contact and to eliminate potential teeth or gum injuries. Lower-arm buckles give the decoy full elbow flexibility. They also allow easy rotation of the cover for a greatly extended cover life (about 4-5 times longer than a high-buckle cover).

Some manufacturers equip their sleeves with loops so that the covers can be attached with a belt (no interchangeability between buckle and belt-type sleeves/arms).

Friction-fitted sleeve covers do not need straps because of their tight fit. They are compatible with a variety of different sleeves, regardless of buckle arrangement.
Friction holds these covers securely in place as long as the dog bites normally (not trying to pull the cover off at the tip). The covers can be rotated in small increments for a greatly extended useful life (5-10 times over regular covers).

SLEEVE COVERS
Proper sleeve covers are made of jute fabric or jute strands, braided covers are preferable.
For beginning dogs a burlap sack can be fastened over a used regular sleeve cover.

Burlap covers are less durable, they are appropriate for young and beginning dogs only. Domestic burlap covers stuffed with (medical) absorbent cotton are impressive for police dog demonstrations but useless as training tools.

Jute covers should be "broken-in" by experienced dogs to become readily accepted by beginners. Many clubs prefer to use a "broken-in" jute cover for a trial.

Braided (rope) covers allow the dogs to get their teeth readily into it yet the material gives and does not cause any discomfort. Beginning dogs as well as advanced ones like the feel of it. Braided covers are the most durable ones and the best buy for the money.

Composite covers where nylon is braided in with jute are very durable. They have no place in training except for very hard biters, and then only when the dog owner is willing to risk gum/tooth injuries to his dog. One has to give, either the cover or the dog.

HIDDEN SLEEVE
Hidden (or civilian) sleeves have a rigid leather forearm and a flexible leather joint and upper arm. The sleeve should be worn under loose fitting civilian clothes, to TEST and not to train a dog.

OVERALL
Overalls should be made of leather, double layered and quilted. They should be flexible and have high square front and back bibs.

Square bibs provide protection to vital parts of the body. Double-layered, padded and quilted overalls give better protection against the "unclean" dog. Custom-made thin "protective" pants are comfortable to wear and to move in, yet they offer little protection. Knee joints should be flexible (special sewing/quilting arrangement), zippered legs make changing easier.

Pants without bib or those with a V-shaped bib and/or open sides should be combined with a separate jacket. Pants and jacket can be bought separately at double the expense. We find this "suit" less comfortable to wear and not necessary for all but the most unusual training situations.

COLLAR
In some situations, a wide leather collar for the decoy might be advisable. It offers additional protection for the throat / neck area.

GROIN COVER
This is a leather shield of a preformed cup made from hard plastic or metal, protecting the genitals of male decoys. This cover is held in position by leather straps, fastened either around the hips, or to the leather pants. It is worn under the overall.

GLOVES
Heavy duty leather gloves (mittens are preferred over gloves) may be required for civil agitation, in the "guarding of an article" exercise, or for other special applications.

STICKS
Sticks should be selected so that they break before a decoy can do damage to a dog. We prefer bamboo sticks up to 3/8" in diameter about two feet long. They can be treated with a preservative to prevent rotting when left outside. Reed sticks can be used too.

WHIP
Some European companies manufacture whips for dog training. They consist of several thin reed sticks in a leather sheath. While this whip looks and sounds fearsome, it is much gentler than a bamboo stick on the dog when used properly, and with the same force.
Horse whips, however, are unsuitable, especially the longer variety, with or without the streamers.

MUZZLE
Good muzzles are made from leather and have a tightly criss-crossed basket with a leather covered steel band in the frontal position (for advanced, civil agitation).
Wire-cage muzzles, plastic muzzles and wide-mesh leather muzzles can not prevent an excited dog from biting. In addition, they are likely to cause injuries to dog and decoy.

SPRING CHAIN
We suggest a metal chain with integral spring of proper tension. This is a safeguard against having a loose dog in case of spring failure.
Steel cable arrangements either have no spring or a coil spring which is subject to breakage under stress.
Leather, rubber, web or plastic tie-outs are unsuitable since they can break or be chewed.

4. SUPPLIERS

It is generally recognized that the best protective gear and dog training equipment comes from Germany.
A few American companies have entered the market, principally trying to duplicate German models. Yet even the one American company that for many years held a monopoly on domestic protective equipment has now switched to importing protective equipment from Germany.

On his rounds, the mailman enters this office which is totally deserted, except for a big dog emptying wastebaskets.

The dog noticing his bewildered look says "Well, I can't believe it either, but this is part of my job."

"By golly, and you even can talk. I have to tell your boss what an intelligent worker he has in you!"

"Please don't. If he finds that out, the bum will make me answer the phones too."

V. THE COMPONENTS

A. GENERAL TRAINING

Successful dog training requires a structured, systematic approach. It should, however, not be carried to the extreme where an inflexible, ritualized training routine creates programmable robots. This would not only take away the fun - from both dog and handler - it would also result in a "fully trained animal" which fails to react properly in non-standard situations.

Such failures can be avoided if sufficient emphasis is placed in training on

> Agility
> Versatility
> Variety.

1. AGILITY

Agility training should be done with a great deal of enthusiasm since it is and should be a very enjoyable part of training for dog and handler. As a side benefit, it gives the handler a chance to show off his dog in public.

A regular obstacle course would be the ideal training place, and it might feature:

> hurdles, brush hurdles, walls
> fences
> window jumps
> barrel jumps
> broad jumps
> water ditches
> ladders
> stairs
> ramps / slides
> tunnels
> car tires
> planks
> logs
> unusual footing, etc.

If an obstacle course is not available, the individual elements can often be found at home, in parks, at play grounds etc.

Trick training also belongs into this category.
Sitting on a chair, rolling over, fetching the car keys from the ignition, taking a message to another family member, carrying a large shovel, carrying a fruit basket, opening a door with European-type door handles, etc. are different, and useful, tasks a dog can be taught fairly easily.

2. VERSATILITY

- Do you occasionally terminate a regulation recall by skipping the finish?
- Do you track in pouring rain, sometimes?
- Do you do protection work at night, once in a while?

Versatility is of great importance in training an animal to be useful. It will prepare
* the service dog to pursue the fleeing criminal rather than being distracted by bystanders,
* the sheep dog to tend his flock next to a heavily travelled road,
* the bomb detection dog to concentrate on finding the explosive in a confusing environment,
* the guide dog to safely steer his owner rather than pursuing his own interests,
* the companion dog to respond to his owner's call rather than running off,
* the "natural protector" to defend his master rather than hiding behind him.
All these are examples where dogs would not perform well if they had not been trained with sufficiently varied distractions.

It requires some ingenuity, and some courage too, to correct the situation.
It is not to everybody's liking, for instance,
- to do a long sit in a crowded shopping mall,
- to stage a courage test at a family reunion,
- to practice the recall near a school yard during morning break,
- to try the retrieve near the bus station,
- to enlist the help of several cats (and their owners) for a training session,
- to hire a friend for a staged burglary at the dog owners home (notify the neighbors beforehand !!),
- or even to track in pouring rain.
The more distractions the handler can think of, the more reliable the dog will become eventually.

Deviating from the training routine will initially confuse the dog. The handler must be patient and persistent to overcome such problems. Soon, however, the dog will become more confident, more proficient, and severe distractions can be introduced.

3. VARIETY

Confronting a dog with unusual, unexpected situations will serve to build his confidence and to stabilize his interactions with the world around him.

Reactions to the exercises described below will differ from dog to dog, and efforts must be made to tailor the situation to the mental make-up of the canine.
For soft (nervous, shy) dogs, the assistants should spread farther apart, their movements should be less sudden, the sounds they make should be more subdued.
The hard (bold, outgoing) dog does not require such a cautious approach. Although he may be startled at first, he will recover quickly, and he will be able to handle the situation without problems. The following description is given for such a type of dog.

Ideally, there are at least five handlers with their dogs, and at least ten assistants.

a) SUPER - GROUP

The handlers with their dogs form a line, side by side, leaving about five feet spaces between teams. They all move forward in the same direction, at the same time, while trying to maintain the line formation.

In the meantime, the assistants have formed the 'super group', wandering aimlessly around and keeping maybe ten feet spaces between themselves.

The dog/handler formation moves through the super group. Then they do an about turn and come back.

The super group now has crowded a little more, getting closer together. Again, the handlers and dogs walk through the group. This is repeated a few times, until the crowd is so dense that the assistants make almost physical contact with the dogs when they pass through.

The assistants must be instructed to watch out for the dogs and not to bump into them. The assistants do not have to get out of the way of a dog/handler team, but they may have to stop momentarily to make passing easier.

b) WHEEL

The handlers with their dogs walk in a large circle, counter clockwise. On command, they all make a left turn and move on imaginary spokes to the center of the wheel. When they are all very close together, the command "about turn" causes them to move out again, on the imaginary spokes of the wheel.

Another "about turn" brings them back to the center, and at the very last moment a "halt" is given. The dogs must sit, and the group forms a very tight circle this way. Another "forward, about turn, right turn" sequence brings all the dogs and handlers back into a circle.

c) CIRCLE

Forming a circle, facing the center, and having the teams separated by about six feet, the handlers now command their dogs to "down". With the dogs remaining in this position, the handlers turn left and step over their own dog. They continue stepping over every dog in the circle until everybody has returned to the starting point next to their own dog.

d) TRADE

The dog/handler teams form a circle as described above.

The training director (or an assistant without dog) approaches one team, inquires about name and special habits of the dog, and takes the lead. The now dog-less handler moves to the right, inquires about name and habits of that dog and takes the lead. This exchange continues until the last handler in the circle takes his charge from the assistant. Then all handlers heel their newly acquired canines in circle formation, using lots of praise and as little corrections as possible. The switching process can be repeated, or everybody can claim his own dog, on directions of the training director.

e) CHANNEL

The assistants form two lines about eight feet apart, facing each other. Each person has another one opposite him.

Dogs and handlers form a single file and walk through the channel.

With the last dog having passed through, the two lines of assistants move a little closer together. This is repeated a few times until in the last pass there is just enough room for the dog/handler team to walk through.

f) TUNNEL

Maintaining the formation from above, each pair of two assistants facing each other now grasp each others hands (right for left and left for right) and hold them up high. The group forms a tunnel this way.

After all dogs have passed through, the assistants may lower their hands, to "lower the ceiling". Again, dogs and handlers file through.

g) NOISES

Still maintaining the channel formation, all assistants clap their hands while the dogs and their handlers are moving through. This can be done loud for one pass, not so loud for another pass. As a modification, the assistants can say "boooo" instead of clapping hands, or they can make other sounds at their discretion.

h) OBSTACLES

The assistants still maintain the channel formation. One of them, however, goes flat on his tummy across the channel. The dogs and their handlers pass through, over the obstacle. For the next turn, one more volunteer goes down and so on, until it becomes difficult for dogs and handlers to negotiate the course.

i) CIRCLE

The assistants form a tight circle, leaving very little space (maybe 6 inches) between each others feet.

One dog is held by a volunteer on a slip leash, about 30 yards away. His owner is let inside the circle and stands in the middle of it. Then he calls his dog.

The volunteer releases the dog which now wants to get to his owner. Many dogs first try to find an opening in the human wall, then they will force their way through it. The assistants should not discourage the dog from going through, but they should not voluntarily create an opening either. All the while the owner is encouraging his dog to come to him.

k) FRIENDS

Once inside the circle, the owner praises and pets his dog and then stands upright again, not giving his dog any attention.

The assistants squat and keep their shoulders together, trying to prevent the dog from leaving. The dog should now be encouraged to investigate the circle and the people forming it. For that purpose, each assistant has a few tidbits in his hands or pockets. Once the dog comes to him he pets him and lets him have a treat.

l) STARTLING

With handler and dog (loose) in the circle, all assistants will squat suddenly, on command of the leader. With the next command they will stand up again, just as quickly. This is being repeated a few times until the dog has gained confidence.

m) CORNERING

In unison, all assistants move backwards, enlarging the diameter of the circle. On command they close in again. This can be repeated a few times.

Then the assistants clap their hands while opening and closing the circle, or they make other distracting noises.

n) CONCLUSION

In conclusion, the assistants form a circle again, standing upright, shoulder to shoulder. The handler leaves the circle. His dog remains behind and is prevented from following through the tight human wall the assistants are forming.

From a distance of about 30 yards the handler calls his dog which is now allowed to force his way through the barrier.

4. GAMES

Games are very important in dog training. They serve both the physical and the mental development of young and of mature dogs, and they provide you with a powerful motivator which you can use to reward your dog.

Running after a thrown ball (or a stick, a frisbee, etc.) is something every dog should be taught to enjoy. Play it with much enthusiasm, run with your dog after the ball, compete with him. Once he plays the game you just have to throw the ball, giving him much needed exercise without wearing you out. Sometimes you should seek out an area with hills. Throw the ball uphill, to increase the difficulty, and to stimulate development of your dogs front assembly.

Chasing a rolling object provides much fun also.
Ask your dog to bring the ball back to you. Practice in unfamiliar locations if he does not cooperate, and/or run away from him.

Many dogs enjoy searching for thrown objects in high grass or in underbrush. Use small potatoes or wild apples - if available. They can be abandoned if the dog is not successful. Throw them first small distances, farther away later on.

Short fun tracks can be a game too.
Hide something the dog really wants, at the end (see chapter on "Tracking"). Be enthusiastic about it, and do not turn it into a "job".

Games of pursuit are another favorite.
Run away with a flapping sack or a piece of cloth tied to a string or your leash. Encourage your dog to pursue the prey and to take hold of it. End with a happy tug of war.
Let a stranger carry the prey later on, move to unfamiliar locations, etc.

Groups of five or more strange dogs playing together is a rare sight in our society.
If you are the typical one-dog owner, you should seek out training classes and clubs that can provide such playful interaction between dogs. While on leash, the strangers will often be uneasy, or even hostile, toward each other, yet usually there is no need to be alarmed.
The group should gather in a small fenced-in area, maybe 50 by 50 feet, and release one dog. He will most likely say "hello" to everyone there. Then we clip the leash off the second dog, let him make the rounds, and after a while we release the third dog. This process continues until every dog is freed. We always wait until we see that the newcomer gets along with the others before we release the next one. Initial caution and apprehension will almost always change into curiosity and playfulness.
Do not be overly protective of your dog, and do not be too concerned when they roughhouse. Be prepared, however, to step in when a dog gets out of control or when open hostility breaks out (fortunately, this is very rare). If it does, then quick interference is called for. A well-aimed whack with the leash for the aggressor by whoever is closest (preferably by the training director who should have anticipated the occurrence and positioned himself properly) usually takes care of the initial problem. The owner of the troublemaker then puts his dog on leash and watches him very carefully. Any further aggression calls for a quick and not-to-gentle correction by the owner. After a few sessions the dog will probably have gotten the message that it is more fun to run around with the others than to be bossy.

Chase and play-fighting between canines help to build their muscles and to develop their fighting strategies. At the same time, a dog learns to submit to the stronger one, and to fairly deal with the submission of a weaker partner.

Play-fights with humans should also be part of a dogs early training.
At first, carefully grasp, and immediately release, the dog by his scruff (do not intimidate him). He probably will seize your arm and hold it in his mouth in a play-like fashion. If he bites too hard, act as if you were badly hurt. Exaggerate, release an outcry of pain, he will be gentler from then on. In time, you can play a little rougher. Also, others in the family, or another club member, can take your role.
Most dogs will play this game with much enthusiasm, others first have to overcome some inhibitions. Exercise some restraint, however, if the dog develops a passion for it.

Another important game involves the dog as a watch dog. Let the puppy have a nice juicy bone. Stand right next to him to give him moral support. Then get another person (but not the owner or a family member) to approach him and to act as if he wants to steal the bone. As soon as the dog starts to growl the game is over, the dog has won and receives praise.

If the dog does not react, the bone should be taken away from him. Repeat after a couple of days or weeks. In time, even a young, shy or insecure dog will learn to defend his possessions. The objective of the game is to teach the dog that his warning (growl) will be respected.

By the way, dogs like to play this game among themselves with objects that are often completely uninteresting, to them.

(We should mention here, that the owner must always be able to approach the dog during feeding time and to take the food away. Sharp corrections should be given if the dog resists.)

Use these games to establish a closer relationship with your dog, to help him to become more self-confident, and to reward him for a job well done.

5. GUN SHYNESS
(see also Temperament Testing)

Most gun shy dogs are man-made.

In preparation for a trial, a novice trainer might, for instance, have over-exposed his dog to the banging noise, by firing too often, too loud, or too close to the dog.
Don't do it!

Children or adults might have teased, upset or even harmed a confined dog, in connection with firing a toy pistol, a pellet gun or a real fire arm.
Restrict access of nasty people to your dog.

A dog might have been harmed or injured by a gun fired at close range.
Prevent further incidents by taking precautions - provide sound barriers, confine the dog to "safe" areas etc.

A higher ranking pack member (mother dog, other dog in the household) might have transmitted his fear of noise to the other pack members.
Separate the gun shy dog from the rest of your dog family, at least during times of noisy activities.

Finally, a startled handler might have subconsciously transmitted his uneasiness or fear to his dog when a gun was fired unexpectedly during training.
Inform handlers of planned gun shots in advance.

All these examples have in common that in the dog's mind undesirable associations have been formed between the gun shots and another unpleasant experience. To correct the problem, these earlier, undesirable associations must be replaced with new, desirable ones. The process requires understanding, time, patience. To repeatedly discharge a gun close to the dog is as harmful in this process as avoiding loud noises al together in the hope that the dog will have "forgotten" by the time the next trial comes around.

Other suggestions, aside from the ones given above, are to never expose the dog to loud noises while he is left to himself.

In training, his handler should be close by when a gun is discharged, and the dog's mind should be occupied with something else, something pleasant. Playing ball or tug-of-war, retrieving, jumping, heeling with lots of handler enthusiasm and praise (for the exercise, not for enduring the noise) will serve to push the gun shots in the background.

Another important point to remember is that the gun should be fired far away from the dog, for several weeks, maybe for months, until the dog pays no attention to the gun shots anymore. Only then can this "background noise" be spiced with an isolated shot at closer distances, once in a while.

It helps to have several guns and several people available. The shooters should be instructed to discharge the firearm without any commotion behind their back, into the ground (always using blanks, of course).

Some handlers have successfully used cassette tapes with prerecorded noises. Gun shots, fire crackers or noises recorded in the kitchen, in a shop, in a factory, at an airport, bus station, street corner etc. are played at a low volume setting for several months, later on at a somewhat increased loudness. Conditioning puppies to such noises is especially helpful.

We suggest to play a 30 minute tape twice daily, not always at the same time of the day, but always when the handler and/or other members of the family are around.

It is foolish to assume that gun shyness can be prevented or cured by repeatedly firing a gun close by whenever the dog is fed. This is over-kill, don't do it. Dogs have a very fine sense of hearing, and loud noises are painful to them. After a time of suffering the dog will have had enough and he probably will become really gun shy.

"Your dog does not have a nose? How does he smell?"

"Terrible! "

B. TRACKING

1. BASIC PHILOSOPHY

Humans rely on their eyes when investigating unfamiliar surroundings, dogs use their nose.
Nose work is the domain of dogs.

The objective in training a dog to track is not to teach him to use his nose, but to tell him what odorous trail we want him to follow.

All dogs can track, although some do it better than others. The trainer just has to channel their talents in the right direction.

An adult German Shepherd Dog has an estimated 500 million of olfactory sensory cells occupying an area of about 26 square inches, compared to about 10 million and 1/2 square inch in a human. Experiments have shown that dogs can detect the presence of butyric acid (a component of sweat) diluted at a ratio of 1 gram to 1 1/2 million cubic yards of air, an amount too small to be registered by the most sensitive gas chromatograph, a highly sophisticated analytical instrument.

Olfactory acuity, then, is directly related to the quantity (and the quality) of the detection equipment. A long-nosed dog, like a German Shepherd, generally can handle a tracking job with much less effort than, for instance, a Boxer with his short nose and fewer olfactory sensory cells. There are many examples of Boxers who track extremely well. Yet observing them and an average German Shepherd, one can easily tell who has to put forth more effort to finish the track.

Teaching a dog to track is rather difficult since the handler is left in the dark, so to speak. He can not see or smell where the odor is, he has to rely on indirect means to control the performance of his dog. Very serious training problems will occur if the dog is working properly on the track but gets corrected by mistake, or if he gets praised at the wrong time.

Furthermore, the dog can not be forced to track. Too much pressure from the handler, or too harsh a correction have ended the tracking career of many a promising dog.
Yet, there are also those dogs that lead their handlers by the nose, literally. If the dog refuses to work (excluding justifiable reasons) or if he is taking advantage of the handler, then a properly timed and well balanced correction from an experienced trainer is quite in order.

A ten week old puppy can negotiate a mini-Schutzhund I track without problems if he was started and trained the right way.
An older dog requires more effort, more teaching, more skill
of the trainer, to accomplish the same, especially if he, in the past, has been discouraged from sniffing the ground.
In any way, start simple and pick the best conditions you can find: flat terrain without bushes, trees, buildings, ankle-high grass, little wind, track laid into the wind, track well scented, lots of rewards and lots of praise. Proceed from here to more difficult conditions by changing one variable at a time. Let the dog become confident and proficient with the new variation, then move on to the next step.

In all instances, however, motivation is the key to a good tracking performance. For best results it should be linked to one (or more) of the three basic instincts, in the order listed here: the survival instinct (food reward), the retrieve instinct (play reward) and the pack instinct (scent of handler or another dog on the track, handler at the end of track).
Using the protective instinct (a bite as reward) is counter-productive for nearly all dogs (see the section Training Theory: Arousal).

2. OBJECTIVE

The dog must retrace the path of a tracklayer, involving various track ages up to three hours, various ground covers, various weather conditions, various distractions, and he must find several well-scented articles "lost" by the tracklayer.

3. SUGGESTED COMMAND: "Find it"
SUGGESTED RELEASE COMMAND: "OK"

4. GENERAL

SCENT
A "track" is a semi-continuous ground disturbance, caused by animals, humans, or things (e.g. cars). In finding the track, the dog is guided by vapors, or "scent" as we call it, which can originate from four different sources:
1. ground scent (ground disturbance, release of entrapped gases, crushed vegetation, etc.)
2. body odor (sweat, shedded skin cells)
3. deposits (personal belongings, clothing)
4. contaminants (rubbed-off particles from shoes, spills of oil, blood, urine, feces etc.)

Of these, the ground scent is of the greatest importance (>95%). Body odor is highly volatile and will disappear, for all practical purposes, before the dog goes on the track. Shedded skin cells are too few to be of any consequence. Air currents as well as Brown's molecular movement dilute and distribute the body odor and the odor from the decaying skin rafts so fast that normally all identifiable traces have disappeared after about twenty minutes. Except for articles or contaminants left behind, there is nothing that could replenish or regenerate the body odor once the tracklayer has left.

This, however, does not hold true for the ground scent. The initial foot step of the tracklayer is only the beginning of a long series of continuing processes, generating more and more scent and reaching a maximum after about 20 minutes (because of this "hump", a SchH I track is started at that time in a trial).

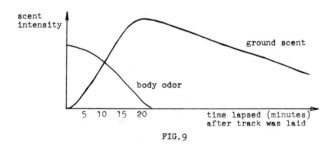

FIG. 9

There is a slow liberation of gases that were entrapped in the ground or that were generated by the crushing and the decay of vegetation, bacterial action etc. It generates little invisible "clouds" which - under equilibrium conditions - hover just above the ground. The "clouds" from several footsteps delineate a corridor (the track) which a dog is able to recognize and to follow long after any body odor has disappeared, up to maybe a couple of days under ideal conditions (European service dogs are working 48 hour old tracks for distances over 10 miles).

This theory has been proven experimentally. Dogs would, for instance, readily follow a trail made by a machine with porcelain feet (Most's wheel, weighs about 150 lbs.), dogs would quit the track at the point where the tracklayer was lifted off the ground by a cable system and hauled away without touching the ground, dogs would at intersections with a second track readily switch to the other trail laid by a second tracklayer of the same weight and at the same time, and so on.
These findings indicate (and millions of dogs substantiate the fact) that a dog can be trained on his owner's track, even in advanced tracking, provided the track has aged more than twenty minutes. They also indicate that dogs do not need an article from the tracklayer to "take scent" in order to follow his trail - a widespread misconception.

TRACKER TYPES
Tracking is hard work for the dog, weight losses of several pounds have been recorded during advanced tracking tests.
The demands vary, however, depending on how the dog works.

The **FRINGE FOLLOWER** proceeds at the edge of the scent corridor, comparing presence and absence of tracking odors as his guide. This leads him often a considerable distance away from the track (sideways), especially with fresh tracks through lush vegetation. This requires a lot of additional physical activity. It is undesirable tracking behavior and it should be discouraged.

The **STEP TRACKER** seeks out every individual footprint, sniffs it out, and analyses the odor emanating from it. This is hard labor, and very tiring.
The dog could be considered to be a perfectionist.

The **LINE TRACKER** proceeds at a reasonable speed on the track, inhaling and exhaling normally. Since he advances while exhaling (when he can't sniff) he is more likely to overshoot an article or a turn, yet he is less tired, and therefore more alert than the step tracker, allowing him to recognize his mistake in time. While his counterpart would "die" on a long track, he can go on and finish the job.
He could be considered to be an effective 'energy saver'.

METEOROLOGICAL FACTORS

Canines don't mind tracking in rain, handlers usually do. The true working dog can not wait for nice weather while on duty, and neither can a competitor in a trial. So one might as well get ready for the inevitable.

It is helpful to understand the various meteorological conditions and their influence on the scent "clouds" comprising the ground scent. The rise and fall of these "clouds", their lateral movement, their compression and expansion is a result of various weather conditions, and it has a decided influence on the dog's tracking performance.

Fog
Fog provides favorable tracking conditions because of high moisture environment. It discourages tracking by sight and limits visual distractions. Orientation is difficult for tracklayer and handler. The teaching aspect, therefore, is reduced to a minimum, the dog is more or less in control.

Dew
Dew on the ground is associated with a situation similar to the one described above, the orientation problems, however, do not exist.
This condition is advantageous for beginning dogs and handlers. Since the track is often visible, fewer chances exist to correct the dog wrongly. It also gives the handler the unique opportunity to analyze his dog's behavior when on and off the track, and it tells the handler how closely his dog is following the actual ground disturbance.

Rising sun will let the track scent rise slowly and intensify it, making the conditions for tracking even more favorable.

Rain
There is - in general - no need to refuse going on the track while it is raining.
> Light rain after a dry spell will actually improve tracking conditions. Light rain onto already wet ground will do little to change the scent pattern, for the better or for the worse.
> Medium rain will "dilute" the guiding odor, and a heavy downpour will wash it away and make tracking quite difficult.
> If a heavy rain stops within a short time after the track was laid, tracking can proceed successfully. If the track is laid after a heavy rain, tracking - in general - poses no serious problem (dogs can follow a track even through a shallow body of standing water).

Snow
Lingering odor in the refrigerator is a favorite subject of TV commercials. During the winter months, nature provides us with a giant ice box and - like in the small one at home - scents are extremely well preserved.
One could probably not ask for more ideal tracking conditions than cold weather, a little sunshine and one to two inches of snow on the field.
Tracking in snow is actually made so easy that advanced dogs can be spoiled for work under normal conditions. The visible trail is only partly responsible for that fact.

Frost
Frost without snow and bare, packed ground create very difficult tracking conditions. Plowed fields or sufficient vegetation, even if dead or dormant, are needed to make tracking tolerable. While any scent is preserved rather well, biological decay processes are at a near standstill with such low temperatures.

Dryness
The olfactory process needs a solvent to function, the dog's nasal tissue must be moist. Experienced handlers water their dogs and wet their dogs' noses before starting on a track. For the same purpose they take some water along on the trail.

In a dry tracking area the dog will be faced with scarce or dried out vegetation which is incapable of producing a generous amount of scent by the biological decay process. Tracking is difficult but not impossible. It just requires additional effort by the dogs and by the handlers.
Dogs trained in such an area and then brought to a tracking test in more northern regions usually score very high. The opposite, unfortunately, is true also: dogs from northern regions competing in the southern states often do poorly without extensive retraining.

Extended Sunshine / High Atmospheric Pressure
The scent-producing biological decay processes are accelerated at higher temperatures. On a sunny day, therefore, more scent is generated more rapidly. The scent "reservoir", however, depletes more rapidly also.
A beginning dog can benefit from this situation. Because of the more generous supply of scent he should do well on a sunny day when allowed to work shortly after the track was laid (10 to 20 min.).

An experienced dog, on the other hand, might not perform well in the same situation. The abundance of scent will very likely cause him to track with high nose, or to follow the fringe of the scent path.
The situation changes as time passes by:
An aged track under the same conditions is much more difficult to work (see "depletion", above). This has an impact on dogs entered in advanced tracking tests (FH, TDX). For training purposes, however, clever handlers use this phenomenon, to correct dogs that track with high noses. When these dogs are presented with a "sunny" track maybe 3-4 hours old, they will have to change their habit very rapidly - or they won't go any place, literally speaking.

Morning Hours

During early morning hours the air is usually much colder than the ground, and this condition is associated with a high moisture content (dew). At that time the tracking scent lingers in a very thin layer just above the ground. This provides the dog with a constant, reliable guide to follow. The intensity of the odor and its dissipation will increase as the air starts to warm up.

Noon Hour

At high noon, with sunshine, the ground can accumulate considerable heat. Convection currents then spread the tracking scent widely, mostly upwards if there is no wind.

Air and vegetation are often dried out, and the heat interferes with the physical activities of the dog. In the wild, the animals would normally rest under these conditions. The higher temperature does, however, accelerate the biological decay processes which produce the scent. Tracking, therefore, is not made impossible at that time of the day, it is just made more difficult.

Evening Hours

In the early evening hours, a fairly even temperature balance between the ground and the lower layers of air will generate stable tracking conditions. Everything else being the same, more scent is generated than in the morning. The scent, however, is not concentrated as much in the very low layers above the ground. This may cause the dog to track with high nose, or to air-scent.

Nighttime

Noticeable increases in tracking performance and reliability are possible during darkness. This is not surprising since the loss of one sense (sight) sharpens the others (nose ability). A problem arises, however, since the handler is very limited in his guiding or assisting the dog, and he can do little to control or even monitor his dog's actions.
For service dogs, special harnesses have been designed that are fitted with a low-current light on the dog's back. This does not serve to shine on the dog's path, it just lets the handler know where his partner is.
Blindfolding the dog is a trick to create night for the dog yet leave daylight for his handler. Just like a dog can be conditioned to wear a muzzle before it is needed, he can be conditioned to wear a blindfold.
Some trainers have reported better tracking results with this method. They also like being able to use flags alongside the track to indicate its direction. One wonders, though, if a sportsman can really justify such a drastic measure as depriving the dog of one of his senses. If this method finds acceptance, the logical extensions would be devastating.

Wind

High winds make tracking difficult, they can even make it impossible under adverse conditions, like scarce vegetation or old tracks.
Moderate to light wind will shift the scent clouds and cause specific responses from the tracking dog.

A dog at the beginning of the track and facing in the track direction can encounter three conditions, basically:

a) frontal wind

The wind comes from straight ahead, picking up the scent "clouds" and blowing them right into the dog's face.
Since more scent is generated all the time (see above), this odor stream is continuous.
Also, the total scent carried by the wind is stronger than the scent developing at the individual footprint just in front of the dog. Therefore dogs have a tendency to lift their head while tracking into the wind (air scenting).
The first few tracks for a beginning dog should always be laid into the wind. The scent cone loaded with track odors

FIG.10

will help to get the idea across what tracking is all about. An experienced dog, however, may be turned off by this heavy scent, or he may get into the habit of air scenting. As a corrective measure we can let the track age longer, we can use ground with scarce vegetation, we can use a light-weight tracklayer, we can ask the tracklayer to take large steps or we can take advantage of atmospheric conditions which have been discussed above.

b) back wind

The wind blows in the direction of the track and carries the scent "clouds" away from the dog.The dog must put his nose down to the footprint, to catch the freshly generated scent before it gets blown away.This condition is ideal for teaching a dog to keep the nose on the ground. The dog must, however, already be familiar with the tracking concept.

c) side wind

The wind blows at an angle to the track, from the left or from the right.
The guiding scent path will be on the downwind side of the track and most dogs will follow the trail in this fashion. The dog's path, then, is parallel to the track, slightly to the left in the above example. The distance between the path of the tracklayer and that of the dog will be dependent on wind velocity, track age, kind of vegetation, presence of windbreaks (shrubs, trees, other obstacles) etc.
During the teaching phase, the dog should be encouraged to stay on the track, to prevent him from becoming a "fringe follower".

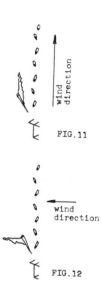

FIG. 11

FIG. 12

In a trial, a side shift of the dog up to two feet is usually not faulted, depending on the weather and ground conditions, and on the experience of the judge.

Since the wind direction is a factor that can be taken into account more easily than others we would like to re-emphasize the following points:
- Consider the wind when laying a track.
- Go into the wind when teaching a novice dog.
- Go with the wind in order to force a knowledgeable dog to keep his nose on the ground.
- Use sidewind to train a dog to stay on the track.
- Try to keep a distance of at least 150 ft between adjoining tracks.

THE TRACKLAYER

The tracklayer and his technique have a significant effect on how well the dog performs on the track. In a trial, he can help the dog to pass a tracking test, or he can make him fail. Tracklayers should be selected carefully, and they should be trained thoroughly.
- The intensity of the "scent path" is directly related to the weight of the tracklayer who causes the ground disturbance. A heavy person will be helpful for the beginning dog, a light person will sharpen the skills of the advanced dog.
    In a trial, an average-weight person is called for. For a cross-track, however, a light-weight person should be chosen, to make the difference more noticeable to the dog.

- Proper footwear, preferably water-proof boots, should be used so that the tracklayer does not have to take detours around wet and rough spots. Leather boots are recommended by some instructors. Under regular tracking conditions, however, their advantage (inherent odor) over rubber boots is either non-existent or negligible.
- Although all kinds of objects can be located by the tracking dog, leather articles of neutral color and about the size of a wallet are preferable. Several hours before the tracklayer goes to work he should place them in an inner pocket of his clothing, to allow them to become scented properly. For a trial, 30 minutes is the recommended time; advanced dogs can be tested with shorter conditioning periods, still.
- Before going on the track, the tracklayer should be given a sketch of the proposed trail. Start, turns, article drops, crosstracks and end are indicated on it. In advanced tracking it is a good idea to take along a few flags for marking the intersections of the crosstrack. This will guide the second tracklayer who removes these flags in passing. Portable radios or walkie-talkies greatly aid in the communication between tracklayer and instructor/judge.
- At the starting place, the tracklayer stomps down a cone-shaped area of about 1 square yard for about 30 to 60 seconds. He then remains there for another minute or so before leaving in the indicated direction.

FIG. 13   STARTING A TRACK

- For the first six to eight feet, short steps and heavy impressions, maybe even triple-laying (going forward, coming back on the same line, going forward again) are recommended. After that, the track should be walked at a normal pace. Large strides before, and short steps after a turn are recommended also. Angles should be rounded very slightly.
- When an article is dropped, it should not just be tossed to the ground. The tracklayer should instead bend down in his knees and place the article right behind the heel of the foot moved last, without much hesitation or breaking his stride. Some handlers prefer to drop the article in front of them and to step on it.
- Under windy conditions, a weight might have to be secured to the article, to prevent it from being blown away. There are also known instances of squirrels and birds having stolen the article.
- At the end of the trail the tracklayer may want to leave the area with a few leaps, to clearly indicate to the dog that the job is finished.

ORIENTATION IN TRACKING

When teaching a dog to track it is absolutely necessary to know EXACTLY where the track is.
Artificial markers like flags, poles, discs may cause the smart dog to hunt by sight. Likewise, tracks laid alongside natural boundaries, furrows, mower lines etc. will teach the dog to use his eyes rather than his nose.
A well laid track is, therefore, more difficult to trace for the tracklayer and for the handler, and both have to learn to properly orient themselves in the field.

TOP WORKING DOGS

The following exercise demonstrates this point very well:
Novice handlers (without their dogs) are sent about 25 paces straight ahead and then into a right or left turn. After a few more paces they are asked to place a match on the ground. Then they are called back.

A few minutes after their return they are sent to retrieve the match, of course without the assistance of their dogs. The rate of success is usually very small even when the exercise and its objective were explained beforehand. People count their paces, scrutinize the vegetation and try to memorize details, stomp the feet in the ground etc., without success. Maybe dropping a fifty dollar bill instead of the match would bring better results!

The only way to approach this exercise - and to lay and to find a track - is to walk a straight line toward a distinct object in the distance, one that preferentially lines up with another permanent marker (don't pick a parked car, they have a tendency to disappear).
To walk a straight line without orienting oneself on such a marker is impossible, and it is very difficult to do it without having the second marker. A friend standing behind the tracklayer, and in line with him, will confirm that quickly.
However, if the tracklayer keeps one marker superimposed over another one in the distance (just like a rifle sight), then there is only one straight line that he can go.
In the sketch, the tracklayer would move right and left until he can find a suitable line-up, here the telephone pole and the corner of the house. This is the spot where he puts his starting flag into the ground.
When moving out, the tracklayer will keep his eye fixed on the telephone pole. He will be all right as long as the pole and the corner of the house line up.

Only once in a while, and then only very quickly, does he glance at the ground in front of him, to make sure it is safe and suitable for a track.
If he would take his sight off the marker for more than a very brief moment, a substantial deviation from the straight-line course would occur, forcing him to make a correction and causing a wavy track pattern.

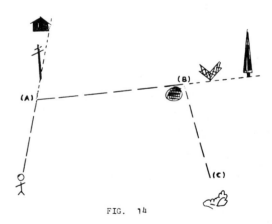

FIG. 14

In the vicinity of the intended turn the tracklayer will be on the lookout for two other objects that can be lined up. When he reaches point A where the fence corner superimposes the distant tree, he will make his turn and proceed toward point B.

There he can not find another suitable line-up. So he makes his turn at point B around a spot of dry grass (or a unique flower, or a fallen tree branch, or another natural, untouched marker) and proceeds toward a group of bushes at C.

Later on, when the dog works on the track, the handler knows exactly, to the inch, when the dog is on or off the track. He can influence and guide or praise his dog according to performance.

USE OF EQUIPMENT

Training problems are sometimes related to the use of unsuitable equipment, or even to the improper use of good equipment. An entangled leash is one example, articles blown away by the wind is another one.

Many trainers prefer to use a harness. They feel that it will prepare the dog for the upcoming job and that it will allow the dog to perform better in the field. Other trainers are concerned about dependence on excessive equipment, and they maintain that tracking with the leash attached to the dead ring on the choke collar is actually beneficial.

As long as there is no correction (jerk) given with the leash, either method is acceptable.

In any event, we suggest that the dog be tracked on lead. Free tracking (off lead) forgoes a vital communication link, the leash. It is permissible, even in a trial, but it invites problems. Without a restraint, dogs will often track too fast and superficial, overshooting turns and missing articles. In addition, control over the dog is difficult to maintain if he decides that chasing or hunting is more fun than tracking.

During practice sessions, 90% of all tracks should be done on the six foot lead. The 30 foot regulation leash should be used very sparingly in training, mainly in preparation for a trial.

Working properly with the long line requires some practice. The following conditions should be met:
- The line must be of suitable, user-friendly material.
- The line must be free of tangles. Gather up the line in your hand in wide loops (like sailors and cowboys do), or wind it on a rack (like a clothes line), or gather it in a large coffee can (like a long wick in an oil lamp). Stretch out the line close to the starting flag, prior to the beginning of tracking.
- The line must be handled delicately on start-ups.
     Since the handler is required to remain at the starting place until all 30 ft. of the leash are reeled out, a smooth transition from feeding the line to following the dog is of great importance. Most handlers are not properly prepared when the dog reaches the end of the line. The resulting jolt (snap) is unintended, nevertheless it causes the dog to interrupt tracking and to check back with his handler.
     To allow for a smooth transition from feeding the line to following the dog
     -tie a knot in the line five feet ahead of the end,
     -keep your hands far apart and let the line run through them,
      straightening out any tangles with the "first" hand,
     -hold arms close to the body and stretch them out when the knot comes up,
     -have one foot in front and step right out when the knot comes up.
- Hold your end of the line high, maybe at eye level or higher.
- The line must be taut while the dog is tracking.
     The tension should be such that if a handkerchief were fastened to the middle of the 30 ft. leash, it would be just short of touching the ground.
- Come to an immediate stop and reclaim the line with both hands as soon as the dog backs up, circles, etc. The gathered-up loops of line will pile on the ground naturally and reel out without problems once the dog gets going again.
- Cut the corner once your dog has negotiated a turn, to maintain proper line tension.
- Speedily advance to any obstacle that has caught the line.
     While one hand holds that part of the line that goes to the dog unobstructed, the other hand tries to free the line as quickly as possible, hopefully without letting the dog feel any restrictions or jolts from the rescue operation.
- Let go of the leash if the dog negotiates an obstacle that   is too difficult to handle for humans (hole in fence or thicket, a narrow passage way, a creek etc.). Go around the obstacle as fast as possible so that you can pick up the dragging leash at the other side.

Proper line handling can be learned in practice sessions, with the trainers taking turns in playing dog or handler. For the most benefit, participants should describe their sensations, actions and reactions to the person at the other end of the leash, and to the rest of the class.

5. TEACHING PROCEDURE

MOTIVATION
In tracking, the handler has to rely on the dog's willingness to work. And the more fun it is for the dog to track, the more willing will he be to do it.
Depending on the type of dog, one unpleasant experience may well spoil the effort of many training sessions. It is therefore essential that the handler maintains a pleasant attitude and that he avoids active punishment (harsh scolding, physical punishment etc.), if possible at all.
If corrections have to be given they should preferably be of a passive nature, like restraint.
In a situation where a dog wants to run after a rabbit, there is a significant difference between yanking the dog back with a "no, bad boy" - and quietly holding on to the end of the leash until the dog has calmed down, followed after a while with an excited "let's track".
The first approach may bring the dog back to the track, not because he wants to track, but because he has to.
The second approach maintains the happy attitude that should be connected with tracking, and once the distraction has disappeared the dog actually enjoys tracking again.
There are a few exceptions to this rule. They apply mostly to advanced dogs who want to take advantage of their handlers. In these situations a proper correction from an experienced trainer is in order.

Three universally accepted forms of reward are: praise, play, food. Each one of these motivators becomes more effective when the dog has been (partially) deprived of the basic need to which it relates.
If you decide to use the first two motivators, you should pay very little attention to your dog for a day or two: not playing with him, not throwing the ball or stick for him, not taking him for a walk, a ride or a swim. Some handlers even board their (mature) dog at a kennel for a few days before going into an important trial. After that time, however, when the dog performs well on the first training day, his favored toy (ball) etc. must be ready and waiting for him. Generous praise after each successful exercise and playing HIS game will be the reward (motivator) he has been craving for.

In teaching the dog to track by this method, the dog would be allowed to watch you going out and hiding a favored toy. Although less desirable since less effective, you or your dog's playmate can hide at the end of the track as the attraction (instead of the toy).

Using food as an incentive is probably the most effective way to teach a dog to track.
Puppies should be worked on a track just before feeding time, and they should be fed at the end of the track.
For older dogs we suggest to cut the dogs ration down to 50% for two days and not to feed him at all the third day. Training with food reward starts on the forth day. (Don't be afraid that you will harm your dog. In nature, wild dogs and wolves don't live on a strict feeding schedule either.)

TRACK BAITING
There are two requirements that have to be met when using food as the motivator in tracking:
1. the dog must be REALLY hungry
2. the food must be something the dog REALLY craves.

Both points require some work on your part: you must study your dog and find the right procedure. You must, for instance, find out what kind of food the dog likes best: raw hamburger, sausage, broiled liver, fried chicken, meat, fish, etc. Regular dog food certainly would be a poor choice for baiting, although establishing the habit of feeding the dog his daily meal at the end of the track will be quite helpful, too.

If food does not seem to work, the pupil was either not hungry enough, or the wrong bait was used.

Frequent food drops on the track, with the major portion of the bait at the end, will catch the dog's interest.

A piece of meat rubbed on the ground, in intervals, serves the same purpose. Some trainers successfully drag the bait (fresh meat, rotten meat, rotten fish etc.) on a string behind them, some dab the bait on the ground in intervals. Others use canned cat food, meat powder, or broth of meat, chicken, fish or shrimp, to sprinkle on the track.

Some trainers scent their shoes with urine (urine from a bitch in season is very effective with male dogs).

Some trainers use a length of pipe with a spongy plug at the lower end and fill it with urine from a (healthy) dog. Dabbing the sponge end on the ground once in a while gets most dogs (and bitches) interested in the track. (One trainer used a plastic fire plug on a large plate, to collect the urine from his male dog.)

In general, these latter training methods are combined with a food drop at the end of the track, and they are used mostly when problems occur: loss of interest, turns, cross tracks, dead spaces, etc.

TRACK TYPES

The physical lay-out of tracks contains, conventionally, the following shapes:

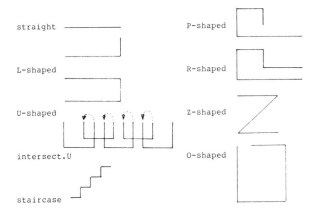

PUPPY TRAINING

The earlier a dog is introduced to tracking the easier it is to make a good tracker out of him.
Right after birth a pup will use his nose to find his way to warmth and food (his mother) since he can neither hear nor see at that time. Quite naturally, this skill is further developed, and at five to six weeks one can already take advantage of it by letting the puppy do his first track outdoors.
We need: a) one hungry puppy
         b) the puppy's mother able to nurse him
         c) two people familiar to the puppy
         d) a grass-covered area with a sudden slope, ditch, bushes, or other hiding place.

TOP WORKING DOGS

The first person holds the puppy at a spot about five to ten paces away from the selected hiding spot. He talks encouragingly to the puppy.

The second person, preferably the owner, holds the bitch by the collar and leads her away from the puppy. While moving in a straight line to the hiding spot, dog and handler create a path by purposely trampling down a lot of vegetation. Then they go into hiding - it does not have to be perfect.

All this time the puppy has been watching. Now he is released, encouraged and praised by his original captor, to move forward toward the hiding place. Upon arrival, the puppy is given a "grand reception", lots of praise from the owner, love and food from his mother.

In this exercise the puppy is not doing a real tracking job. He probably goes more by memory and sight than by scent. His olfactory system, however, is being conditioned. In time, the "funny smell" of the disturbed vegetation will be recognized consciously as a guide to pleasurable, enjoyable experiences.

The exercise should not be repeated until the next day.

As a variation to this method you can
- have the bitch and the rest of the litter at the end of the track (the "tracking" pup wants to get back to his family)
- ask the puppy's most favorite person to hide (without the bitch)
- release TWO puppies at the same time (they will encourage each other, and compete with each other).

After practicing for about a week, the distances can be increased gradually. At 7 or 8 weeks of age, more conventional conditions can be used, like offering ground beef as the food reward at the end, baiting or bait-scenting the track, letting the track age a little longer, and introducing a slight arc, then an obtuse angle (the second leg should lead into the wind, initially).

Further training should proceed according to the guidelines given below, but at a slower pace.

TRAINING MATURE DOGS

To start mature dogs in tracking we suggest several alternatives as modifications to the above procedure:

Take the dog along when laying the first few tracks. This creates a mixed animal/human scent (in addition to the ground scent) which the dog might follow more willingly.

At the end of the track:
- place a FAVORED piece of food (liver, sausage etc.).
  This works for any hungry dog.
- the owner hides alone (provided a close relationship between dog and owner has been established). This works well for dogs that orient themselves to, and depend heavily on, their owner. The one-man dog.
- hide another family member to which the dog is attracted.
  This is suggested for the typical family dog.
- hide another dog to which the trainee is attracted, his playmate.
  This works well for dog-oriented pets.
- hide a favored toy, a ball for instance.
  This approach shows best results for dogs that love to retrieve and to play.

In general, older dogs take longer to adopt the new principles, but then they can advance to more difficult conditions at a faster rate than a puppy.

a) Beginner-level Training

The so called "Intensivmethode" is used extensively by German Service Dog agencies, lending itself nicely to the simultaneous training of several beginning dogs in tracking. It offers
- to the dog the chance to work on a variety of different scents generated by other dogs and humans
- to the dog handler the opportunity to use several tracks although he lays only one himself
- to the instructor the advantage to guide several dog/handler teams with a minimum of effort and time.

STEP 1: Prerequisites
The group secures a suitable tracking area.
The field must be large enough to space the tracks sufficiently apart.
For novice dogs the following conditions should be met:
- The ground cover should be well established. Lawn areas, meadows or farmers' fields would be desirable.
- Dry ground or scarce vegetation, intense heat, heavy rain or high winds should be avoided.
- The group assembles on the up-wind side of the field so that the tracks can be laid with the wind.

STEP 2: Securing the dog
Three to ten handlers and their hungry dogs participate.
They line up, spaced about 100 ft apart.
The dogs are secured in these positions, to a fence, trees, posts or stakes.
Use a tie-out chain/cable with a quick-release snap and attach it to the dead ring on the choke collar. Clip the regular leash to the dead ring on the collar also.

STEP 3: Starting place
Let your dog have a small piece of meat and tease him with the rest of it. Then move forward (in a line formation, with the other handlers) about 10 feet away from your dog, taking with you two flags and the meat, of course. Push the first flag into the ground.
Stamp down the grass in the area to the right of the flag, about one square yard in size and slightly cone-shaped toward the front.
Deposit a few pieces of meat on this scent pad.

STEP 4: Orientation
On instructions from the training director all handlers move out at the same time in a line formation, each toward an individual aim point in the distance.
(If sufficient aim points are not available, an assistant can approach the finish line in a big circle from the rear. He then places the second flag from each handler opposite the first (starting) flag, to mark the endpoint of the track.)

When laying the track keep your aim point in sight, CONSTANTLY. Do NOT look to the ground (only once in a while, and then only briefly).
The tracks of the group should run parallel to each other, roughly maintaining the 100 ft distance between them.

STEP 5: Tracklaying
Total length of the track is about 150 ft.
Take small steps during early training stages.
Deposit a piece of meat directly on the track after 5 ft, another 5 ft and then approximately after every 15 ft.
At the end of the track push the second flag into the ground and deposit a somewhat larger amount of food.
Rush back to the dog on your own track, aiming for the first flag in order to not create an additional scent path.

STEP 6: Start

Everything should have been prepared beforehand (e.g. a quick-release snap on the tie-out chain) so that the following steps can proceed rapidly.

Slide your left hand into the dog's collar.

The folded-up (regular) leash is held in the left hand also, or (less desirable) drags on the ground.

Excitedly move with your dog to the starting place.

With the dog on your left side, bend down and move your cupped right hand (fingers pointing to the dog) in front of the dogs nose to the ground and then 10 to 15 inches along the track away from the dog.

Almost all dogs will follow the meat-scented hand to the ground and start investigating it.

At this time encourage your dog and tell him to "find it".

STEP 7: Tracking

Make sure that the dog keeps his nose down while you are moving along the track at a reasonable speed right next to the dog. If the head comes up, stop. Do not move another inch until your dog's nose is on the ground again.

You can easily prevent running and circling since you still hold your dog by the collar.

Give frequent, but subdued, praise when the dog has his nose on the track.

Do NOT use your dog's name in this connection since it usually distracts the dog and causes an interruption in tracking.

Once the dog finds a piece of meat, give him time to swallow it while praising him at the same time - then continue tracking right away.

Although you may guide your dog to the next food drop, NO action should be taken if he misses it. Tracking just continues to the next marker. The dog should NOT be scolded or made to go back to pick up the treat.

STEP 8: End Marker

Earlier, you had deposited a larger portion of meat at the end of the track. Now give your dog time to enjoy this meal.

Show him your satisfaction and happiness about a job well done (praise, play, petting, rough-housing, etc.).

After the very last track in a session romp around, or throw a ball or stick, or do whatever the dog enjoys most. This will make the training a memorable event for the dog.

STEP 9: Return

Casually return with your dog on your own track, being careful not to create a new scent path.

Discourage tracking on the way back, but do not use punishment.

During the return, drop pieces of meat on the track as replacement for the ones your dog had found. Try not to let him become aware of this.

STEP 10: Switch

Wait with your dog at the starting flag until all teams have returned to their original position.

Then everybody moves one position to the right: team 1 is now at the starting flag of team 2, team 2 advanced to the start of team 3, team 3 waits at the old #4 starting flag and so on. The last team in the row goes to the beginning of the line (position #l), of course.

Since all tracks are baited, tracking can begin right away.

This switch can be repeated until all dogs had a chance to work on all tracks.

Once the dog does well on the straight tracks, you can guide him on the short (1-2 ft.) leash snapped to the dead ring on the choke collar. Longer tracks, turns, articles, U-shaped tracks and intersecting U-shaped tracks can be introduced and worked out in the same manner.

When working the U-track, for instance, let the first team start and then wait until it has reached the first turn. At that time, the second team starts on the same track, and so on.

The "hot" scent, curiosity, and the desire to imitate usually make for good tracking performances.

More advanced work, however, is best done on an individual basis rather than in a group.

If no other dogs are available to participate in the basic group training, you can adopt the principles and make them suit your own requirements.
You can also consider circle tracks.

** CIRCLE/LOOP TRACKS
Circle tracks are a very efficient way to practice tracking. The end of the track brings you right back to the start, relieving you from having to "walk a mile" to pick up the dog or to get back to the car. It also allows you to work the dog on the track and to bait the track for the next run, at the same time.
The principle is actually so simple and effective that one wonders why not everybody uses it.

Novice dogs which have successfully run a few straight line tracks can be introduced to circle tracks.

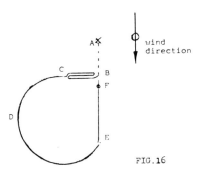

FIG.16

- Secure your dog at point A.
- Walk to point B and start laying the track in a circle, proceeding to C and then to D and E.
- The stretch B - C can be triple laid to assist the dog.
- The last stretch E - F must be a straight line. Most dogs will speed up here in anticipation of the reward.
- Food can be deposited along the track, with the biggest reward left at the end (F).
- Get your dog and start him on the track between B and C.
- Coax him along the track and give him time to swallow the goodies on the way. At the same time, replace the food, without letting your dog know about it.
- The dog gets the big reward and a lot of praise at F.

- After a brief pause urge your dog to go on the track again.
   While the dog moves out, deposit another portion of food behind him at point F, the same way you replaced the smaller food drops in the earlier parts of the track.
   It requires preparation and some skill to not let the dog become aware of this food replacement technique.

Theoretically one can run the circle forever. We suggest, however, to terminate the exercise after about 2 to 3 passes.

Repeats on subsequent days should vary between right and left circles.
Also, straight legs can be used to form a square or a rectangle.
The orientation of the track with regard to wind direction should be changed too.

For variety
- the track length should vary between large and small circles (diameters of 60-200 ft correspond
    to track lengths of about 180 to 600 ft)
- the time between laying the first track and finding it should be longer (20 minutes),
- the distances between food drops should be increased from every 15 ft to about every 100 ft,
- the rewards should be combined with the articles,
- the longer tracks should only rarely be run a second time around,
- switch between short and long tracks, fresh and old tracks, lush and scarce vegetation, all kinds
    of ground cover.
In general, the wind should not carry the scent from the last food drop to the starting place. Occasionally, however, the dog may even be shown where the reward is placed and then be taught that the only way to get it is to follow the track.

b) Intermediate-level training
Introduce one change at a time:
- Use a four foot leash on the dead choke.
- Space the food drops farther apart (double the distances once a week, advancing from about
    15 ft to about 120 ft).
- Use each track only once, then move on to fresh ground.
- Don't return on your fresh track, take an alternate route back to your dog (single track).
- Let the track age 30 minutes.
- Lay all tracks at an angle, never parallel, to any natural boundary (fence, tree line, furrows, mower
    lines etc.)
- Introduce a non-restrictive harness, if you wish.
- Switch between short and long tracks, fresh and old tracks, lush and scarce vegetation, all kinds
    of ground cover.

c) Advanced-level training
Introduce one change at a time:
- Use a six foot leash on the dead choke, or harness.
- Eliminate most intermediate food drops in favor of a larger portion at the end.
- Increase the distance gradually (add about 50%, one change per week).
- Let the track age for 40 minutes.
- Introduce an obtuse-angle turn, with the first leg long, the second leg short: place a small food
drop about 1 to 2 feet past the turn, and have the second leg lead into the wind.
- Introduce articles (glove with food in it).
- Use several articles on each leg initially.
- Start with larger objects, progress to small ones in time.
- Switch between short and long tracks, fresh and old tracks, lush and scarce vegetation, all kinds
    of ground cover.

All tracks in all three levels end with a large portion of food (one to two hand-fulls). Also, praise the dog lavishly at the end of the track, and play with him. Throw the ball, throw the stick, do whatever the dog likes best. He must come to realize that it is of great benefit to him to get to the end of the track. He should develop the desire, and look forward, to get the final reward. Only then will the trainer be able to count on performance.

It can happen to the best handler, and to the best dog, that they don't find the end of the track. You must be prepared for this rare occasion, having an extra reward and an extra article in the pocket. Inconspicuously placing these items on the ground and giving the dog a chance to find them allows you to end the tracking session on a happy note.

The basic training is time consuming. We recommend tracking every other day (1 to 2 tracks per day). Training more often (up to 6 days out of 7) can be advantageous during the initial phase, yet advanced dogs often show a decline in interest with such heavy involvement.

d) Training experienced dogs

Frequent refresher courses are necessary to maintain a dog's tracking performance.

Training once a week would be the bare minimum. Providing variety with regard to location, ground cover, track age, track length, track lay-out, weight of tracklayer, weather conditions, articles, distractions etc. will keep the dog interested.

Acute angles, two tracklayers who separate at one point and join again later, crossing roads, or creeks, or streams, or parking lots etc., provide challenging opportunities to test the dog's and the handler's capabilities.

ARTICLES

In tracking, several "lost" articles have to be found. You have the choice between letting your dog indicate the article, pick it up, or retrieve it. For most dog/handler teams, indication with the dog in the down position would be preferable since this can be taught easily, and there are few chances for a poor performance. Indicating by standing or sitting lends itself easily to misinterpretation and to incidental mistakes, like not remaining perfectly still.

We recommend that the dog assumes a down position upon finding an article on the track, facing the article. You then drop the leash, rush up to the dog, praise him briefly, and waive the article over your head (to show it to the judge). Look at your dog at this time, to prevent him from getting up prematurely. You can hold up the article with one hand, and pet your dog with the other hand. Then encourage him to continue tracking in the direction indicated by the outstretched leash (remember: an article is not supposed to be dropped close to a turn).

Choosing the second option, to pick up the article, you can teach the dog to remain sitting or standing at the spot of the find. A nervous, excited, playful or sloppy dog might drop the article. This costs points in a trial.

You can also teach your dog to retrieve the article. In addition to the possibilities of a sloppy and faulty retrieve, you also lose the direction indicator (the outstretched leash), the dog has to re-do 30 feet tracked already, and he can get distracted when passing the place of the find for the second time.

It is advisable to teach the indication of articles independently of tracking.

During obedience work, or during a casual walk, you can drop a well-scented article without letting the dog notice it. You can also spread out several scented articles on a small field before bringing your dog onto it.

When the dog approaches the article, a firm "down" command will teach him the correct response. You must prevent the dog from touching or mouthing the article, as well as from laying on top of it. Control can best be exercised with the six foot leash: hold him back so that he stops just short of the article. Then you claim the article, waive it over your head and praise and reward the dog.

Teaching the dog to properly indicate an article can be done with the help of the "refrigerator effect" also. The following story describes the supposed origin of it:

" A dog and his master would frequently visit another family. Upon entering the house the dog would head straight for the kitchen and sit quietly in front of the refrigerator, staring at the handle. The dog would not leave his position until the home owner came and gave him "his" piece of meat. "

Applied to tracking, the "refrigerator effect" can be taught as follows:

Obtain a glass or plastic container with a tight lid and put some food in it. As described before, the food must be of the right kind, and the dog must be really hungry. The container is then positioned on the training field or on the track, together with, or even inside of, an article. As soon as the dog has arrived at the container, teach him to go down and to wait for it to be opened on the spot. After a few times, the dog will automatically assume the correct down position. Not taking an eye off the container in front of him, he will wait patiently for your arrival, and for his reward. Unpack it, be excited, excite the dog by sniffing on the reward yourself - then give it to him.

Besides teaching a reliable indication of articles, the containers have an added bonus: other animals (wild ones or stray dogs) can not steal the food, and ants can not get at it either.

Once the dog indicates reliably, combine it with tracking:
Lay a 100 feet simple, straight track, and drop an article every 30 ft. Start your dog on the track as usual. Most likely he will indicate the article as taught. Remain calm, praise and reward him, and keep him in the down position for a little while. The restart, and repeat at the next article.

COMMUNICATION

As in other phases of dog training, communication between dog and handler is of vital importance. Since the dog can not speak, the handler has to rely on other clues.

A smart handler will learn to read his dog during practice sessions. Watch how the dog carries his head, his ears, his tail when on and off the track. Analyze the manner in which the dog moves, the steadiness, the pull in the tracking leash, the breathing rhythm and intensity, etc. Each dog behaves somewhat different, but still, there are distinct patterns each dog exhibits when on and off the scent path. Using this information in a trial with an unfamiliar track will enable you to guide your dog skillfully.
Encouragement ("that's a good boy, go on") is given as long as all signs indicate that the dog is on the track. Some dogs need little reassurance from the handler, others require more. When the dog signals 'loss of track' yet still searches for the lost scent, encourage him again but with a different tone of voice ("find it, where is it"). If the dog is attracted by something else, stimulate him to continue tracking ("look what I have found here", point to the track).
The clues for guidance should always be taken from the dog, not from the terrain layout, or from visible trails in the grass, or from helpful friends, etc.

COMPETITION

The tracking portion in a Schutzhund trial is usually considered to be the one where the handler has the least control over the performance of his dog. There are, however, many things that the trainer can do to improve or worsen that situation.

Get your dog ready.
Take your dog out of the car at least thirty minutes before he goes on the track, to replace the fuel fumes (present in every car) with the local scent environment. Let him relax and eliminate. Prevent contacts with other dogs, especially dogfights or attraction to the opposite sex, and avoid other excitements as well. Don't let him watch protection work, for instance. Don't do any obedience work with him either, even a "heel" or "down" might inhibit his initiative. If he sniffs on the ground, don't discourage him. He probably knows what is coming up next.
Give him some water that you have brought from home, or splash some of it over his nose just before tracking starts. This will moisten the nasal tissue and make it more receptive for the scent.

Get your equipment ready.
If you use a harness, place it close to the starting area. Unroll your leash and stretch it out on the ground, hook next to the harness.
Do you wear gloves on the track? Do you have them?

Where is your numbered armband/vest? Wear it.
Make sure that you have the reward ready, a ball, a toy, a tidbit, either at your car, or in your pocket. If you take it with you, have it well concealed and tightly wrapped. If the dog smells the meat he will probably concentrate more on your pocket than on his track.

Report to the judge.
Get your dog, your equipment, and report to the judge to begin tracking. Remember that precision heeling is not required at this time. Skip the "heel" command if at all possible, in order to keep the dog's mind free of any restraints.

Approach the starting flag.

While approaching the starting flag, search for clues that will tell you the initial direction of the track. The experienced judge should know where it is, he should not stand on it, nor should he let anybody else get close to it, spectators or even you, while you approach the flag. (Watch out for the judges, though, who do not know where the track is. I have seen one in a championship who let the spectators trample all over the track.)

A close-by wall, house, river, fence, road, starting pole from another track etc. will also limit the directions your track can go. Sometimes dew lines, trails in high grass or snow etc. can be seen. However, all these clues should be used to reassure the handler, not to let him take over the tracking job of his dog.

Start tracking.

Once the dog gets close to the starting flag, encourage him to pick up the scent. Some handlers prefer to down their dog at the flag yet this is not always the best choice. It might switch the dog's mind from tracking to obedience, as explained above. Holding him short on the leash would be preferable. Requiring a dog to stay for a given number of minutes at the start is another fallacy. A good handler reads his dog. He lets him go out on the track once he sees that the dog has acknowledged the starting scent and is straining to go from there. Holding the dog back at such a time is like telling him to forget about tracking. Feed him the lead and follow him as soon as the end comes up.

6. PROBLEMS

** LOSS OF INTEREST

At one time of another, most trained dogs go through a phase where they seem to have lost interest in tracking.

The following causes may apply:

a) CAUSE   Medication.
           Certain medication interferes with a dog's ability to analyze scents.
   TRAINING   Wait until medication is no longer needed or until its effect has worn off.
   SUGGESTIONS   Consult with your veterinarian.

b) CAUSE   Saturation.
           The dog was tracked too often, and the (small) reward was not worth the effort, in the dog's mind.
   TRAINING   Track less often, use shorter, simpler tracks, provide variety, motivate your dog.
   SUGGESTIONS   Try bigger, better, different rewards.

c) CAUSE   Exhaustion.
           Past tracks were too difficult, the handler advanced too fast in the program.
   TRAINING   Back off, work on simpler, shorter, fresher tracks.
   SUGGESTIONS   Use track baiting.

d) CAUSE   Boredom.
           The dog is not sufficiently motivated.
   TRAINING   - Try a different kind of motivator: food, urine, play, decoy.
   SUGGESTIONS   - Use the motivator only in connection with tracking, withhold it at all other times.

e) CAUSE   Failure.
           In earlier training, the dog lost the track and could not earn the reward.
   TRAINING   - make sure that you know where the track is. Guide your dog if necessary.
   SUGGESTIONS   - Always carry an extra glove (and reward). Once it becomes clear that you can not finish the track, drop the extra glove inconspicuously, then help your dog to find it. Praise/reward him.

** LOSS OF TRACK

Your dog works steadily, yet suddenly he indicates loss of track, maybe by lifting his head up, checking left and right, circling, moving erratically. Most likely a stretch of weaker or faded scent, unfavorable ground cover, unusual climatic conditions, an old gasoline, oil or chemical spillage, gas leaks, other natural or artificial masking odors might have created a "blind spot".

You should stop instantaneously, maybe even move back a little on the track, and give your dog a chance to work it out on his own.

A clever handler will know when his dog has recovered the scent. The nose will most likely be glued to the ground again, his body and head carriage indicate confidence, he moves in a straight line, and he pulls in the harness. At that time you should let him take the lead, but only then. Do not follow if he is not sure.

On the other hand, overly long circling just worsens the situation and it requires that you make a decision.

Rather then to give up, advance somewhat in the direction where the track is most likely to continue. In doing so cast the dog to the right and left, hoping to recover the lost track on uncontaminated, more favorable grounds.

In a trial, you will certainly lose points for such unscheduled assistance, however, you still have a chance to find the track and to complete it, harvesting the points assigned to that portion.

It is always a good idea to prepare your dog for the worst conditions:

Locate a large tree or a wide underpass (bridge), or stretch a sturdy cable between to elevated points (buildings, poles, trees etc.). Tie a strong rope to the overhead and secure the lose end near the envisioned track path. No sooner than four or five days later lay your track and let the tracklayer aim for the rope. Once he reaches it, ask him to swing away from the track Tarzan-style. Upon reaching the ground again, let him continue the track.

You have created the perfect "loss-of-track" situation and can practice with your dog recovery.

A less dramatic (and less effective) variation of this jungle exercise is to have the tracklayer make a few leaps sideways at the point of the intended loss-of-track, or to let the track cross a road etc. (see the section "Dead Space" below).

** HIGH SPEED PURSUIT

You should slow down your dog to a comfortable walking speed since too fast a pace in tracking causes him to miss turns and articles:

a) Tire him out somewhat before going on the track (running, playing).

b) Use physical restraint, hold him back with steady, constant tension on the tracking leash.

c) Guide the leash over your back and lean into it.

d) Use Boettcher's harness.

e) Use a regular choke collar on the live ring (steady pull).

f) Use a prong collar (steady pull).

g) Let him drag some weight while tracking (a good pulling harness and suitable weights, for instance an old car tire, must be secured beforehand).

h) Track under less favorable conditions (see meteorological factors).

** TURNS

Often, dogs have difficulties to negotiate a turn. As soon as he overshoots and indicates loss of track you should stop, hold on to the leash and give the dog a chance to find the continuation of the track. Give encouragement and keep the leash reasonably taut to prevent entanglement. Follow when your dog is pulling steady in the new direction.

In training, practice for a perfect turn in the following way:

a) Let the new direction lead into the wind.

g) Place a reward just past the turn.

f) Rub meat on the ground along the first four to five paces in the new direction, e.g. *after* the turn, or use another desirable scent source (meat powder, meat broth).

b) When laying the track, take large strides just before the turn.

c) Triple-lay the first four to five paces in the new direction, using small steps.

d) Round the corner, or make an obtuse angle. Then, in subsequent tracks, make the angle smaller and smaller, until it becomes an acute angle (20-25 degrees).

e) Do as many left turns as you do right turns (many handlers practice right turns only).

h) Work with a short leash (6 ft.), or shorten the leash just before a turn comes up.

FIG. 17

i) Don't let the dog overshoot the turn more than a couple of feet.

j) Make sure that you stop soon enough. Don't end up standing on the turn that the dog is supposed to work out.

k) Avoid signaling your dog that a turn comes up by tightening the line. He should be able to work out the turn on a loose lead.

l) Do many (rather) short tracks with one turn only. The first leg is the longest, the second leg terminates with the reward ten to twenty paces past the turn.

m) Praise your dog only while he is on the track, not while he is off or searching for it. Be sensible about it.

Some trainers suggest that the tracklayer takes very *short* steps for the last few yards before the track changes direction. This, unfortunately, is the surest way to make the dog miss the turn. The opposite should be done: the tracklayer should take very big strides for the last few yards before changing direction of the track. Then, past the turn, he can place the footprints closer together, for a few paces.

A few facts that everyone can verify for himself:

* Reaching a turn, all dogs will continue to go straight, the beginner dogs for a few feet or yards, the advanced dogs maybe for a couple of inches. This is partly due to an inertia (they can not pull their brakes that fast), partly they want to make sure that the track does not continue in the most likely direction, namely straight ahead.

* All dogs working on a track become alert when they lose the scent. Efforts to find the continuation of the track are increased at that time.

* Heavy (overwhelming) scent density as it is found in fresh tracks or on stretches through lush vegetation like alfalfa fields causes dogs to track with a high nose, in a more casual manner.

* Very heavy scent can be objectionable to dogs. This can be confirmed by using freshly mashed vegetation (plant soup) on a track.

* The experienced (and successful) tracking dog is a 'line tracker', as compared to the 'step tracker'. He does not sniff out every footprint. He exhales and inhales normally while following the scent path, paying attention mainly to changes in the scent composition which indicate loss of track. At that time he puts forth additional effort to find the continuation of the track.

What happens if the track is scented heavily just *before* the turn?
The dog relaxes upon reaching this area. There is no doubt that he is still on the track, he can verify that even with his head up in the air - which he will do. In addition, the very heavy scent may be objectionable to him, one reason more to lift the head off the track.
With so much reassurance of being still on the track, and with some of the heavy scent generously distributed in the vicinity of the critical turning point, the dog is almost forced to continue straight ahead, and to overshoot the turn.

What happens if the track is scented scarcely before, but heavily *after* the turn?
The dog experiences a disruption of the scent path, or an 'almost' loss of scent BEFORE he reaches the turn. This activates his brain cells and he spends additional effort to find the continuation of the track. In doing so he puts his nose to the ground. He also keeps going straight forward, as explained above. At that time he reaches the actual 90 degree turn and encounters the heavy scent to the

right (or left) of the track. Since he was expecting loss of track anyway, he has no problem to change direction, in an almost perfect trace of the original trail.

One more comment:
Each dog has a different inertia, so the length of the scarcely scented portion just before the turn must be tailored to the animal.
Ideally the dog should be just short of the exact location of the turn the very moment he has reconfirmed that the track is still there. Considering timing elements, allowances should be made for the dog's way of thinking:
   a) the surprise period (where is the track ?)
   b) the period of recovery (the track is still in front of me but fading)
   c) the period of willingness to change the track direction (I thought so, the track now
     turns right, or left).
Observing your dog closely, you can fairly accurately determine the length of parts a), b) and c). You can then instruct the tracklayer to do a couple of big steps for a distance of ' x ' yards, before negotiating the turn.

** ARTICLES

a) PROBLEM   Article ignored.
    CAUSE   The dog did not recognize/acknowledge it.

    TRAINING   - Work him slower, do not let him run on the track.
    SUGGESTIONS   - Use a greater variety of articles with regard to shape, size, material, and where
                   you store the articles between usage.
               - Scent the articles better. Carry them for a couple of hours on your body before
                   you deposit them on the track.
               - Practice finding independently of tracking. Use the techniques described earlier.

b) PROBLEM   Wrong articles indicated.
    CAUSE   The dog hunts by sight.

    TRAINING   - Collect many small articles made of glass, metal, wood, paper, leather, fabric
    SUGGESTIONS   etc., and spread them out in the open where nobody will touch them for 2-3
               weeks. Then collect the pieces with tongs and drop them into a paper bag. Lay
               your track and deposit the "garbage" near it (use the tongs!) and a few well-
               scented real articles as well.
               Discourage your dog when he steers for the garbage, praise him as soon as he
               acknowledges the real article. Clean-up afterwards, reuse the junk.
              - Hide the article from sight, dig a shallow hole for it, cover it with some grass or
               dirt.

** CROSSTRACKS

Advanced tracking dogs must be able to follow a track without switching over to another intersecting trail. Investigating the crosstrack for a few paces is not faulty, as long as the dog returns to, and pursues, the original path.
Experiments conducted by German Police Canine Units have shown that well-trained and talented dogs can differentiate between the tracks of two equal-weight tracklayers, provided there is a time lag between the two tracks of more than five minutes, at a total track age of about three hours.

The following conditions are suggested initially, for starting the crosstrack training:
    primary track: 300 paces, straight, 2 hours of age
                       food reward on main track 5 ft. past the cross track, and at the end
                       heavy weight tracklayer (more than 30 lbs. difference between the two
                       tracklayers)

crosstrack: intersects primary track near the end (at about 280 paces), at a 90 degree angle
5 minutes of age (e.g. laying it almost 2 hrs. later than the main track)
light weight tracklayer.

Hold your dog back if he wants to investigate the crosstrack for more than three paces to the right or left. At the same time you should verbally, but casually, discourage the dog from following the crosstrack any further. Give lots of praise and encouragement as soon as the dog gets back on the main track. If necessary, guide the dog onto the main track, and to the reward which is just 5 ft. away from the intersection.

Practice similar tracks for five to eight more training sessions during the following weeks. Then introduce difficulties, one at a time, like turns and articles on the main track, other tracklayers, more crosstracks, intersections other than 90 degree etc. Increase the main track age to three hours, the crosstrack age to thirty minutes (for instance: main track laid at 6:00 AM, crosstrack laid at 8:30 AM, tracking started at 9:00 AM).
Crosstracks must be sufficiently separated from articles.

The following diagram shows situations with increasing levels of difficulty:

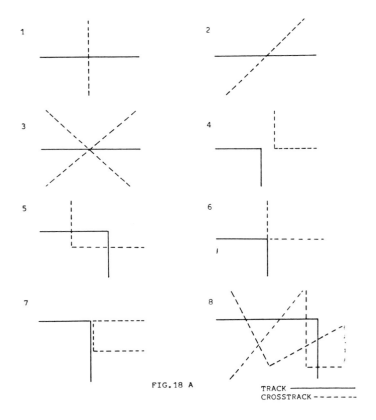

FIG. 18 A

TRACK ——————
CROSSTRACK — — — — — —

For training purposes it is also quite helpful to create a super-saturated crosstrack situation: five to ten assistants, each about 20 ft. away from their immediate neighbor, are asked to walk in a line formation across a U-shaped main track.

The dog is worked on this track in the usual manner, with assistance from his handler, if needed (see Fig.18 B)

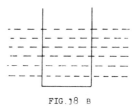

FIG. 18 B

** DEAD SPACES

Hard surfaces like rock, sand, concrete and asphalt do not generate or hold sufficient amounts of ground scent since physical disturbances cause only minor changes to their inherent scent patterns. Bodies of water severely complicate tracking as well. Beginning dogs, therefore, should not be trained on such grounds. If an experienced dog is able to pick up any track scent, then it is most often from material carried with the footwear onto the hard surface.

The basic training concept for crossing a road or a body of water consists of following the track up to the edge of the dead space and then sending the dog ahead in a straight line, with an obedience command. After reaching suitable tracking ground, the dog is directed to cast to the right and left until he picks up the scent again.

During the teaching phase, you should know the continuation of the track. You should send the dog, intentionally, at a slightly different angle so that the casting can be practiced. Give encouragement and verbal praise once the dog picks up the track.

It might be advisable to bait the continuation of the track, initially.

** MAKE BELIEVE

Some dogs appear to be working, nose on the ground, pulling in the harness, yet they are definitely not on the right track.

a) CAUSE	The dog is following an undesirable scent. There are, for instance, cases where dogs have followed the track of the judge who instructed the tracklayer on the day before the trial.
TRAINING SUGGESTIONS	a) Retrain your dog (see crosstrack techniques) b) Don't show anymore under that judge, pick a better qualified person (a good judge will stay off the field and direct from a suitable observation point).
b) CAUSE	The dog has learned that he can please his master and avoid punishment by faking the track.
TRAINING SUGGESTIONS	a) Ease off on the pressure and on the corrections and b) re-start basic training, knowing EXACTLY where the track is.

** CASTING

A tracking dog ideally retraces the path of the track layer, step by step, as it was laid.
In practical terms, however, occasional checking to the left and right is quite natural and acceptable, especially in the vicinity of turns.
Yet excessive circling, excited running from the left to the right border of the scent path, and other departures from the track cause the dog to put in considerably more work than necessary and tire him out prematurely. Lack of success then leads to frustration with dog and handler, and to further deterioration in training and trial performance.

The problem develops most often with hyperactive, easily excitable dogs, those that are eager to work and/or anxious to please. Quite a few Dobes fit that description in their beginning stages of tracking.

The basic idea in channeling this excess energy into more desirable behavior patterns is to gain better control of the dog.
The six-foot tracking leash is therefore essential. Hold it taut for a steady pull, yet avoid jerking it under all circumstances. Aside from that, you should observe closely and determine what makes the dog behave in such an undesirable manner.

The more common causes are listed below. If they apply, one (or several) of the given training suggestions can be selected to eliminate the problem. If you diagnose a different cause you must use your own judgement and find a solution.

a) CAUSE — The scent is too strong (offensive) - the dog needs to make wide sweeps to determine where the tracklayer has NOT been (fringe follower).

TRAINING SUGGESTIONS
- change to a different ground cover (alfalfa grass, for instance, seems to generate a scent that is offensive to some dogs)
- change to a location with scarce ground cover
- employ a light-weight track layer
- instruct the track layer to take large strides
- let the track age longer
- bait and/or scent the track.

b) CAUSE — The scent pattern is too weak, the dog has trouble finding it.

TRAINING SUGGESTIONS
- change to a location with lusher vegetation
- employ a heavy track layer
- instruct the track layer to take smaller steps and to drag his feet
- soil the track layers boots with manure, fish etc. before he goes on the track
- don't let the track age as long as before
- bait and/or scent the track.

c) CAUSE — The scent pattern is confusing (the scent may be blown away in some places, trapped in others, like ditches, holes, vegetation and high ground cover).

TRAINING SUGGESTIONS
- practice more often under similar, adverse conditions
- help and guide your dog over the rough spot
- use more articles on the confusing stretches

d) CAUSE — The dog shows a desire to track but he is too excited, too jumpy.

TRAINING SUGGESTIONS
- use more articles
- use smaller articles
- tire him out somewhat before going on the track (running, playing)
- use physical restraint, hold him back with steady, constant tension on the tracking leash
- if the dog is uncooperative when using the physical restraint, consider
  a) Boettcher's tracking harness
  b) attaching the tracking leash to the live ring on the choke collar and guiding the leash between his front legs
  c) as b) but using the prong collar
  d) letting him drag some weight while tracking (a good pulling harness and suitable weights, for instance an old car tire, must be secured beforehand)

d) CAUSE — The dog is not interested in tracking, he wants to plays or to hunt.

TRAINING SUGGESTIONS
- if this is an isolated instance, the dog may just need a stern verbal correction
- if it happens on more than one occasion, the dog needs to be retrained from the ground up. Motivation is the key word.

There are numerous other factors that can cause a seemingly erratic tracking behavior. For instance:
- Illness.
- Conflicting tracks made by other people, animals or vehicles can cause a dog to ignore the trial rules.
- Chemicals, oil or gas spills may not be obvious to a human, yet the dog's performance will be affected by them.
- Ground disturbances, buried chemicals or leaky pipelines, sulphur or hot springs in certain parts of the country can cause the dog to respond differently.
- Automobile exhaust fumes during long car rides may have temporarily impaired a dog's scenting ability.

In short: Dogs do not always perform as expected, but there is always a reason for it.

The sensible handler tries to find the reason.

Concentrate on the causes rather than on the symptoms.

If one approach does not cure a problem, try different remedies until the undesirable behavior patterns are eliminated.

Then gradually change over to standard tracking procedures.

7. SUMMARY OF TRAINING SUGGESTIONS

- Track regularly, at least once a week.
- Know exactly where the track is so that you can monitor your dog's performance and help when necessary.
- Select the method and the motivator (reward) that is best suited for your dog.
- Don't give obedience commands (heel, sit, down) before going on a track. You don't want to cripple your dog's initiative.
- Tie your dog to a tree when laying the track and tease him with the bait, instead of giving the down command. You want him to lunge forward, to be anxious for going out on the track.
- Give your dog some fresh water (brought from home) just before he goes on the track. This will moisten and activate the nasal tissue and make tracking more comfortable for him.
- If you use a harness, put it on just before you go on the track. Take it off immediately afterwards.
- Read your dog at the starting place and let him go when he is ready. Don't remain there too long or too short.
- In practice, use a short leash and keep your dog on the track at all times.
- Use positive reinforcement (encouragement, praise, reward).
- Avoid Punishment, if possible. Use restraint instead.
- Start simple: short grass, short track, no turns, lots of rewards.
- Introduce difficulties gradually.
- Always have a spare article and reward with you so that you can fake the end of the track if the dog can not find it.
- Provide variety, like longer and shorter tracks, older and fresher tracks, lay tracks with turns, without turns, track in a variety of ground covers, track during all seasons, in all weather conditions, change tracklayers, or carry some weight occasionally to alter your ground impressions, provide distractions during training like other people, dogs, cars, traffic noise, wildlife etc.

"Do you know that
your dog barked all night?"
"Yes, but don't worry.
He sleeps all day."

C. OBEDIENCE

1. BASIC PHILOSOPHY

Obedience work is the yardstick for the talents of a dog trainer.
A spirited, happy, joyful and accurate performance of the dog working in unison with his master attests to the high qualifications of the handler. Listless, dutiful, sloppy compliance, on the other hand, indicates the need for a change in training style.
This chapter aims at developing the rapport between dog and handler that makes training an enjoyable pastime for both, and which necessarily leads to a superior training style.
To accomplish this goal:
- start preliminary obedience training during puppyhood
- pay attention to the needs of the individual dog
- use rewards in various forms, in connection with compulsory guidance
- have short, lively, spirited training sessions, followed   by play.

2. PUPPY TRAINING

Playful obedience training should start at an early age, as early as six weeks perhaps. The puppy is very receptive at this time, and very easily impressed, too. He learns fast, yet his attention span is short. Do not insist on drill routines, or on perfection. For the pup, showing a desire to comply is more important than performing like a robot.
Patience, tolerance, forgiveness and gentleness are qualities that you need at this time. Enthusiastic praise, play and tidbits as reward for good work, as well as very short training sessions, are other requirements.

Coming when called is probably the first exercise a trainer wants to teach his puppy.
Reserving the "come" exclusively for occasions to which the puppy looks forward anyway (feeding, going for a walk etc.), calling the pup in a very pleasant, excited tone of voice (as an invitation, rather than as a command), always rewarding and praising him when he comes, never connecting anything unpleasant with the recall (scolding, punishing, confining, attaching the leash etc.) will lead to a reliable performance of the recall in the adult dog.
The front sit and the finish should not be practiced in connection with the recall, at this stage.

The sit and down commands can also be introduced at an early age.
A tidbit held above and slightly back over the dog's head will cause the puppy to sit naturally and voluntarily. The command "sit" (short, emphasis is on the "t") should be given at the same time, and through repetition the dog will learn to follow the verbal instruction.
If the dog backs up, you can try to
     - move your hand with the tidbit quicker
     - hold the tidbit a little lower, or a little further back
     - do the exercise in front of a wall which prevents the puppy from backing up
     - hold the tidbit in the right hand and use the left hand to stroke the puppy's back with
       very gentle pressure on the croup.
During early training, the sit-stay is practiced for very short durations only.

A similar approach can be taken to teach the down. The right hand holding a tidbit is moved in front of the dog's nose toward the ground, and then a few inches away from him. More likely than not the dog will follow it and lay down. Your left hand can assist in this maneuver by physically manipulating the pup into the down position, sliding the front paws out, for instance, or applying very, very slight pressure on the shoulder. Initially, the hand can be left on the shoulder for a while, to insure the down-stay.
Uncooperative pups can be flipped on their sides, quickly, but still gently. As with the sit, a verbal cue is given. The appropriate "down" is truly a command, it should be given firmly. The exercise down-stay is terminated after a very short duration.

Another task would be to condition the puppy to collar and leash. Initially the leash is just attached to the collar and he drags it around, later you should hold on to it and encourage him to accompany you. Use a lot of verbal encouragement, and select a destination the puppy favors (the local park, for instance, and not the veterinarians office). This will help to avoid the pulling contest that many dog owners have to live with.

It is also a good idea to start leash training away from home. For the first few times, take him to an area he is not familiar with, and attach the leash to his collar there. While the new surroundings will capture his attention, they will also increase his dependence on you, and as a result he will be more cooperative than at home.

On these first excursions the pup should not be told to heel, he should just learn that you determine the direction of travel. If he disagrees, you should slowly continue in your path, encouraging him to follow. Leash corrections are NOT given at this time, the leash is just used to restrain the puppy.

It is very important that a puppy understands the meaning of the word "no". Proper timing, at the moment when he gets into mischief, and an outburst of displeasure (e.g. an animated display of anger, without physical contact) convey the message best. Rarely is it necessary to physically punish the puppy, the startling and the scolding usually are sufficient. This, however, must be followed immediately by praise, provided he interrupted the mischievous behavior.

A young dog needs much attention, and much interaction with his trainer. Just opening the back door and wishing him a good time in the yard will not be enough. In living with his owner, doing things together, being around, the puppy can best, and most easily, be taught to behave well, and to adopt to the peculiarities of the "human pack".

3. OBEDIENCE TRAINING FOR MATURE DOGS

Serious obedience training should start when the dog has reached about six to eight months of age. Up to that point, training should have been conducted in a somewhat playful manner, putting more emphasis on cooperation by the dog than on precision of the execution of exercises.
If the dog is much older than a year, more patience and skill is required of the trainer, but here too, progress can be satisfactory. You CAN teach an old dog new tricks.

As preliminaries teach the dog to come when called, and to accompany you for a walk (not heeling!). Both items have been described above under puppy training.

Further training lessons should provide a balance between movement (e.g. retrieve) and rest (e.g. long down), and between exercises the dog considers to be attractive (e.g. jumping) and unattractive (e.g. heeling).
Individual exercises must be broken down into parts and practiced separately (e.g. sit-stay + come when called + finish = recall). Progress from simple to more complicated tasks must be made gradually (e.g. holding the dumbbell, getting the dumbbell, bringing it back).

Group training (similar to "Intensive Method"/Tracking) offers many benefits to instructor, handler and dog. If available, it would be the preferred method of instruction.

Some handlers will select the "down" as the first exercise with which to strive for perfection. Other handlers will pick another important and easy routine. Each dog requires a slightly different approach, and you are encouraged to compile your own program, and to proceed at your own pace.
The topics covered in this chapter are arranged in groups of related exercises, therefore the sequence of presentation does not necessarily coincide with the sequence of teaching.

•• HEELING ••

GENERAL
Heeling is the most basic, but also the most easily boring exercise in obedience training.
It requires more skill, more involvement and better preparation from the handler than most other exercises.

Many trial rules specify that the dog keeps his shoulder "in line with the left knee of the handler". This would result in a rather discontinuous movement, and for all practical purposes "knee" should be (and actually is) interpreted as "hip", or "shoulder".

OBJECTIVE
The dog will remain at the handler's left side, keeping his shoulder in line with the handler's left knee (hip) at all times, regardless of changes in pace or direction.

SUGGESTED COMMAND:	"heel "
SUGGESTED RELEASE COMMAND:	"OK "

PSYCHOLOGY
To walk at the heel position is completely unnatural to the dog, he was "programmed" to scout ahead of his master.
While physical restraint and punishment can force a dog to remain at his handler's left side, the sight of such a duo is usually a rather pitiful one: the dog with lowered head, drooping ears and in a depressed mood, the handler tense, grim, uncoordinated.

Now look at this team: the dog responds excitedly and happily to his masters every movement, glued by an invisible bond to the handler's left side, ears alert, head up, monitoring his master's facial expression so that he can anticipate the next movement. The handler himself is relaxed, friendly, responsive and constantly stimulating his dog's interest. They move in unison, as a true team.

Training philosophy is the difference.

The first team is a typical "drill sergeant" example: the "soldier" had not much of a choice.

The handler in the second team, however, practiced "applied canine psychology".
He recognized three basic facts, and he followed three basic rules:

Three facts:
1. Roaming ranks very high on the dog's list of desirable activities.
2. Force alone may get compliance but never happy performance.
3. A motivator displayed but withheld too long will lose its effectiveness.

Three rules:
1. The handler must capture, and constantly stimulate, the dog's interest.
   This will be possible for relatively short periods only.
2. Correction for inattentiveness and undesirable responses must be lightening fast and pronounced.
3. Genuine praise must be given immediately after each correction, and for each special effort the dog makes. The most effective level of praise and correction have to be determined for each dog individually.

Do not practice heeling in combination with another exercise.
If you want to teach your dog to do a "down out of motion" then you should not correct him for forging just a little, at least not at this time.

The best results in heeling are usually obtained when you conduct a short, spirited training session which is concluded by an enjoyable play period.

PREREQUISITES
None, except a well-established dog/handler relationship.

ACCESSORIES
a) Collar
One end of the extended choke chain is pushed through its own ring and pulled through until both rings meet (Fig   a-d).

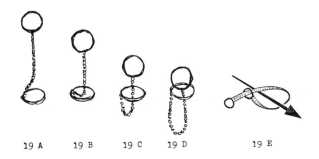

19 A   19 B   19 C   19 D   19 E

Orient the collar so that it forms a "P" in front of you, then slide it over the dog's head (Fig.19 e; the point of the arrow is the dog's head). The collar will free itself (by gravity) when the tension is released . Having the collar up high, just below the dog's ears, gives better leverage.

b) Leash
For initial training, hold the excess length of the leash in your right hand, neatly bundled like ribbon-candy. A loop with very little slack hangs in front of you, giving the dog enough freedom to move without feeling pressure on the collar, yet allowing you to tighten the collar instantaneously. Your left hand should be on stand-by, swinging normally (and more freely than the right hand) as you walk. If the dog leaves the heel position, then reach with your left hand for the leash (but only then !) and administers the correction. Immediately thereafter, the left hand releases the leash and pets the dog for being now in the correct position.

c) Leash Correction
Although some people consider it cruel, a forceful leash correction with the choke collar is much more humane than the slow self-strangulation of dogs who drag their owners around.

Each leash correction requires some preparation. You must learn to read your dog and to anticipate what the animal will be doing one half of a second later. If trouble lies ahead which requires a correction, you should execute the following patterns in rapid succession:
   a) Feed the dog more lead. There is no tension on the line, yet.
   b) Give the command "heel". If the dog responds, then steps c) to f) are omitted.
   c) Balance and brace yourself, feet securely positioned on the ground.
   d) Pick up the slack in the leash and give a forceful correction. It is ineffective to just gradually tighten the leash - this will accomplish nothing but a pulling contest. You must suddenly and forcefully snap (yank, jolt, jerk, slam) the leash, comparable perhaps to the effect the dog would experience in a powerful lunge. The correction should be strong enough to physically manipulate the dog into the proper position.
   e) Instantaneously release the tension and take your left hand off the leash.
   f) Continue walking, speeding up to recover the ground lost while giving the correction.
   g) Praise the dog enthusiastically for now being in the proper position, touch him (left hand).

COMMANDS

The "heel" command must be given a split second before the correction. This is very important from a teaching standpoint. It offers the dog a chance to avoid the correction, if he stays alert, and if he responds instantaneously. (If he does, the correction is not given, of course).

Sometimes it may be necessary to give a second command, but a command must never be repeated more than once.

The first time the dog has a chance to comply, the second time the dog should be made to comply. If you are not able to enforce the command, then you would be better off not to give it in the first place.

TEACHING PROCEDURE

Recommendations (obedience training from a-z):

a) Brief but regular training sessions are advisable (one to two minutes, 2-3 times daily). The dog should not be bored to death with endless repetitions.

b) Before a work-out, let your dog explore and sniff out the training area - on or off lead.

c) Use a light-weight leash and a choke collar.

d) A brisk walking pace (short steps, fast rhythm) will keep the dog's attention focused on you.

e) Show enthusiasm, give lots of encouragement and much praise when he earns it.

f) Talking to the dog will make him comfortable at your side, and anxious to stay there. How, how much, how often you need to talk depends on the dog. Don't talk him to death.

g) You must CONSTANTLY observe your dog, giving praise or correction the instant it is needed.

h) Directional and pace changes should be made in rapid succession. This leaves the dog little time to concern himself with other things. Then, a few long stretches are done, until the dog becomes inattentive again.

i) Give timely, quick, snappy leash corrections when needed, and always follow with praise.

j) Tempt him to make a mistake whenever he is not paying attention, then apply your correction. Praise him afterwards.

k) Ask for perfection. Give a correction even for minor "violations".

l) Do not follow a set heeling pattern, improvise instead.

m) You should never wait for your dog, nor should you adjust your pace or your position to accommodate the lazy or rambunctious dog. A steady speed is important, it should be maintained even when giving corrections or praise.

n) Never let your dog lead you. When he pulls left, you go right. When he slows down, you run. When he forges, you make an about turn without hesitation.

o) Occasionally hold a favored toy (ball etc.) or a piece of meat in front of your chest (with the right hand). This stimulates the dog to look up to your face. Let him have the reward after a short period of practice (feed the meat, throw the ball).

p) Encourage the dog to look up to your face, by rewarding him EVERY time he does so on his own. For the reward, start your left hand below the dog's left ear and slide the hand -under the chin- up to the tip of the muzzle. This gentle stroking will lift the head up still further.

q) Heeling alongside and close to a wall or a fence teaches the dog to stay close to you.

r) If the dog heels wide, you can hold the left hand "glued" to your left knee and pet the dog near the neck, while heeling. Affectionate dogs will seek contact and stay close.
If this method fails, you can quickly yank the dog toward you and praise him afterwards. Walking past a post so that the leash between you and the dog gets caught on it is quite educational to the dog, especially when you continue with not too much hesitation.

s) If the dog crowds, goose-stepping might help.

t) Forging and lagging will be discussed below under "Problems".

u) Very brief off-lead periods should be introduced early in training. Select a fenced-in area initially, and do not change your habits or your behavior when making the transition from on to off lead. Walk in a straight line for about 50 feet, do not make any turns at that time. Clip the lead on and off frequently so that the dog can never be sure when it is safe to take liberties.

v) During the on-lead / off-lead transition, a short piece of nylon cord permanently attached to the dog's collar may be helpful. After demonstratively removing the regular leash - but inconspicuously holding on to the string - give a harsh correction if the dog slacks off.

w) Attach a light-weight 30ft line to the collar and let him drag it (he needs to get used to it first). You, or an assistant, can quickly grab it in case of training problems.

x) The nape-grab method is very effective for a correction during off-lead work.

Quickly grab the skin fold on the dog's neck and pull, shake, and/or scold the dog, depending on the age, the size, the situation and the temperament of the dog.

y) In off-lead heeling you should use both hands
   - to get your dog's attention (clapping, moving them in front of the dog's nose, maybe holding a toy or a tidbit)
   - to reward or reassure (petting, stroking)
   - to guide (channeling in turns, keeping the dog close)
   - to correct the dog.

z) Each training session should be concluded with an exercise the dog can do well. This gives you a justification to lavishly praise your dog and to happily play with him afterwards. The dog will remember, and look forward to the next training session.

REFINING PROCEDURES

a) Precision Heeling

In training, precision heeling should be done as a challenge to the dog: how well can he follow abrupt changes in pace or direction, how neatly does he sit after a halt from a run, how eager is he to stay at heel when you make a multiple right-about turn (twice around on the spot, or 720 degrees: the dog should almost wrap around your legs in doing that turn).

You must help, of course, using verbal stimulation and encouragement, verbal correction, hand contact to guide, correct and praise your dog, as well as teasers (tidbit, ball) or a leash correction, if needed.

The sit after a halt should be incorporated into the heeling routines and the various turns must be practiced.

Much of the practice should still be done on leash but the lead is now generally held in the left hand, the excess length neatly folded up.

In some trials, the judge requires execution of the commands as he gives them. You are not expected to respond instantaneously, a little lag time is perfectly all right. Taking one or two more steps after having been ordered to stop will allow for a much smoother halt and a much more accurate position of the dog. This must be practiced, however, and in training, a friend should call the shots, once in a while.

In a Schutzhund trial, you are working on your own.

Some judges insist that a particular heeling pattern be followed. While this request may or may not be justified according to the rules, it is suggested not to argue with the judge on the field.

A heeling pattern does have certain advantages: you are less likely to forget any parts, and you will cover the required distances. In training, however, you should deviate from the standard often enough so that the dog can not anticipate and learn the sequence.

b) Sit

Whenever you stop during the heeling exercise, the dog is supposed to sit automatically. The dog has to be next to you, and on your left side, sitting straight and squarely, sitting close and facing the same direction.

To teach the sit:
   - Walk forward.
   - Keep the dog on your left side.
   - Continue walking and fold up the leash in your right hand, as short as comfortably possible - but not taut. For large dogs you may have to have your right hand near the buckle of the leash. This gives you control over the front end of the dog.

- Come to a halt, and while doing so bend down in the knees, way down, but keep the upper part of the body straight, nearly vertical. This brings your left hand down to the level of the dog where you can guide him, without changing directions, without shifting position, and without leaning over him - all of which could create undesirable associations.
- You should not turn toward your dog, you must both face the same direction.
- Give the command SIT.
- A split second after the command, tap the dog with your left hand on the croup. If the dog does not sit, hit him harder. At the same time give a tug with the leash, up and back, or up and forward, depending on the reaction and position of the dog.
Hold the leash up straight and reasonably taut, above the dog's head.
- While the dog is preparing to sit, guide him into a straight position.
If the dog swings his rear end behind you, use the left hand to slap him on the right flank, to push him away. However, if he swings his rear end away from you, then the left hand slaps him on the left flank and guides him into a straight sit.
This guiding must be done while the dog is *in the process* of sitting down, NOT afterwards. Also, both dog and handler must continue to face the same direction, namely forward.
- Straighten up the knees.
- Praise your dog calmly.

c) Start up
Some trainers suggest to move the left foot first, others say to move the right foot first when starting to heel. It does not really matter since most likely the dog will lag in both instances, initially. What the dog really needs is an "early warning" system.

For the start-up in heeling:
- Get the dog to sit at heel, straight.
- Visually check ring, ground, stewards and judges position.
- Check your dog again.
- Count slowly 1 - 2 - 3 - 4 - 5 - 6 and do one of the following things on each count:
    1. Straighten your body, concentrate your thoughts.
    2. Move your feet unobtrusively up and down a few times, as if you were walking in place. This should not be overdone. To an observer it should look like restlessness, rather than like an exercise.
    3. Bend one knee slightly forward, the one you will be using in taking the first step. It does not matter which foot starts.
    4. Give the command "heel".
    5. Maintain the posture from position 3 and fall forward, feet together, body straight. If it was not for the next step (6), you would fall flat on your face.
    6. Step out.

The preceding sequence helps you to standardize one of the most tense spots in an obedience trial. Being sure what to do there - because so much attention was given to it in practice - makes the rest of the trial easy.
The routine forces you to concentrate on a sequence of events which leaves little room for other worries.
Your restlessness causes the dog to pay attention and to be ready for the moment of the start. Steps 3, 4 and 5 above actually cause the dog to believe that you are already moving, giving him a little head start. This is needed to have the team perfectly lined up from the very beginning.

d) Turns

Left Turn
Tighten the leash (held in the left hand) to slow the dog down just a little while stopping the forward movement with the extended left foot. Bring the right foot up to the left foot (both feet are side by side now) while turning the body 90 degrees to the left. Then stride out in the new direction, logically with the left foot first. Notice that during this maneuver the outstretched left leg blocks the dog's path, to guide him into the new direction.

Other foot techniques are possible, but common to all of them is the slight hesitation during the turn, and the sharp, 90 degree angle the handler executes.

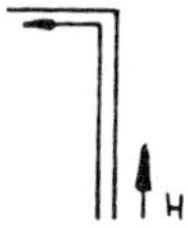

Later, the exercise is done off leash. If needed, you can slide the left hand along the left side of the dog (front to back), to push his rear end around, to line it up with the new direction. Such assistance is eliminated gradually.

FIG. 20

Right turn
Stop forward movement with the right foot extended to the front. Give little tugs with the leash (held in the right hand) while at the same time petting the dog on the neck with the left hand, encouraging him to speed up and to stay with you during the turn. In the meantime, the left foot has been brought up to the right foot (both feet are side by side now). Stride out in the new direction, logically with the right foot first.
Other foot techniques are possible, but common to all of them is the minute hesitation during the turn (very important here since the dog has to walk the larger outside circle), and the sharp, 90 degree angle the handler executes.

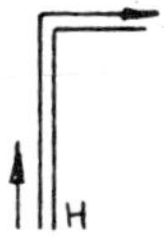

Done off leash, both hands should be used to pet, stroke, and encourage the dog to speed up during the turn. If necessary, a tug on the collar (if you can get a hold of it quickly enough), or the nape grab can be employed to get cooperation. This must be followed with praise, of course.

FIG. 21

About turns
There are three ways to do an about turn:
    Right About Turn (AKC style)
    Left About Turn (Schutzhund style)
    Left About Swing (flashy style).

Right About Turn
This is really an extended right turn. Stop forward movement with the right foot extended to the front. Give little tugs with the leash (held in the right hand) while at the same time petting your dog on the neck with the left hand, encouraging him to speed up and to stay with you during the turn.
In the meantime, the left foot has been brought up to the right foot (both feet are side by side now). Stepping in place (don't overdo it), continue to turn until you have completed a half circle (180 degrees). Then stride out in the new direction, most likely with the left foot first.

It is important
- that you hesitate just long enough to give the dog a
    chance to walk the larger outside circle
- that you keep your feet together while turning, to avoid
    tripping the dog
- that you move and simulate walking while turning on the
    spot, otherwise the dog will come to a halt also
- that you resume a brisk pace walking in the opposite
    direction as soon as the dog has completed the turn.
Done off leash, both hands should be used to pet, stroke, and encourage the dog to speed up during the turn. If necessary, a tug on the collar (if you can get a hold of it quickly enough), or the nape grab can be employed to get cooperation. This must be followed with praise, of course.

FIG. 22

Left About Turn
This is really an extension of the "finish" from the recall exercise.
Stop forward movement and turn left, facing the broadside of your dog. With the leash (short) in the right hand, encourage the dog to turn right, around you. Stepping in place to indicate motion while

slowly turning to the left until you face the opposite direction, change the leash behind your back into the left hand. Encourage your dog to keep going around, and resume a brisk walking pace in the opposite direction as soon as the dog has completed the turn.

During off lead training, both hands can be used to guide and praise the dog.

FIG. 23

Left About Swing

This turn is seldom seen. It is best left to the owner of a lively, eager animal. In training, keep the leash very short in your right hand, and use the left hand on the canines left flank, teaching him to back up and to swing backwards into the new direction while turning to the left yourself. For an eager retriever, a ball can be used to excite and manipulate the dog to jump into the proper position. During the initial training it is important to have complete physical control over the dog's front and rear end, to avoid confusion and frustration.

FIG. 24

e) Normal, Fast and Slow Pace

"Normal Pace" is by no means a leisurely stroll. The suggested speed for most working dogs is a rather brisk 5 - 6 MPH.

The length of the strides should be adjusted for harmony in movement of dog and handler (it almost always means shorter strides). Walking briskly helps to focus the dog's attention on you (it also provides you with some physical exercise).

Changes to Slow or Fast Pace should not be too abrupt, and in Schutzhund training, you are allowed a "heel" command to alert the dog to the change. Some dogs interpret the slow pace as a signal to come to a halt and to sit, especially when a leash correction is given to slow the dog down. To avoid this confusion, you should try to eliminate the leash correction, and you should generate some additional body movements, for instance by swinging the front foot out with every step, like in a military parade step. If done within reason, the technique will not be faulted even in a trial.

For the fast pace, running speed is required. Training for it, you must excite your dog sufficiently to get cooperation, for instance with verbal encouragement, or by clapping the hands, or by using treats or a toy, etc.

f) The Group / Figure Eight

As part of the Schutzhund Trial, the handler/dog team must move in and out of a group of people milling about. There is at least one halt required in this group, and the judge usually asks the handler to circle one of the people in the group to the right, and another one to the left. A sit, down, stand out of motion may also be requested. Although somewhat more difficult, this exercise is similar to the FIGURE EIGHT required in AKC obedience. The training suggestions given here apply to both forms of competition. It must be understood, however, that the exercises recommended below do not constitute the actual requirements in a trial.

For practice purposes, two objects (barrels, chairs, cartons etc.) can be placed four feet apart. Beginning close to the connection line, circle the object on the left first. This is the preferred choice since it gives you a chance to easily control the dog: he is between a rock (the post) and a hard spot (the handler) when YOU take the outside circle. A good start often means a good exercise.

Proceeding at first with the Figure 8 pattern, deviations should be incorporated occasionally. You may want to circle one object twice, reverse directions, round both objects as a unit in O-type fashion etc.

In training you should slow down on left circles. This forces the dog to pay attention and to adjust his pace. Leash correction for forging dogs, and hand as well as verbal contacts for encouragement, are recommended.

For right circles you should speed up intentionally. Most dogs will lag here since they have to negotiate the larger turn. Forcing them to be alert and to accelerate whenever there is a right turn will change that behavior into a habit.

TOP WORKING DOGS

A metronome or a tape recorder with march music have been used successfully by some trainers to maintain a steady pace in this exercise.

In time the objects should be changed to smaller ones and finally be just sticks which have to be circled at close quarters.

As another variation change the speed, going fast all the way at one time, and rather slowly at another time.

Furthermore, the objects should be placed farther apart, and sometimes even closer together, for variety.

Distractions

Distractions can be introduced once the dog performs well under the conditions outlined above.
- Stewards with and without dogs take the place of the objects suggested above, for practice.
- Spectators stand around and keep a noisy conversation going - or they may clap their hands, or say "boooo".
- Other dogs are worked at close quarters: the retrieve, the send-out, or a few protection exercises are always attention getters. A caged bird, rabbit or cat are almost irresistible temptations for a dog.
- The exercise can be done in public places. Shopping plazas, schools, bus and railroad stations, airports etc. are ideal for this purpose. Inquire first, since local laws may prohibit the use of these public places for dog training.
- Food distractions can be introduced also. Meat dropped on the floor or in the hands of the stewards may attract the dog's attention.

In all these instances you should insist on perfection. Quick corrections, verbal and physical encouragement, praise for good work, short and happy training sessions will accomplish the most.

On Leash vs. Off Leash

Heeling on lead can not be stressed enough. Even dogs in higher classes of competition should be trained on lead frequently. As soon as the dog becomes inattentive or lazy, a few turns on lead should be inserted, followed by short off-lead periods.

A short piece of nylon cord (or nylon fishing line with a handle) attached to the dog's collar in addition to the regular leash works well in the transition period from on to off leash heeling. Once the regular leash is removed and thrown to the side with much fuss, you are still able to surprise your dog with a leash correction by holding on to the short string.

Circle Weave

All handlers and assistants form a circle, leaving about 3 ft. spaces between them. The handlers keep their dogs sitting at heel position, in this circle.

One dog/handler team leaves its place and weaves its way in and out of the circle, around the stationary other members of the group. Upon return to their spot, the next dog/handler team proceeds.

The handler of the moving team encourages his dog to stay in a nice heel position. The stationary members of the group must keep their dogs under control.

Instead of just weaving, the team can also do a "Super Figure Eight": circling the first "post" to the left, the next to the right, the next to the left, etc.

Reverse

All dog/handler teams form a queue, one team behind the other at a distance of about 10 ft.

The queue moves out, at a normal pace.

The first team at the head of the queue makes an about turn and weaves its way (right, left, right, left etc.) through the group. Having passed the last member, they turn around and join the moving queue at the end.

During all this time, the queue had continued to move straight ahead.

The second team then repeats the performance of the first team and so on, until everybody had a chance.

Line Formation
Several assistants form a line, leaving about 4 ft. spaces between them.
The line moves forward at a steady pace.
One dog/handler team moves in and out of, and through, the line in an irregular pattern.

Group
At least four assistants form a group. They slowly mill about and keep a conversation going. They are not supposed to get out of the way of a dog/handler team but they may have to stop momentarily to let them pass.
One or two dog/handler teams work inside and around this group, taking right, left, about turns and right and left circles around a group member. A few halts should be included also.
During such a halt the handler may want to shake hands with an assistant, pat him on the shoulder and start a brief conversation.

Crowd
Four stakes and a rope (or other boundary markers) are needed for this exercise.
An area of sufficient size (maybe 40 x 40 ft for four dog/handler teams) is staked out.
All handlers with their dogs practice heeling within the boundaries of the ring. Halts should be included.
Assistants slowly decrease the size of the ring by moving the posts closer together. After a while the space should be so crowded that dogs and handlers have a difficult time to move at all.
Then the exercise is terminated.

PROBLEMS

a) Take-off
Some dogs say "good bye" as soon as the lead is unclipped.
To get him back, wait a little until the initial excitement is over - then sternly command "down" (a "come" will, most likely, not work at that time). Go and pick him up - don't call him.
A less glorious way to catch your dog is to ask everybody on the training field (that is people and dogs) to join you in walking to your car. Tell your dog you leave him there, and that you will have a marvelous time without him. To convince him, you may have to start your engine, or even to drive a couple of yards, but it works - as long as the dog is watching.
You can try to bait your dog with food, a ball, a stick, but only a few dogs will fall for this trap.
Never run after your dog to catch him - he will enjoy this game, for hours on end.

The next step would be to resume leash training, for quite some time (re-read the "heeling" section).

b) Forging
Heeling correctly, a dog should always have his shoulder lined up with the left knee (hip) of the handler. When staying farther back the dog is 'lagging', when moving farther ahead the dog 'forges'. Of the two, forging is much easier to correct.
Forging clearly is a matter of the handler not having the dog's attention. He must get it, and keep it.
For the first two approaches outlined below you need a leather leash and a small-link choke chain, or - if the dog is stronger than you are - a prong collar. For the correction, you must also determine the minimum amount of force required to get the dog's attention.

A secluded training field is best suited for initial training, later on a busy place with distractions should be selected.

Corrective Turns
This procedure is most suitable for dogs in the beginning stages of training, or for those dogs that forge ahead badly.
Heel your dog at a normal pace, on a loose leash. Wait until the dog forges ahead, not paying attention to you. Then do the following in rapid succession:

- give your dog more lead, not restricting him at this time
- turn to the right (90 degree)
- brace yourself, feet set apart, and hold the leash securely with both hands
- command "heel"
- hesitate a little
- give a sudden, snappy leash correction which should propel the dog toward you
- turn another 90 degree to the right and proceed in the opposite direction of your original travel (back to the starting place)
- praise the dog for having made the turn with you (although you did all the work yourself) and for being on your side now.

The total sequence of events should require no more than one second.

After a few times, the command and the preparation for the correction will cause the smart dog to dash to your side. If this happens, then the correction must NOT be given.

Bump
The following applies to working dogs with moderate forging habits.

Heel your dog at a normal pace, on a loose leash, and wait until he is forging approximately one foot ahead. Then make a sudden left turn on the spot, swiveling on the ball of the left foot. While turning on the left foot, raise your right foot to the back, bend your knee, swing your right, extended knee around and connect with the right shoulder of the dog. If done properly, the dog gets thrown off balance. He was forging ahead far enough so that he could not see the correction coming. To be better prepared the next time, the dog will try to stay just a little farther back which, of course, equals better heeling.

During the whole procedure the dog is held on a very short, but not taut, leash. This enables you to better aim for the dog's shoulder and to pull him back to your side after the collision. Genuine praise should be given afterwards.

A word of caution: You should abandon the collision attempt when you realize that not the dog's shoulders but instead his rump or the head will be hit. Try again.

Verbal Correction
The third approach applies to dogs that only occasionally forge a little. These dogs are usually in an advanced training stage, or they belong to the group of soft, sensitive dogs.

Both types respond readily to a voice command if given properly. A short, crisp, sharp 'hey' or the like will redirect the dog's attention, away from whatever he was interested in at the moment and back to you. To maintain the regained control praise him. A follow-up with rapid changes in pace and direction will keep his mind busy and focused on you.

c) Lagging

Lagging can occur for several reasons: fear, shyness, habit, boredom, laziness, distractions etc. You must determine the cause first, before you can address the problem.

Comparing heeling on lead to off lead might give a clue. Dogs lagging more on lead than off lead usually have had traumatic training experiences, like too much pressure or force in leash training. A better, more empathic dog/handler relationship must be developed where gentleness, encouragement, praise and reward can help the dog to overcome his shyness or fear - in time. Make training sessions very short, and very pleasant, for instance.

If heeling on and off lead do not differ much, another approach must be taken.
Dogs lagging out of boredom, inattentiveness or habit have to be awakened. A moderate but snappy leash correction followed immediately by lots of praise and encouragement, a faster walking speed, sudden and rapid changes in pace and direction will usually do just that. A ball, a toy, or a tempting tidbit held in front of your chest during very brief training segments (and then offered to the dog) will often accomplish the same. It is important that you get the dog's cooperation.

In addition to these suggestions, the following points should be considered:
- Off lead heeling should be started early in the training program, for brief periods.
- On lead, as well as off lead work should be done during brief training sessions for advanced dogs.
- The dog should be encouraged to move up to you (faster pace, coaxing, baiting, teasing with ball, toy or tidbit, clapping hands, bending down, praising - all this while still walking). You must never slow down or wait for the dog to catch up.
- Just that minimum amount of force should be applied in a correction that is needed to get this dog's attention. Much praise is offered after each correction.
- The dog must feel comfortable while in the proper position. Give reward, praise, petting while you continue walking.
- For advanced work, you should practice in areas with lots of distractions (check local laws first), like shopping plazas, downtown areas, bus and railroad stations, airports, stores (many pet stores will allow dogs inside !), school yards and factory entrances at quitting time, or in dog obedience classes. It is more likely that lagging will occur in these places which you then can correct.

d) Inattentiveness

An inattentive dog reflects very poorly on his handler, pointing to a lack of team spirit. Correct the situation right away, do not let it become a habit. You probably will have to change your attitude, become more enthusiastic, more spirited, more animated, more "peppy".
Surprise him with short BURSTS of enthusiasm, walk faster, make changes in direction and speed after every 4-5 steps, do sudden halts from fast pace, do running starts from a stand still, move into the opposite direction when he is not paying attention, etc.
In doing so, use forceful leash corrections - and praise afterwards.
Try to get the dog to look at you, to watch your face. Use food, toys, animation, pet him spontaneously, slide your hand from his throat to the tip of his muzzle.
Make the training sessions short and fun.
Do not go through the same training routine every time, concentrate on a different exercise for each daily session.

e) Jumping

Dogs who jump up while heeling must NOT be punished unless you want to turn your eager, happy, spirited animal into a "drag along". You should instead speed up for a few paces whenever the dog jumps. This forces him to keep all four feet on the ground in order to stay next to you.

•• SIT ••

GENERAL
Besides being useful by itself, the sit is a part of many different exercises. It should be practiced early in training, and the dog should be made to sit quickly and squarely when told to do so.

OBJECTIVE
On command, the dog will sit, instantaneously, fast, reliably, under any condition, and he will remain sitting in that spot until released by his handler.

SUGGESTED COMMAND: " Sit"
SUGGESTED RELEASE COMMAND: "OK"   (or "heel")

PSYCHOLOGY
The "sit" is a transitory state: the dog wants either to relax (lay down) or to get up (walk away). The handler must, therefore, be prepared to correct instantaneously and firmly if the need arises.

The "stay" command is not needed.
The purpose of a command is to solicit some response from the dog. The "stay" command defeats this purpose: NO action is wanted.

PREREQUISITES
None, except a well-established dog/handler relationship.

TEACHING PROCEDURE
During initial training the leash should be clipped to the collar - mainly to prevent an escape. Later on, off-lead training is recommended.

Options available:

a) Inducive Method
It was described earlier under puppy training.

b) Show & Tell
Teaching the sit is best done with the dog on the left side of the handler. The exercise begins with the dog standing.

Hold the leash in your right hand, as short as comfortably possible - but not   taut. For large dogs place the right hand near the buckle of the leash. This gives you control over the front end of the dog.
(Control over the rear end is exercised with the left hand).

Then give the command SIT. A split second after the command, tap the dog with the left hand on the croup. If he does not sit, hit harder. At the same time, give a tug with the leash, up and back, or up and forward, depending on the reaction and the position of the dog. Then hold the leash up straight and with some tension, above the dog's head.

While the dog is preparing to sit, guide him into a straight position:
If he swings his rear end behind you, the left hand should be ready to slap him on the right flank. However, if he swings his rear away from you, slap him with the left hand on the left flank to make him slide him into a straight sit. This guiding must be done while the dog is in the process of sitting down, NOT after he is sitting already.
During the sit, praise him calmly only. Offer lots of praise, however, after the release command has been given.

REFINING PROCEDURE
Practice the exercise in various locations, with various distractions, even during a casual walk. The dog may be close by when given the command, or he may be further away. Always insist on an immediate response, using correction and praise as needed.

a) Sit out of Motion
This should be practiced after the dog reliably executes the regular sit command.

In preparation for it, fold the lead in your right hand as short as comfortably possible, while heeling. Wait until the dog heels parallel, then give the command "sit", firmly, followed immediately by a snap on the lead upward/backward and a tap (do not push) on the dog's croup with the left hand. All this is done while you slowly continue walking in the original direction. However, in passing the dog's head you turn gradually to the left to face your dog. Come to a halt in front of him. Hold the tight leash in your outstretched hand straight up over the dog's head.
After a while return to the heel position and release your dog.

In subsequent training sessions eliminate the tap and the snap with the leash. Successively, drop the leash to the ground, move farther away, do the exercise off lead, discontinue the turn to face the dog and pretend not to watch your dog anymore once the command "sit" is given.

In training it is a good idea
- to tell the dog that he is doing fine as long as he remains sitting
- not to release the dog immediately after your return
- to practice the sit out of motion on various occasions, especially when he is NOT heeling.
If the dog does not perform well or breaks, you should rush back to him and position him properly, not being too gentle, too friendly or too talkative at that time.
Give him a lot of praise at the end of a successful exercise, however.

For reliable performances, practice the "sit out of motion" and the "stand out of motion" as the more difficult exercises more frequently, the "down out of motion" (see below) less often, but all under a variety of conditions, and always as a surprise to the dog.

b) Long Sit with and without Distractions

Procedures are identical to the "Long Down w & w/o Distractions" (below).

PROBLEMS

a) No Sit
When commanded to sit, the dog remains in place but he lays down or he stands.
To correct the problem you should physically manipulate the dog into the sit (see above), making sure that your commands for "sit", "down" and "stand" sound sufficiently different.

b) Slow Sit
If the dog sits slowly, quick corrections are needed. The tug on the leash and the tap on the croup must come a split second after the command was given. The dog will try to avoid the correction the next time and sit faster.

When the sit is practiced in connection with heeling, you can hold a stick (maybe 2 ft. long) in the right hand behind your back, and land one end of it with a flick of the wrist on the croup of the dog very shortly after the command was given. The dog can not see it coming, so he has to associate the hit with the command. Heeding this warning, he will learn to sit quickly, quickly.

c) Changing Position
After a while, the dog may decide to lay down or to get up.
Close supervision to detect the dog's first muscle movement to change position, and a verbal correction given in time, may prevent the problem. If not, you must rush to the dog and physically put him back into place. This is best done silently (except for an angry "sit") and firmly.
If the dog has a tendency to run off, a leash or a light-weight line can be attached to the collar. (see also DOWN, below)

** DOWN ••

GENERAL
The down is a life saver in more than one way.
It can be used to control the hyperactive, the obnoxious, the evasive, or the aggressive dog, and it can be used to keep the dog out of the way - your way, or that of an automobile.
If a dog is set on pursuing a cat, no "heel", "here" or "come" will get him back. Only the "down" - if it was practiced properly - will prevent him from going onto the road and getting hit by a car.

OBJECTIVE
On command, the dog will drop to the ground, instantaneously, fast, reliably, under any condition, and he will remain at that spot laying down until released by his handler.

SUGGESTED COMMAND:	"down"
SUGGESTED RELEASE COMMAND:	"OK"

PSYCHOLOGY
The "down" is one of the two commands that the dog has to obey out of fear ("out" is the other one). We utilize a natural response where the animal seeks cover to avoid a threatening situation. A dog understanding the meaning of the command yet not complying with it should receive instantaneous and forceful correction, given in a threatening manner.
This approach does not allow for more than very low-key praise during the down. Afterwards, however, heap praise on your dog, to make up for, and release, the pressure your dog was subjected to during this exercise.

PREREQUISITES
None, except a well-established dog/handler relationship.

TEACHING PROCEDURE
Initial training is best done with the leash clipped to the collar - mainly to prevent an escape. Later on, off-lead training is necessary. Options available are:

a) Inducive Method
It was described earlier under puppy training.

b) Show & Tell
Kneel, with the dog sitting on your left side. Reaching over the dog's shoulder, grasp the left front paw with your left hand, and the right front paw with your right hand. Then slide the feet out to the front, giving the "down" command at the same time. Place the left hand on the dog's shoulder with gentle pressure to prevent any attempt of getting up. Don't give any praise at this time, the dog would take it as a sign to get up. A little reassurance is all right, however.

There are a few other, less desirable methods that have limited applications in certain instances:

c) FLIP #1
With the dog standing on soft ground, broadside, kneel next to him and reach for the feet on the opposite side. Then quickly pull the feet out from under him and command "down" the same time.

d) FLIP #2
Quickly grab the loose skin near the shoulder with your l (r) hand, and the loose skin near the croup with your r (l) hand. Pull towards you and flip him to the ground. If this procedure takes longer than 1/2 of a second, then the dog will prepare himself and fight - and you can not win.

e) TUG #1
Reach for the live ring on the choke collar, give a tug downwards and tell the dog to go   "down".

f) TUG #2
Hold the leash in a short loop and hang on to your end. Place one foot over the buckle which is attached to the dog's choke collar, and quickly step on it, giving the "down" command at the same time. Watch your balance.

REFINING PROCEDURE
Once the dog understands the command "down", you can work on perfecting the exercise:

a) Reliability
Practice everywhere (quiet and busy places), anytime (day or night, rain or shine), at home, on the street, in a mud puddle, during casual walks etc. Give the down command as soon as the thought occurs to you. This prevents the dog from preparing for the down by reading your (unintentional) gestures or facial expression.

b) Speed
A fast response is desirable. It can be accomplished by giving an angry, sharp, short, stern command, then waiting a quarter of a second, then quickly bending over the dog with both arms

outstretched - a very dominating posture - and flipping him with both hands to the ground ("Flip #2", above), provided he did not comply already.

Be quick with your correction, prepare yourself for it, avoid the wrestling contest.

You may have to push him sideways if he has planted his feet to the ground. After a couple of times the dog will want to avoid the push, and he will go down quickly by himself.

c) Distance

Teaching the down should at first be done with the dog on your side, then a few feet away, then a few yards away etc. A very effective means of practice is to give the dog a chance to roam and to wait until he is far enough away. Then all of the sudden he is commanded to go "down". If the dog does not respond well, he is made to obey (long line, assistant, throw chain, sling shot, shock collar - note that the dog will run away if he sees the projectile coming his way), and you must go back to practicing at closer range.

d) Sit

Before releasing the dog and rewarding him, he can be asked to change into a sit. This does not only look professional, it is also a requirement according to some trial rules:

Return to your dog's right side (the proper heel position, dog still down), give the command "sit" and then, after a short moment, praise him.

e) Down out of Motion

The down command is given during slow, normal and fast pace heeling, first on lead (the lead is just dropped), then off lead. You continue walking while the dog lays down and remains behind.

Initially, stay fairly close to your dog and observe his response to the command. A quick, well-timed correction (if needed) is essential.

In a trial, however, you may not turn the head to check on your dog, and you must continue without hesitation for a specified number of paces.

f) Long Down w & w/o Distractions

Gradually increase the time during which you ask the dog to remain in the down position, maybe to 20 minutes. Stay close by, move farther away, or even hide in the vicinity. Disappearing at one end of a building and sneaking back behind it to the other side will allow you to watch the dog without being noticed yourself. A large mirror in an elevated position, or a reflecting store window may accomplish the same trick.

Distractions during the long down, like people, dogs, cats, vehicles, noises (incl. gun shots) should be introduced sensibly and gradually. A stranger calling the dog or offering some food, and protection work by another team done during the long down are quite a temptation for any dog.

In all these instances, you should be prepared to correct (or sometimes to reassure) the dog as soon as he indicates that he wants to move. Ideally, you or an assistant should check the dog the very moment he moves the first muscle to get up. A long check cord may serve this purpose.

If the dog has already gotten up, then you must rush back. Bring him firmly and quickly (but silently) back to the original spot and yank him down not too gently. Don't give any praise until sufficient time has elapsed to conclude the exercise.

Some handlers believe that screaming the "stay" command at their dog will prevent him from leaving his position. This is not only offending a dog's intelligence, and his delicate sense of hearing, it is also a public announcement of a handler's doubt in his and in his dog's capabilities. Besides, it does not work. Not the loudness, but the determination standing behind a handler's command impresses a dog. And determination can be whispered!

PROBLEMS

a) No Down

When commanded to go down, the dog remains in place but he sits or stands. Physically manipulate the dog into the down position (see above "FLIP #2", "Speed"), making sure that your commands for "down", "sit" and "stand" sound sufficiently different.

TOP WORKING DOGS

b) Creeping
The dog inches toward you, or toward another point of interest.
Close supervision is needed to detect the first muscle movement in preparation for creeping. Give a firm verbal correction at this time, attach a long line to the collar and have an assistant operate it, land pebbles or a throw chain about two feet ahead of the dog's nose, set up a real barrier (a board from the broad jump on edge) or a psychological barrier (scratch line on the ground just in front of the dog's nose), it may cause the dog to abandon his creeping. Practicing just short of a drop in terrain (embankment, small cliff) or close to the edge on a raised platform (heavy sheet of 4x8 plywood, table) may help also. It requires quite a few practice sessions, however, to eliminate creeping.

c) Getting up
The dog gets up and leaves his position.
This is usually somewhat easier to correct than creeping, once the reason for it has been determined.
Practicing the down with you (later on an assistant) nearby, giving reassurance, a forceful correction, a firm verbal correction (timing is very important !), or using the long check cord will help.

During early training stages, you can guide the leash under the heel of your foot, pick up any slack, and step on it forcefully as soon as the dog wants to get up (see above under "Tug #2").
Some dogs will break as soon as the handler returns. To them, the return is the signal to be released (or to be corrected). To break this habit in training, return to your dog and circle him one time, or several times; or return, go away, return again, several times, before you release the dog.
Some dogs will leave the down position in anticipation of a recall. While this is one of the exercises in a Schutzhund trial, in practice you should most of the time (90%) return to your dog, rather than calling him.
Some dogs will get up when the gun is fired. It may help when you stand close by and reassure him. If this does not help, the problem of gun-shyness must be addressed individually (see TEMPERAMENT TESTING).
Methods that should NOT be used since they will aggravate the problem are: electronic collars, throw chains, sling shots.

** STAND ••

GENERAL
The "stand" has practical applications for grooming, examining, carting, backpacking, preventing the dog from sitting in the dirt etc. It is also an excellent control exercise.

OBJECTIVE
On command, the dog will cease to move (his feet, that is) and remain in a standing position until released by his handler.

SUGGESTED COMMAND:	"stand"
SUGGESTED RELEASE COMMAND:	"OK"

PSYCHOLOGY
Standing motionless for more than a very short moment is quite unnatural. The dog wants either to move on, or to get more comfortable (lay down, sit). For that reason, the "stand" is one of the more difficult exercises to teach.
It requires to mildly shock the dog with the way how the command is given, and, therefore, it should not be practiced in conjunction with precision heeling.

To avoid undesirable associations (like anticipating a recall and leaving the stand position prematurely), return to the dog 90 percent of the time, do not normally call him to you.

PREREQUISITES
Long sit and long down

TEACHING PROCEDURE
The most natural approach to teaching the "stand" is to prevent the walking dog from sitting, rather than telling him to get up into a standing position (from a sit, for instance).

With the dog on lead, take a few steps and give the command "stand". Draw out the word: "sta-------nd", raising the voice just a little at the end of it, to become authoritative.
Practice the (AKC) "stand for examination" first.

Stand for Examination
To teach this exercise, bend over your dog, having the right hand on the collar, and the left hand with gentle pressure on the left flank of the dog. If the dog is responsive then the left hand barely makes contact. If, however, the dog insists on sitting then the left hand has to hold up the rear end of the dog as much as necessary.
Male dogs generally do not approve of this procedure, it should, therefore, be used by the owner only, and with much discretion.

When you give the command "stand" be sure that the dog is standing comfortably. There is usually no problem if the dog was allowed to walk into the stand.
Sometimes the front feet are not side by side. Lift up the front end of the dog a little by reaching under the chest, and set him down again.

Initially, the command "stand" can be repeated a couple of times, to accustom the dog to it.
React quickly if the dog moves. Reach for the offending foot and place it back to where it came from, saying "no, stand" at the same time. Don't give any leash corrections, they cause the dog to sit. Harsh scolding usually has the same undesirable effect.

Once the dog understands, another person is asked to step up to him from the front, from the dog's left side, to pet him, and to slide the hand along the dog's back. The dog should be approached in a confident manner. A hesitant, fearful, bold or intimidating assistant usually means trouble.

For the first few times you will have to stay close to your dog, to correct the inevitable foot movements. Later on, you can step back further and observe the examination from a distance.
In AKC trials, you must give the "stand/stay" command and then walk away six feet (not back up !) from the dog so that the judge may examine him. The situation is often tense, especia lly if the judge is tense himself. Prepare your dog for this in training, by asking the assistant to dress strangely, to walk strangely, to act strangely when examining the dog.

Stand out of Motion
For this exercise, the dog has to come to an abrupt halt and to remain standing until released by you. Give the command while heeling at normal, or at running pace, you continuing and the dog remaining behind. You may then either return to your dog or call him to you.
To avoid anticipation, we suggest that you return to him in practice almost all of the time (90%).

As always, early training is best done on leash.
After giving the command, drop the lead and place the outstretched right hand in front of the dog's face, blocking his view without touching him. If necessary, the left hand is held on the right flank of the dog.

To prevent the dog from moving forward you must stay close, initially. In addition you should turn, to face the dog for the first few times.
The primary cues (blocking the vision, contact with the flank) should follow the secondary cue (command "stand") within a fraction of a second.

REFINING PROCEDURE
Once the dog has mastered the basic principles of the exercise, eliminate - one at a time -
- the turn to face the dog
- the touch on the flank
- the outstretched hand in front of the dog.

Still working on leash and in close proximity to the dog, try to refine the exercise with
- a more sudden stop
- a secure and sure stand, until the release is given.

Then
- practice off leash
- move further away from the dog
- move out of sight for a short moment
- do the stand out of slow, normal and fast pace
- do the exercise with distractions, with other dogs, people, machinery around.

PROBLEMS
Each animal is different and requires a different approach in problem solving. The suggestions given below may or may not apply to a particular dog.

Rather than going through the list and trying one after the other, select the most appropriate approach based on the personality of your dog. It is quite likely that minor or major modifications have to be made.

a) The dog is afraid and uneasy
When introduced to the "stand", soft dogs often cringe, back arched, tail tugged between the legs.
1) Be less harsh, back off on the pressure.
2) Practice this exercise only once per session.
3) Give lots of praise, and play with the dog, afterwards.

b) The dog sits when coming to a halt
4) Practice on leash.
5) Do not praise your dog during the stand, only afterwards.
6) Stay close to your dog and repeat the stand command.
7) Together with the "stand" command gently put your left hand into the right flank of the dog.
8) Catch his rear end on the way down with your left foot under the belly, gently lift him up.
9) As 8) but use your left hand.
10) As 8) but quickly grab the loose skin on the back, near his croup, and pull him up.
11) Lay a short piece of rope loose over his back, or tie it loosely around his belly.
12) Make a large choke collar out of your leash by sliding the buckle through the loop handle. Put this "collar" loosely around the dog's belly/groin. Hold on to the buckle and tighten the choke if the dog wants to sit.
13) Give the "stand" command when your dog has just stepped over one of the boards from the broad jump, set on its edge. The board is between the front and the hind legs, but closer to the rear. On the way down (to sit) the dog will make contact with the board - which tells him to stand.

c) The dog sits when the handler returns
14) The suggestions 4-11 from above can be tried.
15) Leave your dog, return, leave, return, leave etc. for several times before you release him from the stand.
16) Before finishing the exercise with the sit command, heel your dog a few paces straight ahead.

d) The dog does not stand right away
He continues forward for one or more steps after the command to stand:

17) Try suggestions 4-6 from above.
18) Together with the command "stand" quickly put your cupped left hand over his snout and push it toward his chest. Release immediately.
18) Together with the command "stand" quickly grab the loose skin around his neck. Release immediately.
19) Rush to him and put him and his feet back into exactly the same positions where they were supposed to stay.

e) <u>The dog leaves his position when the handler returns</u>
20) Try suggestions 4 5 6 15 16 20 from above.

** RECALL ••

GENERAL
The FORMAL recall should be one of the last exercises taught in a basic obedience program. The INFORMAL recall, however, can be practiced as soon as the handler obtains his dog.

OBJECTIVE
On command, the dog will come to his handler, fast and reliably. He will stop for a sit in front of him and go to the heel position when asked to do so.

SUGGESTED COMMAND: "come"   "heel"
SUGGESTED RELEASE COMMAND: "OK"

PSYCHOLOGY
Motivation is the key element in teaching the recall.
1. The dog must WANT to come to you when called
2. The dog must EXPECT something pleasant when he is called,
      Then everything else will fall in place easily.

To avoid confusion, the command "come" should be reserved for the occasion where the dog is expected to perform competition-style. The dog must be able to count on the reward, and on the fun, in connection with this command.
On the other hand, if you just want the dog to be closer, then another command should be used, for instance "here". Then there is no need to follow through with the praise, the games, etc.

PREREQUISITES
None, except a well-established dog/handler relationship.

TEACHING PROCEDURE
Two rules apply, and they must be followed religiously:
1. The "come when called" must ALWAYS be an enjoyable experience for the dog, it should ALWAYS end on a happy note.
2. The dog is NEVER, never reprimanded when he comes to his handler of his own free will - regardless of what happened before.

Introduction:
In compliance with these requirements, and to psychologically prepare the dog for the reward, the dog is invited, not commanded, to come.
A pleasant tone of voice sets the stage for happy things to come. There must be no doubt in the dog's mind that when he dashes in, his master will be happy and pleased.

The exercise ends, and the fun begins, when the dog gets within your reach. Do not practice the formal front sit and the finish in connection with the recall, at this stage. Instead, reward the dog immediately: friendly words, praise, petting, playing, roughhousing, etc.

                    TOP WORKING DOGS

Food rewards are very effective, especially when the dog is hungry, and when the treat is truly a delicacy in his eyes.

After rewarding the dog for coming, set him free again. The dog must not form the undesirable association between being called and being put on a leash.
If he has to be restrained, then you should first give praise lavishly, before clipping on the lead in an inconspicuous and casual way. Furthermore, for a short time thereafter, you should not give any leash corrections.

For progression, call from close distances at first (tease the dog with the reward), from larger distances later on.

Squatting, clapping hands, excitedly calling and backing up or running AWAY from the dog entice a reluctant pupil to approach his master.

To reinforce the recall, take your dog to a remote field which is unfamiliar to him, far away from cars and other people.
Set him free and allow, even encourage, him to roam. Hide quickly once he is far enough away and not paying any attention.
Call him from hiding, once only. Then remain silent and motionless until the dog finds you.
It will take some time on the first try, it may even require a second call. You should, however, not reveal your location prematurely. The dog, having ignored your call, must experience the feeling of being left behind. This will teach him to respond quicker to the call, and to keep an eye on you while roaming.
After two tries, you will probably have a tough time to ever hide again without being seen by your dog.

Completion:
Practice the front sit and the finish independently of the recall.
Teaching a straight sit, or a smart finish, requires some correction, and if it were connected to the recall it would spoil the fun for the dog.
In addition, the "come when called" can be practiced even with a very young puppy, while the front sit and the finish should be introduced to a more mature dog.

Front Sit:
Use a different command when teaching the front sit, for instance "front". This will leave the "come" reserved for an exercise of pure fun.

During a casual walk, with the dog on lead, give the command "front". At the same time quickly walk backwards, away from the dog, and encourage him to follow. Stop after a few paces and guide your dog into a sitting position in front of you, using, as needed, the leash, both hands on the sides of the dog's neck/cheeks, and maybe an outstretched foot (to prevent him from sitting sideways).
Once the dog is closer, reach with one hand for the collar, under the chin, and slightly lift the front end of the dog up and push it back a little. Stroke the back of the dog with the other hand, near the croup, to urge him into a sitting position.

This way the command "sit" can be eliminated. If it were given and the dog would not comply, force would have to be used, spoiling the fun for the dog. As suggested here, there is no command, and therefore no harsh enforcement needed.
If the dog does not sit, you must improve upon your technique for coaxing him into a sit.

Food can also be very effective when teaching the front sit.
Skillful teasing gets the dog to come close, to sit close, to sit straight, to sit attentive. To accomplish that, hold the food with an outstretched arm toward the dog. Once he shows an interest, move your hand with the food toward your stomach, and then up toward your face, then slightly above and backwards over the dog's head.

Only then, when the dog has shown an effort to comply (later on only when the dog sits correctly) is the food actually given to him.

Another method is to hold the food in your teeth and release it from there after bending slightly forward. This has several advantages:
- the dog is being taught to look up to you
- the dog is being taught to sit close (otherwise he would miss the food when it is dropped)
- you can keep your hands in a natural position (you must, however, learn to speak with a full mouth).

The trainer can also fasten a clothes pin to his belt which holds the meat. This leaves his hands and his mouth free, yet the dog should be taught to take the meat on command only.
Some trainers suggest to practice straight sits with two barriers, one each to the right and to the left, in front of the handler. This chute leaves the dog not much of a choice but to sit straight - as long as the barriers are in place.

The chute, the long line, or even the leash are very inefficient training tools if the aim is to establish a secondary behavior pattern. They are unreliable by nature, as long as the dog is aware of their presence, or rather their absence.
Skillful use of the long line or the leash can leave the dog in doubt if he at the moment is restrained or not. This benefit never occurs with the chute, the dog can determine its presence or absence without fail.

Finish:
There are at least three permissible ways to get the dog from a front sit to the heel position.
One is for the dog to jump up and just land in the heel position.
Another one requires that the dog makes a fairly large sweep to his right and then comes back to the heel position via a left circle.

The third approach is more practical and more reliable then the others:
The dog advances forward, along the handler's right side, around and behind him in a close circle, and then shows up on the left side for a straight sit, in heel position.
In preparation for this exercise you should practice leash handling WITHOUT the dog:

a) Loop the leash into a neat, compact bundle, hold it in the right hand.
b) Go into a slight knee bend (the smaller the dog, the deeper the bend).
c) Move your right hand straight back and then to the rear.
d) Pass the leash to the left hand, behind your back, at about the height of your (bent) knees.
e) Move the left hand forward, at the same time bring the right hand QUICKLY in front your body to the left hip.
f) Both hands meet at the left hip. The right hand then accepts the leash (still in a neat bundle) and moves forward in a straight line.
g) Use the left hand to guide your (imaginary - at this stage) dog into a straight sit and to praise him.
h) Straighten up.

Practice this sequence to perfection without the dog, it should go fast and smooth.
Then clip the leash to the dog's collar.
a) Give the "sit" command and step in front of your dog, so close that there is almost contact. Face your dog. Fold the leash into a bundle, as short as comfortably possible. With the larger breeds the leash is completely folded up so that your right hand (which holds the leash) touches the end of the collar.
b) Go into a slight knee bend (the smaller the dog, the deeper the bend).
c) Give the command "heel", and with the right hand (which holds the leash) snap/tug the leash. This motion is horizontally. It gets the dog on his feet and moving forward.
IT IS IMPORTANT NOW to keep the dog in motion up to the completion of the finish, therefore all of your subsequent actions must be performed swiftly.

d) Guide the dog around you in a tight circle. Keep the leash still very short, and change it from the right to the left hand behind your back, as described earlier.

e) Continue the steady pull on the leash with your left hand, at the same time move the right hand quickly to your left hip.

f) Transfer the leash (still short) and continue to pull, but forward at this time.
By now, the dog should be on your left side, ready for the sit at heel.

g) Use the left hand to guide your dog into a straight sit and to praise him.

h) Straighten up.

The inducive method to teach the finish would require food, or a ball. It is best done off leash. Step in front of your dog and show him the treat in the cupped right hand. Then lead him "by the nose" forward, around you, and to the heel position at your left side. Change the food quickly from one hand to the other, just as described for the leash above. Give the reward to your dog only after he sits straight at heel, not before.

With this last approach the dog has a tendency to swing around too far, almost to the front again to face you, since he wants to see you and the reward. Your left hand should be ready to prevent this and to guide him into a straight sit. The correction must be fast since it is necessary to catch him in motion, not after he is already sitting.

REFINING PROCEDURE

After the initial training, the three parts:

> calling
> front sit
> finish

can be combined into the complete recall exercise.

However, practice the individual parts frequently in random sequence, for maintaining a happy recall, and for preventing anticipation.

Practice the recall as the last routine in a training session, most of the time. A good trainer will play with his dog after a work-out. In anticipation of this, the dog will be anxious to come to his handler, fast.

Dogs have a competitive spirit, too.
The novice dog, having watched another dog do a couple of fast recalls and receive a reward, often is quite eager to come quickly when called.
Two dogs, called at the same time, may also do a better recall if a small but tasty treat is offered as a reward. However, this does not work with all canines, since the desire to compete is influenced by the pecking order, by experiences from past competitions with this rival or with other dogs, as well as by other factors.

There is still another approach to firmly establish a fast, happy recall. It utilizes an isolation effect which increases the desire in a dog to be with his master as he gets farther and farther away (pack instinct).

Sit your dog at one end of a field 300 to 400 feet long, free of obstructions - somewhat isolated from other people and other dogs.
Then walk away from him, but watch him constantly and very closely. That moment is critical where the dog moves the first muscle to get up. You must recognize it and call your dog in a friendly, inviting tone.
Call him even though you may have gotten away only a few steps, and praise him lavishly when he arrives.
A moment later repeat the same exercise.

Quite naturally and without any additional effort, the distance between you and your dog, before he breaks, increases gradually yet rapidly. Within a week or so you should be able to walk away 200, 300 or even 400 feet before the dog breaks.

Again, it is important to call the dog at the first sign of getting up, and to reward him for coming with lots of praise. Offering a favored tidbit helps to get speedy recalls and straight, attentive front sits.

By the way, we have never found any difficulties with the long sits and downs because of this training approach.

PROBLEMS

a) The dog does not want to leave his position

Probably the "stay" command was too forceful, or the "come" was given too harshly.
- Give the "come" in a more pleasing tone, as an invitation.
- Run away (away from the dog).
- Have an assistant inconspicuously throw a throw chain or a tin can behind the dog. Then quickly call your startled dog.
- Attach a long line to the collar. Snap it once, together with the "come" command.Then drop the line, clap your hands, excite the dog to come.
- Restart with the motivation process: food, toys, praise.

b) The dog comes too slowly
- Make him stay longer before you call.
- Call him from farther away.
- Run backwards, away from the dog.
- Kneel.
- Clap your hands.
- Excitedly call your dog.
- Show him the treat.
- Call from a spot that is of interest to your dog (stand next to the exit, your car, other people or other dogs).
- Restart with the motivation process: food, toys, praise.

c) The dog wanders off

All the suggestions that were given for the slow dog can be tried. In addition, the following comments may help:
- Attach a long line to the collar and haul him in, a few times.
- Withhold food and/or ALL attention to the dog for at least 24 hours (with adult dogs only). Then tease him with the reward and call him. Give genuine praise when he comes.
- Exclude distractions, initially.
- As a temporary measure, sternly command "down" so that you can fetch your dog (refer to the "down" section).

d) The dog slows down when coming close to his handler

All the suggestions that were given for the slow dog can be tried. In addition:
- Give little praise during the first part of the run,   more praise and excitement during the final stages as the dog gets closer.
- The "drop on recall" (AKC) may interfere here, too. Practice the "drop" less frequently, the straight recall more often.

e) The dog does not sit in front, or sits crooked
- Practice the sits independently of the recall.
- Nudge the dog into the proper position, if necessary. Never give a harsh correction after, or in connection with, a successful recall.

f) The dog anticipates the "heel" and finishes on his own
- Do most recalls without the finish, practice the finish independently.
- Let the dog wait (maybe 20 seconds, but vary the time) before you tell him to heel.
- Do the finish yourself. Keep the dog sitting and walk around him, to end up in the heel position.

** SEND AWAY ••

GENERAL
The "send away" (or "go out") has various useful applications. The dog can be asked
- to scout ahead (quartering in protection work)
- to retrieve articles from a location known only to the handler (directed retrieve in Utility work)
- to deliver a message or an item to a specific person or location
- to move out (conformation show ring).

Herding dogs, police dogs, military dogs, customs dogs etc. must go out in the direction indicated by their handlers to accomplish certain tasks.

OBJECTIVE
On command, the dog will leave the heel position and move away from the handler, at a fast pace and in a straight line, in the indicated direction.

SUGGESTED COMMAND   "go" or "go out"
SUGGESTED RELEASE COMMAND: "down" or "sit"

PSYCHOLOGY
A dog wants to be with his handler, not to be sent away by him. Proper introduction of the exercise at an early training stage, and sufficient practice (but not endless repetition during any one training session) are needed to avoid problems.

Without an orientation marker, people and dogs can not walk a straight line (close your eyes and walk 100 paces !). The clever handler will, therefore, make sure that the dog has some kind of a goal to go to (maybe a person, a large building, the shade of a lonely tree etc.) to prevent him from "running in circles".

PREREQUISITES
A reliable "down" or "sit", controlled from a distance.

TEACHING PROCEDURE
For the "go out", both a signal and a command may be given. Raise one outstretched arm and give the command at the same time. The arm should be kept up as a signal until the dog has complied with the "down" (or "sit") command. Lowering the arm any earlier can be faulted in a trial as an additional signal/command.

In early training, command the dog to "down" at the conclusion of the "go out". He will be more willing to do that than to "sit", and a refusal to sit would complicate your job tremendously.

Generally, dogs are more willing to go out in an open area, rather than in an enclosed field.

Several methods are available to teach the send away:

Preparation for this exercise at an early age of the puppy may consist of teaching the dog to go ahead of you - on or off lead.

It may consist of teaching the dog to get out of your way, moving forward.

It may consist of playfully running and encouraging the excited dog to move ahead, away from you.

One dog can learn from the other. The "expert" is being sent out first and commanded to go down (or to sit) while the "student" is being held by the collar. When released and sent, the new dog is usually eager to join his playmate out there. If the dog does not want to leave, run with dog #2 to dog #1. Give lots of praise and encouragement during and after the exercise. Emphasis is placed on stimulating the dog to go out happily. If necessary, the concluding down or sit can be skipped during initial training.

Tie your dog to a post and tease him with a reward (food, toy). Walk away. In full view of the dog, and alerting him at the same time, place a large piece of cloth (a jacket will do) on the ground, with the reward on top of it. A chair, or a cardboard box can be used also, to prop up the reward. Run back to your dog, excite, release and send him. If necessary, run with him a few times to the drop point. After several successful attempts fold the cloth in half, later on fold it again until after some time only the food reward, then nothing at all, is left in the field. Carry the reward in your pocket and give it to the dog in these instances. Again, the down or sit can be skipped during initial training.

Family members, or fellow club members with their dogs, might serve as attraction too. The dog is sent toward them, rather then away from them.

Dogs that enjoy protection work can be sent toward a decoy who stands quietly in the field. The decoy moves only if the dog lacks enthusiasm.

An eager retriever can be held by the collar. Throw an article and send the dog after it. Change to smaller and smaller articles until finally only the gesture of throwing, or pointing, remains.

A very common practice is to leave the dog on a long down in the same spot to which he is being sent for the go out. For best results, the send away must immediately follow the long down.

Getting right behind the dog after the command "go" is given - and staying there - to chase/push the dog with both hands ahead of oneself is another method. No dog likes to have someone step on his tail (even if it was docked). You have to be quick, however, to not let the dog evade to the side. Don't stop if he throws himself on the ground, just keep pushing!
You should chase him toward an easily identifiable orientation marker. He will eventually take note of it and move out straight.
This method to teach the go out is most startling to the dog but it is also the quickest, the most effective and the most direct approach.

Methods of questionable training (and/or moralistic) value are:
- a "race track" with little picket fences
- a rope/pulley arrangement (with an assistant running the rope,
- tying the dog to the bumper of a car (which is driven away by a assistant).

Give the "down" or "sit" at the end of the send out while the dog is still moving away from you at a reasonable speed. Do not accommodate him and give the down command when he slows down or hesitates to go out further. If the distance is too short, make him go again, and again, and stop him in motion at your will.

Return to your dog at the conclusion of the exercise. While it is more convenient to call the dog back, it conditions him to anticipate the recall, and problems with the down (sit) arise.

REFINING PROCEDURE
Advanced dogs should go for greater distances, at a faster speed, and in a straight line. Practice on various fields, chose each time a different direction for the go out, incorporate distractions such as people, animals, vehicles, noises etc. All this will help to build a reliable performance.

PROBLEMS

a) The dog does not want to leave the handler
   Refer to "Teaching procedures" above.

b) The dog does not go in the indicated direction
                                    and/or he may change direction.
   - Select an obvious aim point, possibly one of interest to the dog. This can be the shade of a lonely thee, the exit from the field, a familiar person, an unfamiliar person, your car, etc.
   - Line up your outstretched arm with the aim point, next to the dog's head. Make sure he faces and looks in this direction.
   - Build up his expectations by placing food or a play object on the spot where you want him to go to. This baiting can be done in full view of the dog, or still better, unnoticed by him beforehand. The dog must come to realize that there is always a reward waiting for him if he goes in the direction pointed out to him. This requires practice for several weeks, maybe months.

c) The dog goes out too slow
- Run after him, clap your hands, excite him.
- Follow your dog and release him right after the down, then give him his reward (food, play).

d) The dog does not go far enough
- Run behind him, repeat the "go" command as soon as he slows down. Even though you may not be able to keep up with him, the shortened distance is to your advantage.
- Never give the "down" or "sit" command when the dog slows down or stops. Make him go out further, if necessary several times, and command "down" or "sit" while he is at full speed.

e) The dog is distracted
- Put many distracting objects on the field. Send your dog past them.
- Ask a decoy in full protective gear to stand on the field. Send your dog past him.

f) Faulty "down" (or "sit")
The dog does not go down at all, he does go down only part way, he does go down too slowly, he does get up again, he does creep, or he does wander off.
- Practice the "down" independently of the "go out".
- Always return to your dog after a go out, don't call him back to you. He may otherwise come to expect the recall (the same reasoning applies for the "sit").

** RETRIEVE ON FLAT ••

GENERAL
The retrieve is an exercise with many useful applications. It should be introduced very early in a dog's training program so that sufficient time can be devoted to each step in the exercise, without causing frustrations either in the dog or in the handler. The second lesson in the first obedience training class is about the right time.

A regulation dumbbell of the correct size should be used from the very start, to point out to the dog the difference between play and work.
This is not to say that retrieving a ball, a stick or a rag would be improper. These games have their place too, as a reward for good work, and for the dog to have some fun with his handler. When these articles are involved, different, less strict rules apply.
However, as soon as the dog sees the dumbbell he must realize that work is involved which has to be carried out in a precise manner.

OBJECTIVE
With the dog sitting at the heel position, the handler throws the dumbbell. On command, the dog goes out, picks up the dumbbell, and returns to the handler, all at a fast pace. The dog sits in front of the handler, releases the dumbbell on command, and does a smart finish to the heel position.

SUGGESTED COMMAND   "get it"   "out"
SUGGESTED RELEASE COMMAND "OK"

PSYCHOLOGY
Some dogs are happy retrievers, they can easily be trained to do the regulation retrieve. Other dogs show initially a strong disliking for this exercise. They require a little more effort on the part of the trainer.
All dogs of all breeds, however, have the inborn instinct of carrying things in their mouth from one place to another. If you convey to them a feeling of ease, if you relax them by talking in a soft tone all the while, they will be more cooperative. Progress in small steps, take your time.

PREREQUISITES
None, except a well-established dog/handler relationship.

TEACHING PROCEDURE
The retrieve is taught in three separate parts:
1. taking the dumbbell ("take it")
2. carrying the dumbbell ("hold it")
3. releasing the dumbbell ("out").

It is advisable to work on holding and carrying the dumbbell first, before steps one and three are dealt with.

a) Introducing the dumbbell
To introduce a 'green' dog to the dumbbell, the following procedure has proven to be helpful:
* Keep the dog on your left side, leash in the left hand.
* Hold the dumbbell by the bar in your right hand, wedged between the base portion of the thumb and the index finger.
* Slide the free four fingers of the right hand into the choke collar (over the dog's head, pointing to his rear).
* Release the leash and hold the dog with the four fingers of the right hand, as described above.
* Reach with your left arm over the dog's shoulder and, from the left side of the dog, slide the left hand under his head.
* With your left thumb, push the dog's lower left lip onto the lower left teeth near the base of the mouth.
* At the same time, push the dog's lower right lip onto the lower right teeth near the base of the mouth, with your left middle finger.
* The squeeze from the last two steps will cause the dog to open his mouth. (Note that this procedure avoids covering the dog's eyes which would bother the dog and generate additional resistance). At that time release the collar and quickly scoop the right hand with the dumbbell in front of the dog's mouth. The fingers of the right hand point toward the dog's throat, palm up.
* With a push of the palm roll the dumbbell into the dog's mouth, then release the two fingers which had pried the dog's mouth open. At the same time say "hold it, good boy".
* Continue to keep the right hand scooped under the dog's head, barely maintaining contact with the dog's lower jaw.
* Slide the left hand into the dog's collar, fingers pointing toward the dog's head, or just have your left hand behind the dog's head, praising and caressing him. At the same time talk to him in a reassuring tone.
* Do not touch the dumbbell anymore, holding it is now the dog's responsibility.
* Make the dog hold on to the dumbbell. Backing out of it is prevented with the left hand in the collar and/or behind the head. Spitting the dumbbell out is countered by the scoop of the right hand which holds the lower jaw up, and by the lower portion of the right arm which is in an upright position and at a right angle to, and just in front of, the dog's nose.
* Although the dog will balk at this procedure, don't give in. Make him hold the dumbbell for a short moment before YOU tell him to release.
* Heap love and praise on your dog for doing such a marvelous job. Don't repeat the exercise for at least another hour.

This procedure for accustoming the dog to the dumbbell should be followed for several weeks, maybe even months, depending on the response of the dog.
The time for holding the dumbbell should be increased gradually but must be varied, even at an advanced training stage.

Once the dog willingly holds the article, without any assistance from you, ask him to carry it for a short distance. Keep your left hand in the dog's collar and the right hand (just as a precaution) under his lower jaw. Then urge him to move forward and advance a few steps. After taking the dumbbell back from him, praise him lavishly.

This training stage is followed by short heeling patterns first, more elaborate ones later on, all with the dog carrying the dumbbell, without any assistance from you.

b) Taking the dumbbell
The other parts of the exercise should be introduced only after the dog does all the above exercises flawlessly.
Progressing in stages, tell him first to "take it" while you hold the dumbbell in front of his nose. Very rarely will you have to push his head toward the dumbbell, and to force his lips against it (move his head, not the dumbbell!).

In subsequent sessions bring the dumbbell closer and closer to the ground. Then rest one bell on the ground while you hold the other end up. Then drop the dumbbell just in front of him, then kick it a little away from the dog, then throw it farther, etc.

In the beginning it is helpful to send the dog for the dumbbell while it is still moving, 'living' things are, by nature, of much more interest to the dog than inanimate ones.

Do early training on lead. You may also have to push the head of your dog toward the dumbbell. Important is a certain firmness. You must not give in to an uncooperative dog when you know that he understands what is asked of him.

As usual, a command should only be given once. The second time it is pronounced the dog must be made to obey.

c) Releasing the dumbbell
This is the easiest part of the retrieve exercise. It should be practiced on leash.
Reach for the dumbbell with both hands, one hand for each end, and give the command "out" in a pleasant but still firm tone. Unspoiled dogs will release willingly since their attention shifts from the dumbbell to the excited handler.
Praise your dog.
Dogs that have already developed bad habits require a more firm and determined "out", but still without yelling or becoming violent. Praise is given after the release.

d) Combining the parts
When combining the three parts into a complete retrieve exercise, common sense and prior experience in obedience training will help. Working on leash at first, using a proper mixture of firmness and praise, keeping the training session interesting and short, and practicing in a variety of locations and with various distractions will make for a perfect performance in the end.

REFINING PROCEDURE
Training for advanced dogs should include the retrieve of leather, metal and wooden dumbbells. The dumbbells should be of various sizes, shapes and weights: 2000 grams are required in the Schutzhund III retrieve.
Introduce distractions gradually, and insist on an exact performance.
For variety and usefulness, teach your dog to bring a basket, a large shovel, keys, the newspaper, shoes, a purse etc. He can also learn to drag a heavy object (box, tire) by a handle; this is just another variation of the retrieve. Sending him after an object thrown in the water (make sure that he can handle the current and that he can get out of the water by himself) will serve a multitude of purposes: variety, dependability, courage, physical exercise, etc.

FORCED RETRIEVE
Some trainers maintain that the inducive method (described above) is inefficient, and that only the forced retrieve will guarantee a reliable performance. This may be so, but then, if I just want my dog to be quiet I would not shoot him either.
There are various flavors to the forced retrieve. In the true version, two leashes and a prong collar are used. An assistant violently jerks the prong collar and stuffs the dumbbell into the dog's mouth when he cries out loud in pain.

The approach is wrong, for moralistic, and for psychological, reasons. It also attests to the dog owner's inability to properly train a dog. We disapprove of the true, forced retrieve.

A modified approach, however, will benefit dogs who have mastered the retrieve earlier and who now have decided that they do not like it.

The force I want to apply is psychological rather than physical: When the (trained) dog refuses to pick up the dumbbell I want to convincingly play the role of a very angry, violent person who is just about to pick up a 2x4 and clobber his dog over the head. I would not do it, of course, but I want the dog to believe that I would. Rushing to the dog, angrily pushing his head toward the dumbbell and making him pick it up, or shoving it into his mouth if he still refuses, usually does the trick. Then comes the big praise.

PROBLEMS

a) Anticipation

Some dogs dash out to get the dumbbell before the command was given; they have learned the sequence of events.

Vary the sequence in training: throw the dumbbell, do another exercise, then send your dog to retrieve. Or force him to obey: leash corrections; nape grab; varying time intervals between throwing the dumbbell and sending him).

b) Distraction

If the dog refuses to retrieve because of distractions, then prior training was not versatile enough. Practice dumbbell work in busy places, under simulated trial conditions, with a decoy standing motionless next to the dumbbell, or while another dog does protection work. Keep your dog on a long leash, and demand perfection. Be firm, get the job done in a hurry, and then reward your dog lavishly.

c) No Find

The dog may have trouble finding the dumbbell. Painting the bells white so that it can be seen easier, and throwing the dumbbell so that it lands in the desired spot will help.

If the article was thrown too far or too much sideways, the dog may have to search for it. Landing the dumbbell on the ground in exactly the spot where you want it is quite possible. It requires technique, and it requires practice.

* Hold the dumbbell by the edge of the bell, between thumb and the remaining four fingers.

FIG. 25

* Throw it and give it a twist the moment you release it, so that it spins around its center point.

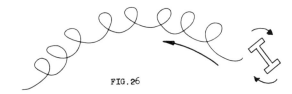

FIG. 26

TOP WORKING DOGS

* Throw it and give it a twist the moment you release it, so that it spins around its center point.
* On landing, spin and inertia of the dumbbell will offset each other and the dumbbell will remain at the spot where it first touched the ground.

d) No Pick-Up
If the dog repeatedly refuses to pick up the dumbbell, you have probably progressed too fast. Review and practice the introductory exercises again, at a slower pace.
If the instance is isolated, then a firm command, maybe a firm correction, will straighten things out. A variety of methods has been used by trainers with varying degrees of success:
- rubbing meat on the center bar of the dumbbell
- tying a glove with the handler's scent around the center bar
- gradually converting from ball to dumbbell in the following sequence:
.. rubber ball
.. rubber ball with dowel pushed through it
.. as before, with small bells on the dowel
.. as before, with larger bells
.. as before, but with portions of the ball removed
.. as before, but with just a little rubber from the ball left on the dowel
.. dowel with bells alone (=dumbbell).
- pinching the dog's ear or stepping on his toes (from a psychological standpoint this is not only useless but also harmful)
- forced retrieve (unethical, should be used only in very rare cases as a last resort, by an experienced trainer).
If the dog objects to retrieving certain objects only, then re-training, variety, a firm command, maybe force, will bring results.

e) Pick-up by the Bells
There is a greater chance that the dog may drop the dumbbell, or mouth it, if he picks it up by the bells. To discourage this, nails with the heads protruding by about one inch can be driven into the bells.

f) Dropping the Dumbbell
Practicing at close range, on leash, and quickly correcting the dog before he can fully eject the dumbbell from the mouth is recommended if the dog develops the habit of dropping the article. Walking with the dog while he holds the dumbbell as a separate exercise (see above) is recommended also.

g) No Return
The dog may decide not to return with the dumbbell but to take off instead.
He wants to play.
Give a firm verbal correction, and practice on a long leash, or in a fully enclosed area, for a while. Another approach would be to use a glove or a small bag/container with meat in it. The dog needs to return it to you so that you can unpack the reward and give it to him (see Tracking: Refrigerator Effect).
You can also drill a large hole into one of the bells and close it with a plug. Let your dog watch when you hide a piece of meat in it, then throw the dumbbell. Without bringing it back to you, the dog will not be able to get the meat (if you did your job right).

h) No Out
The dumbbell must never be ripped out of the dog's mouth, unpleasant experiences connected with this exercise will cause a severe set-back.
Try teasing the dog with food which he can only obtain after releasing the dumbbell.
Practice on lead, press the dogs lip with your thumb over the dogs teeth (dog "bites" itself), press your fingers against the dog's jaw to open it gently, or give a threatening "out" command.

** RETRIEVE OVER HURDLE / JUMPING ••••••••••••••••••••••••

GENERAL
Retrieving and jumping are activities which most healthy dogs enjoy. Why, then, do we see so many poor performances in these categories? The answer lies almost always with the handler who chases his dog over, and over, and over, and over the jump, without reason.

It must be recognized, though, that jumping is a strenuous exercise, requiring the dog to be in good physical condition. The best way to prepare for it is a fitness program: run with your dog, or road work him from a bicycle, for instance. This can be started with a young dog already, if done within reason.

OBJECTIVE
With the dog sitting at the heel position, the handler throws the dumbbell over the hurdle. On command, the dog goes out, jumps, picks up the dumbbell, jumps back and returns to the handler, all at a fast pace. The dog sits in front of the handler, releases the dumbbell on command, and does a smart finish to the heel position.

SUGGESTED COMMAND   "get it" "jump" "out"
SUGGESTED RELEASE COMMAND   "OK"

PSYCHOLOGY
With the retrieve over the hurdle we prepare our dogs for clearing obstacles and barriers of reasonable height. This, however, is not obvious to the dog at the time of training. He only sees a narrow obstacle that can easily be bypassed on the side. In his way of thinking it is ridiculous to go over it.

Since you insist on the jump, and since you (initially) go over it too, the dog will comply to please you, but his cooperation should not be abused. You must make sure that the dog can do a satisfactory performance on the second or third try in a row. To this effect you may have to use more encouragement, more guidance, or you may have to lower the height of the jump somewhat. When the dog finishes properly you should praise him lavishly, quit training for the day and play with him.

PREREQUISITES
Running (roadwork). Retrieve on the flat.

TEACHING PROCEDURE
Jumping can be started very early in a dog's life. A small board placed in a doorway which the dog passes frequently is probably the most convenient solution for you, and the most reasonable way for the puppy, to learn jumping.

Already at two or three months of age you can casually approach a small obstacle while playfully running with your puppy. A tree branch, a board, a long piece of pipe, a miniature creek etc. serve that purpose.

With a friendly, inviting "jump" or "hop" (not a command) both you and your dog clear the obstacle. If the dog is playful and excited enough, if the obstacle is small enough, and if you do not make an "exercise" out of it, there will be no problems. If he wants to, let him explore and sniff out the barrier, initially. The size of the "hurdle" should be kept quite low for many months so that you and your dog can concentrate on technique.

Once the dog masters the long sit, place him in front of the hurdle. Attach a long, light-weight leash to his collar, guide it over the hurdle, hold it and walk to the other side of the jump. Then call the dog (do not command him) and guide him over the hurdle.

In the next phase throw a favored toy over the low hurdle. Jump with your dog (on leash) both ways, let him retrieve. Finally do the complete retrieve on the long leash, later on off lead, with you remaining at the start.

Use a low jump throughout this training. Continue with it for at least several more weeks, maybe even months of daily exercises. After the dog has matured (usually over one year of age), the build-up to recommended heights can be accomplished gradually and quite quickly.

TOP WORKING DOGS

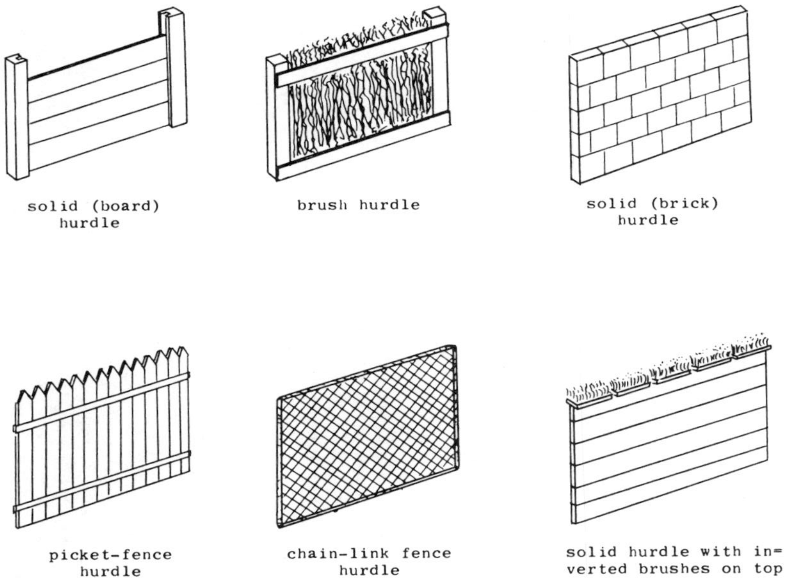

solid (brick)
hurdle

solid hurdle with in=
verted brushes on top

brush hurdle

chain-link fence
hurdle

solid (board)
hurdle

picket-fence
hurdle

Figure 27: HURDLE TYPES

REFINING PROCEDURE

Advanced dogs should retrieve leather, metal and wooden dumbbells of various sizes, shapes and weights: 650 grams are required in the Schutzhund III retrieve over the hurdle. Restrict jumping with heavy articles to an absolute minimum, though, since the forces acting on the joints of the dog upon landing can cause irreparable damage, in time.

Introduce distractions gradually, and insist on an exact performance.
There are several different types of hurdles available to the serious trainer, each one with its advantages and disadvantages (see Fig. 30).
The most common "jump" uses boards that slide into the grooves of two posts. This type is preferred by many for its portability and ease of height adjustment.
The brush hurdle, a framework filled with vertically oriented twigs, resembles more closely natural obstacles but its height can not be changed easily. This is the hurdle required in SV trials.
The board jump fitted with bristles on top (brooms) is a viable compromise between these two common hurdle types.
The picket fence obstacle could be considered a variation of the brush hurdle, it too forces the dog to clear the barrier without stepping on it. Chain-link fence material stretched over a tubular metal frame builds the transition to the bar jump, insofar as the dog can see through it.
The bar jump itself is considered by many the ultimate obedience criterion since the dog jumps on command although he could walk around and even underneath the bar.
Many variations can be found to these four basic types of hurdles, like the solid jump made from stacked logs or from bricks, jumps fitted with a window frame on top, oil drums, railing fence obstacles etc.
Try to use as many of these different types of hurdles as possible, to keep your dog's interest awake, and to train him to become a useful working dog.

PROBLEMS

Refer also to the problem section under "Retrieve on Flat"

a) No Jump

If you, or your veterinarian, have determined that there are no physical or health problems which cause the dog to refuse the jump, then the following suggestions should be considered:

Return to practice on leash for a while.
Start by walking up to the (full size) hurdle, tap the upper edge, climb over it and encourage your canine to follow. Most dogs will cooperate, but if yours refuses and fights, you must shorten the leash and coax/pull/drag him over the barrier. Do not give in, do not release the leash, do not spend all day with it. He must go over the hurdle, now. Reward him royally afterwards and quit jumping for the day. Repeat the procedure once each, for the next 3 or 4 days. Then, during the following session, run with your dog at a rather fast speed straight toward the hurdle, your dog approaching it dead center (this gets you somewhat off to the right). Just before the hurdle (maybe 4 ft. away from it, depending on the jumping technique of the dog) give the command "jump", together with a quick snap on the leash, and run around the hurdle, encouraging the dog to go over.
Repeat this in subsequent training sessions, but instead of running around the hurdle stay on the departure side, feed your dog enough lead for the landing, and then call him back, aiding him with another quick snap on the leash.

It is conceivable that you stand too close to, or too far away from, the jump, or that the dumbbell lands too close to, or too far away from, the hurdle.
Too close means that the dog has not enough room for the take-off, too far means that the dog can see an advantage in walking around the obstacle. Adjust the distances.

b) No Return Jump

The return jump is often refused when the dumbbell lands too far to the side so that the dog can then see you.
The hurdle does not block the dog's direct route back to you, and smart as he is, he chooses the path of the least resistance.

You must prepare for this in practice by throwing the dumbbell purposely to the side (or by throwing the dumbbell straight and then stepping to the side), and then forcing the dog to jump both ways (long line). You should also practice throwing the dumbbell so that you can place it exactly.

c) Stepping on, or touching the hurdle
Stepping on the hurdle, or touching it, costs points in a trial. There are several tricks available to eliminate the problem:
- make the hurdle slightly higher for all training jumps.
- Build the hurdle with a top panel that swings when the dog steps on it.
- Stretch a string or a wire over the top of the hurdle, with or without small flags attached to it (to make it visible).
- Put a loose broom stick on top of the hurdle.
- Fasten brushes/brooms to the top of the hurdle, with the bristles sticking up.
- Use a brush hurdle.

** RETRIEVE OVER WALL / CLIMBING **************************

GENERAL
The "Guinness Book" credits GSD "Danko" with holding the world record in scaling an upright wall: 11 feet and 3 inches.
The six foot wall in Schutzhund competition should then pose no problem for most healthy working dogs.

A few years ago the specifications for the wall were changed from an upright to an incline, because many dogs jumped from the top to the ground and got hurt in the process. They still jump down from the new wall. The change was not really necessary, it just established a new, lower standard.
Dogs can be taught to climb down the upright wall or the inclined wall so that they don't get hurt on the descent. This is described below.

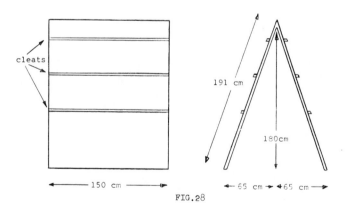

FIG.28

OBJECTIVE

With the dog sitting at the heel position, the handler throws the dumbbell over the wall. On command, the dog goes out, scales the wall, picks up the dumbbell, climbs back and returns to the handler, all at a fast pace. The dog sits in front of the handler, releases the dumbbell on command, and does a smart finish to the heel position.

SUGGESTED COMMAND   "get it"   "jump"   "out"
SUGGESTED RELEASE COMMAND   "OK"

PSYCHOLOGY

With the retrieve over the wall we prepare our dogs for climbing obstacles and barriers of reasonable height. This, however, is not obvious to the dog at the time of training. He only sees a narrow obstacle that can easily be bypassed on the side. In his way of thinking it is ridiculous to go over it. Since you insist on the jump, the dog will comply to please you, but his cooperation should not be abused. You must make sure that the dog can do a satisfactory performance on the second try in a row. To this effect you may have to use more encouragement, more guidance, you may have to make the incline less steep (provided the wall can be adjusted), or you may have to lower the height of the wall somewhat. When the dog finishes properly you should praise him lavishly, quit training for the day and play with him.

PREREQUISITES

Running (road work). Retrieve over the hurdle.

TEACHING PROCEDURE

There are four phases to the exercise:

1. <u>Start</u>   The dog jumps up, in a nearly vertical direction. Most dogs can do that easily and naturally. It is, therefore, wrong to position dog and handler more than, maybe, 6 feet away from the wall for take-off. With a longer distance the dog has a tendency to build up speed and then to crash into the wall.

2. <u>Ascent</u>   Reaching for the cleats with his paws, the dog pushes and pulls himself up to the top. Enthusiasm, encouragement and praise will help the dog. To prevent the dog from sliding back, some gentle pushing from behind (sending), or some gentle pulling from the other side of the jump (calling), for instance by reaching into the collar, may be needed.

3. <u>Climax</u>   Once the front feet have reached the top edge of the wall, the dog brings up the hind feet too and balances himself, all four feet resting on the top edge of the wall for a moment. The dog makes a quick assessment of the situation (how to get down, where to land, location of the dumbbell) while preparing for the descent.
He should not be rushed at this point.

4. <u>Descent</u>   Aided by the cleats, the dog climbs down the wall 2/3 or maybe 3/4 of the way. Then he pushes himself off the wall for a (nearly) horizontal landing.
The dog must be taught not to jump from the top, to prevent injury.

Younger or beginning dogs need all the help they can get.
An inclined wall which is hinged at the top and which can be spread to various angles is very useful.

Spread it to a rather wide angle (secure properly!) and run with the dog on a short leash towards it while showing a lot of enthusiasm and giving encouragement. The approach to the wall should be fast, and for the dog dead center (this gets you somewhat off to the right). Just before the wall give the command "jump", together with a quick snap on the leash. Go with your dog over the wall. (Did you know that the Russian trial regulations require the handler to go with his dog over the six foot upright scaling wall?). This is done once, or maybe twice, then play with the dog and pause for at least six hours.

After a few days of practice the wall is set up at a steeper angle, a longer leash is used, and you run past the wall, guiding your dog over it. For this transition it is important that you make the dog believe up to the last moment that you will go with him over the wall. Execute the detour only after the dog has committed himself to jump. Timing and speed of approach to the wall, and your hesitation and deflection are critical.

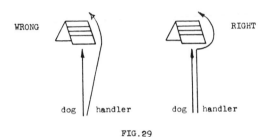

FIG. 29

After several days of practice, exchange the leash for a short piece of string (l ft.), attached to the collar. Let go of it just before the dog jumps.

Then do the exercise off leash.

The next step would be to sit the dog at one side of the wall, to walk around to the other side, to climb halfway up the wall and to call the dog very excitedly. You can tap the wall or tease your dog with a favorite toy or a tidbit, to encourage him to come up the wall. If the dog responds, praise him and get off the wall in a hurry to make room for him.

Then all the parts of the exercise can be put together.

First ask the dog to go over the wall both ways, without, and then with, a toy or a light-weight dumbbell. A long line can be quite helpful if it is handled properly: feeding enough lead for the landing, and then calling him back, aided by a quick snap on the leash.

REFINING PROCEDURE

Introduce distractions gradually, practice on a variety of training fields with walls of different built, and insist on an exact performance.

PROBLEMS

Problems common to the retrieve on the flat and to the retrieve over the hurdle were covered there.

a) Refusal to Climb

Aside from the suggestions offered for "No Jump" (see RETRIEVE over HURDLE) the dog may refuse to take the wall because of earlier unpleasant experiences on the descent. Some trainers have installed a platform on the far side of the wall, about 3 feet down from the top. The dog can then get to the ground easily. These trainers concentrate on climbing technique, and only for about 10-20% of the exercises do they remove the platform to teach their dogs the proper descent.

b) Jump from the Top
- A deflecting chute can be installed temporarily.
- Two people familiar to the dog can be positioned on the
    far side of the jump, to guide him down.
- You can run around the wall during the natural pause the
    dog makes at the top position. Stand close to the wall,
    right in the middle, so that you can receive and guide
    your dog between yourself and the wall. Reach with
    your outstretched hands for the dog's shoulders to
    keep him on the wall. This way the dog is discouraged
    from jumping and forced to climb down. He is allowed
    to jump to the ground the very last moment only.
    This last approach is most comfortable to the dog, and
    very effective too.

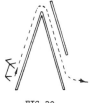

FIG. 30

** SPEAK ON COMMAND ••••••••••••••••••••••••••••••••••••••

GENERAL
Speaking on command is the foundation for many useful means of communication between dog
and handler. A dog that knows how to speak on command can more easily be taught to indicate
a find (hidden person, narcotics, explosives), to announce visitors, to express his desire to go
outdoors or to get water, etc.
He also can more easily be taught not to bark.

OBJECTIVE
On command, the dog will bark authoritatively (even aggressively) and repeatedly, until told to be
quiet.

SUGGESTED COMMAND   "speak" (also use a signal,
                                            the pointed index finger)

SUGGESTED RELEASE COMMAND   "quiet"

PSYCHOLOGY
With the exception of one breed (Basenji), or an ill animal, all dogs can bark. The problem is not to
teach the dog how to bark, but when to do it. This takes time, and starting the training at an early
age will eliminate many problems that normally arise because of time pressure.
The kind of barking we want to reinforce is caused by angry frustration: a forceful, demanding
staccato.

PREREQUISITES
None, except a well developed dog/handler relationship.

TEACHING PROCEDURE
    The simplest approach, but also the most time consuming way, is to wait until the dog barks on
his own and then to praise him: "good boy, speak".
    Learning through imitation is another possibility: ask a trained canine to speak, and then reward
him in front of the novice.
    The dog can also be stimulated to bark by teasing him with a tidbit, a favored toy, the invitation
to go out etc. Holding him by the collar usually has a beneficial effect.
    Restrained by a fence or a chain, many dogs will bark when teased or harassed by a stranger.
Give the command "speak" repeatedly and reward your dog the moment he does.
    Young dogs will often speak when you give a tug upwards on the lead, together with command
and signal.
    Dogs that enjoy protection work can be allowed to watch other dogs on the sleeve, or they can
participate in line or circle agitation. They are encouraged: "speak, good boy", and they are
rewarded after a few barks verbally ("good boy, speak") as well as with a bite on the sleeve.

Another method is to tie the dog up in an isolated area. Walk away and call the dog, also giving the command "speak". At first, you may have to walk quite a distance, but eventually the dog will whine, yelp or bark. This is the moment when you joyfully run back to your dog and praise and pet him. Soon the dog will have found out that barking prevents you from getting away too far.

There is still one other, less pleasant way to teach the "speak on command" which should be used only as a last resort: Hold the dog by the collar and use a stick to lightly hit him on the front legs. Command: "speak" and praise him when he does. The stick is gradually shortened until just the motion of an outstretched finger reminds the dog of the pain and the invitation to speak on command.

REFINING PROCEDURE
Once the dog understands what "speak" means, it is simply a matter of establishing the desired response by repetition. Ask your dog to speak before you throw the ball or the stick, before you give him his tidbit or his meal, or before you take him for a walk. Practicing with distractions is also a good idea.

PROBLEMS

a) The dog does not bark, he just yaps
- There was not enough stimulation. You must excite the dog more, maybe by using a different training approach.
- Try withholding the reward a little longer.

b) The dog does not quit barking when told to do so
- Give the command "quiet" more firmly.
- Change to another activity (another exercise, play, etc.).
- Startle the dog, with exuberant praise, with noise, or with a sudden movement.

"Say, your puppy
just bit me in the ankle."

"Well, you don't expect
a little dog to bite you
on the neck, do you?"

D. PROTECTION WORK

1. BASIC PHILOSOPHY

Protection work is considered by many to be the ultimate accomplishment in dog training.
Some people will disagree, but the fact remains that no other phase of dog training exposes so much of the true temperament, of the working spirit, of the strengths and weaknesses in a dog than properly conducted man work. Obedience tells how good the handler is, protection work tells how good the dog is.

Training procedures for man work depend on the final goal the handler has in mind. A police dog, a military dog, an area protection dog, a personal protection dog, a competition dog - all require a somewhat different approach. The most universal and basic type of training is found in the Schutzhund sport.
Schutzhund protection training benefits practically every dog of the working breeds in a certain way, provided the attitude of the handler compliments that of the decoy/trainer. A shy dog, for instance, gains self-confidence, and an over-aggressive dog becomes more manageable. Optimum results, however, can only be obtained when the dog, as well as the owner/handler and the decoy/trainer meet certain minimum requirements. Improperly done, man work can create tremendous stress for both dog and handler. It can also be the cause of severe injury, it may require financial restitution for damages inflicted, and it can lead to serious legal problems.

A WEAPON
Dog owners who get involved in Schutzhund training expect - at least subconsciously - that the dog will come to their rescue if a dangerous situation should arise. They want a bold, courageous canine. This is quite all right, even desirable, provided the dog has a nice, even tempered, good natured disposition.
Some trainers do not understand that concept. They discourage strangers from approaching their dog and swell with pride when "Killer" growls and snaps at anybody that comes within reach.
They might even TEACH their dog to become suspicious of every acquaintance, to become hostile and aggressive to every stranger. This attitude is borrowed from a trainer of attack dogs and has no place in our sport. The dog owner who can not let his friend and his dog ride in the same car, or who can not have visitors at home without first caging his dog, is not only ill advised, he is a disgrace to the Schutzhund sport.

This is not to say that a Schutzhund must be a lap dog, and that he must be friends with everyone and his cousin. Schutzhund dogs should be alert, reserved, discriminating, but they must be sociable as well. The Schutzhund dog lives with his owner, and while he will do well as a protector, he must never become an aggressor. This is even true for police dogs!

The most desirable result of Schutzhund protection training is the ability of the dog to change from a friendly, likeable pet into a convincing, effective protector as a new situation may require.
Dogs are quite capable of doing that. They are not bothered by personal or moralistic inhibitions like humans who need time for such a change and who often expect dogs to react likewise. Canines sense the sudden necessity to react protective, and with proper training, the working breeds are quite capable to master a threatening situation. Schutzhund training definitely gives them an advantage, especially when situations, locations, decoys and protective gear have been changed frequently.
Owner agitation, on the other hand, would be undesirable in that respect. Although the dog may learn to bite the sleeve, he will not understand the reason for it and may fail in a critical situation.

PREY us. PROTECTIVE INSTINCT
There are two factions in the world of Schutzhund trainers, as far as the introduction of novice dogs to bite work is concerned:
> those who utilize the prey instinct, and
> those who utilize the protective instinct.

The supporters of the first group maintain that Schutzhund is a sport where technique and not motivation is judged. They state that very few of the average dog owners could justify training and harboring a personal protection dog, and that there are few recorded instances where a Schutzhund dog has had the need, or the opportunity, to bite in defense of his master. They also state that the prey instinct is better developed in most dogs, and that man work can be taught much easier and faster on the basis of this approach.

Supporters of the second group maintain that man work becomes a farce if a dog just goes for the sleeve and does not care at all about the person carrying it. They claim that protection work based on the prey instinct becomes unrealistic, and that dogs trained this way will not be able to protect their masters when the need arises.

There is some truth to each one of these claims.
We believe that both instincts can be used as motivators with advantage, each one where it is most suitable and most beneficial. The "Search/Find/Bark" and the "Escape" would be good examples for utilizing the prey instinct, the "Attack on the Handler" should be geared to the protective instinct, on the other hand.
The most successful trainers use the prey instinct to develop the fighting technique of young and novice dogs, to "sharpen their tools" so to speak. During that phase the decoy is merely carrier of the prey. He usually moves away from the dog, and during a bite he usually has the dog behind him, or on his side.

At a later stage the decoy would change from carrier to competitor, struggling with the dog for the possession of the sleeve. This is a natural and logical switch from prey to protective instinct.
As soon as the dog is ready for it, the decoy will employ still more open hostility toward handler and dog. Now the dog is usually worked in front of the decoy, and the decoy moves forward in a self-confident manner rather than moving backward defensively. Yet even at that stage the agitator must solicit the prey instinct and surrender the sleeve as soon as the dog reaches his limits and plans to give up the fight.

It follows than that the ideal Schutzhund dog needs a pronounced prey instinct (usually present) as well as a convincing protective drive (often lacking). The responsible trainer will, therefore, give his dog every opportunity to develop both to the fullest degree.

In Schutzhund training we do want our dogs to bite the padded arm and no place else. Our dogs are not prepared to be service dogs. Schutzhund is a sport, a competitive one. Each sporting discipline has its rules, its standards, to allow comparison and rating of a performance of one individual against that of another one. To this end, and also to avoid any unduly dangerous situations a decoy might not be prepared for, the VDH Rules have selected the (padded) arm as the target (prey). In Ring Sport, the dogs go for the decoys belly and other parts of his anatomy, but then he knows about it and gets prepared.

THE DECOY
One of the most important keys to success in man work is the decoy, also called helper or agitator. A good decoy can make even a poor dog look good. A bad decoy can easily ruin even a good dog.

The decoy should be a kind person. He must be in good physical condition, with quick reflexes and responses. Participation in a fitness program, and regular exercises on the weight bench, or with a chest pull, or with the DEUSER bands (European style exercisers), and practice with the "false dog" (40 lb., later 70 lb. boxing bag, strapped to the sleeve and manipulated like a real dog) is highly recommended.

The decoy is expected to have a certain amount of courage. A fearful person would be unduly concerned about his own safety, and training techniques would suffer as a result. This does not mean that the decoy should play "steam roller". On the contrary, it is his primary job to instill in the canine opponent the belief that the dog can subdue any human aggressor. The secret recipe is for the decoy to display, at the right moment, the proper mixture of threat and fear, advance and retreat, aggression and defeat.

The decoy must have experience in the training of (his own) dogs, and he must be able to read and understand dogs, operate on their level of thinking, so to speak.

He must have imagination, he must be able to improvise. Schematic, standardized routines inhibit the dog's reliability and efficiency.

He must be dependable and self-confident, but he must also be willing to sacrifice his own glory for that of the dog. His calling card is the training performance of the dog. The dog always wins. If a person can not lose, he should not be a decoy.

It takes a lot of experience to become a good decoy, and while learning, we all make mistakes. However, you as the handler have a moral obligation to protect your dog from an abusive decoy. A well-known American trainer and high-ranking Schutzhund official, for instance, teaches the "find and bark" exercise by hitting the biting dog over the snout with a lead pipe. Impressed by this man's credentials, you may hesitate to act. Don't. Take your dog and find better company, don't become an accessory to the crime.

Every dog handler should once in a while get into the leather suit and "take the sleeve". For one, it gives him a better appreciation of what the decoy is doing for him all the time. It also shows him what is going on at the other end of the leash. He becomes a better and more effective handler in the process.

THE TRAINING DIRECTOR
The training director is another person essential to progress in protection work. Not being directly involved in the physical activities, he can observe and analyze the performance better, and he can offer suggestions based on his own experience and knowledge. He can also act as a negotiator between decoy and dog handler if an argument should develop (and sometimes it does).

The training director should see to it that training is conducted in a safe manner.

PLAY IT SAFE
Like any other outdoor activity, Schutzhund training is not without a certain risk to the participants. When riding a bicycle, for instance, the rider can - through negligence - hurt himself and/or others. When training a Schutzhund dog the trainer can - again through negligence - cause harm to himself or to others. "CAP" is the answer: Consideration, Anticipation, Preparation.
Consider the decoy's position:
    Is he properly protected (overall, sleeve, cover) ?
    Does he wear the right kind of footwear ?
    Does he know your dog's age and experience to customize his agitation work ?
    Did you inform him of your dog's unusual biting habits (if any) ?
    Does he work the dog properly ?
    Do you keep a safe distance between your dog and the decoy while he works with another
        animal ?
Consider the position of a bystander:
    Was he directed to a safe observation spot ?
    Was he instructed not to move, especially when a dog is approaching him ?
Consider your own position:
    Can you hold your dog or should you stake him in addition ?
    Can you control your dog ?
    Are you far enough away from the other dogs to avoid getting bitten accidentally ?
Anticipate:
    Watch your dog closely, read him to avoid any close calls.
    Yell "loose dog" when your animal or another one gets off the hook.
    Call your dog off if the decoy should slip or fall.
    Catch and correct your dog when he intends to go for the decoys leg, shoulder, face etc.
        React quickly, before the damage is done.
    Hold your dog securely when the decoy comes back without the sleeve for the civil agitation.

Prepare yourself:
    Read up on the subject, inform yourself.
    Discuss problems with the training director, the decoy, others.
    Get and use the proper equipment, check its condition before each training session.

Use common sense, and "CAP", and you will stay out of trouble.

2. PUPPY TRAINING

Serious protection training should not be started before the dog has matured. It takes about ten months of a puppy's life to fully develop the protective instinct.
The foundation for man work, however, should be laid at a much earlier point in time, and it is here where the prey instinct can be utilized with much advantage. Developing the fighting TECHNIQUES, which at a later time are combined with the motivation to protect his master, gives the dog a definite advantage over others who did not receive this preliminary training.

Some instructors argue that protection training must not be started until the dog is fully obedience trained. Any training, including protection work, benefits greatly when the foundation for it has been laid during puppyhood. As a matter of fact, obedience work improves considerably when combined with protection exercises since corrections given here have a much less depressing, or lasting, effect on the performance of the dog.

The average dog needs about two years to reach a high level of proficiency in obedience performance.
For an all-around training, much valuable time will be lost if you out-wait this period. At that age a dog is less able to adapt to new mental and physical stimuli, he is normally too dependent on his handler, his initiative is often dwarfed and his protective instinct is nearly always suppressed. He has - for too long - been reprimanded when he barked at strangers, or when he was alert and suspicious of them, all of which is supposed to change now on a moments notice.
It takes a very special effort on the decoy's part, a knowledgeable training director, full cooperation from the handler and lots of patience to make a Schutzhund out of such a dog.

STARTING THE PUPPY
    Puppies can be prepared for protection work at a very young age, by playing with them a gentle tug-of-war, using a soft cloth at first, a piece of burlap later on. A couple of socks left with the youngsters can provide hours of pleasure, for them as well as for the owner watching them play with it.
    Older puppies can be taken along to the training field, to let them observe the more mature dogs. When their leads are tied to the fence, or to a post, you do not even have to keep them company. Give them a good vantage point, however, from which they can see the action on the training field. Learning by imitating the "older generation" is important not only for the human civilization!
    Proper upbringing (which includes early conditioning to strange people, to strange dogs, to strange places, to strange sounds, etc., playful fights with litter mates, and an authoritarian master), home and not kennel raising, enough attention, close bonds to their master, feeding regularly meat that the dogs have to tear apart, are all essential prerequisites for the training of top performing Schutzhund dogs.

PROGRESS
Older puppies have much fun with the "Rabbit Chase". This is best played with three dogs held on leash by their owners. The assistant has a leash too, or a piece of rope, to which a burlap bag is fastened. For seasoned dogs a used sleeve cover is more suitable than the rag. The assistant informs one of the handlers that his dog is going to become the winner. Then he teases the dogs with the prey and starts running away, dragging the "rabbit" behind. All three dogs follow close yet the handlers prevent them from actually getting a bite. Once everybody is excited, the handler of the

predetermined winner goes faster and lets his dog catch the prey. At this point the assistant lets go of the string and releases the prey to the dog. It is very important that the dog be allowed to hold and to carry the prey, and to brag with it in front of the other two contestants. This has a tremendous psychological effect on all three dogs which becomes quite obvious when the next (and then the next) dog gets a chance to capture the prey.

RAG AGITATION

With the dog on leash, the decoy wiggles a soft piece of cloth, a towel or a burlap sack in front of himself close to the ground. He moves it away from the dog as to simulate an escaping animal. Most dogs will grab it eventually since there is no threat involved. After a moment of gentle struggling, the decoy will let go of the sack - yet sneakily and suspiciously he tries to grab it back. Supported by his handler's praise, the dog gets to carry the sack off the field.

Once this phase is mastered, the dog must fetch the prey which now moves about 3 to 4 feet above the ground. Usually he will have to jump up for it, and he will have to struggle a little more before he gets possession of it. A considerate, skillful decoy is of the greatest importance here.

3. TRAINING TECHNIQUES FOR MATURE DOGS

At the age of eight to ten months the dogs are normally introduced to the active phase of protection work.

Since the readiness for combat (fighting drive) increases
- in an area with shrubs, trees and/or other objects, as compared to a wide open field
- in the presence of the handler
- on the home grounds (territorial instinct)
- when the dog is restrained (leash, fence), conditions should be chosen accordingly.

BAD GUYS

While most of his contacts with mankind have been friendly so far, the dog must now learn that there are bad guys as well, which need to be dealt with. Some dogs have no problem, others simply can not believe that somebody would threaten or harm them.

An overly friendly, soft dog does not make a good Schutzhund. Yet even most dogs with good Schutzhund potential will initially refuse to bite. Their owners had reprimanded them, usually severely, for any sign of hostility, and now they let their master handle threatening or dangerous situations. The "experts" advise you to get another dog. Fortunately, that is usually not necessary. A good decoy (playing skillfully the role of an aggressor), supported by an understanding handler (playing convincingly the role of a helpless victim) can turn things around.

If this does not work, then "flanking" may turn the dog on.

This requires that the decoy sneaks up to the dog, quickly grips, pinches or pulls the loose skin on the dog's flank between hind leg and stomach, and then runs for cover. If you support your dog properly, the decoy never gets another chance to flank your dog again.

Securing a good, experienced decoy for the beginning protection work is quite important since the initial confrontation may well determine success or failure.

The dog must be challenged but not overpowered, he must be threatened but not defeated. "The dog always wins" is probably the most important rule every decoy has to obey.

Depending on the temperament and the courage of the dog, the decoy can be more or less aggressive. Depending on the personality of the dog, the aggression must be directed against the handler (for many German Shepherd Dogs, for instance), or against the dog (for many Dobermans, for instance). It is a very fine line the decoy has to tread, and he must back off as soon as the dog becomes insecure. The sequence of cowardly approaching the beginning dog and fearfully running away from him at the slightest sign of the dog defending himself or his master, is the trademark of a skillful decoy.

The following diagram shows the response of a dog in time as an agitation exercise gets under way:
-   First, the decoy has to set the stage, and the dog has to acknowledge that a potentially hazardous situation exists (confirmation).
-   Continued harassment will solicit appropriate hostile responses from the dog (conformation).
-   The desire to fight the bad guy increases with each unsuccessful lunge of the restrained dog. At the same time, however, frustration builds up and reaches - eventually - a plateau.
-   If on repeated tries the reward (bite) is withheld, then the dog resigns. A good decoy will sense this stage before it happens and he will give the dog a chance to bite.

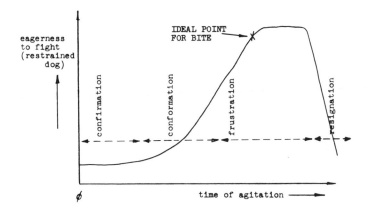

THE FIRST CONFRONTATION
Both you and the decoy have to be good actors to stage a threatening situation where the dog's assistance is needed - and generously rewarded when given (with praise, of course).

The decoy will approach you and the dog, advancing sideways. This projects to the dog a narrow profile rather than the more intimidating frontal "broad side". The decoy acts fearful, suspicious, moving slowly, crouching, growling low and lightly wiggling a burlap sack hanging from his hand. He will not throw or shake the sack into the dog's face, nor will he vehemently move around or actually attack you or your dog.

Most dogs are still uncertain at this time and they have to find the proper reaction that also has the approval of their master. In response to the decoy's suspicious behavior the dog will normally bark and/or take a step forward, but then he will turn his head immediately, to look up to your face to ask for approval. This is the moment where the decoy fearfully runs away, it is also the moment where you must praise your dog lavishly.

In repeating this exercise you should stimulate your dog to participate, by becoming aggressive yourself. Shout at the decoy, make threatening or hitting motions. The dog will most likely "assist" you, and you should praise and encourage him as soon as he does so.
The first training session should be concluded by letting the dog chase the decoy off the field.

Dogs which do not respond should be given another chance at another location. When challenged by an intruder at their own grounds (car, or home, or kennel), the combination of the various instincts (pack, protective, territorial, survival) will often be sufficient to stimulate aggression. A fearful approach of the decoy, retreat upon the slightest response from the dog, and encouragement and support from you are important, to let the dog know what is expected of him.

TEAMWORK

The involvement of the handler is important, especially for those of inhibited or soft dogs.
Much too often do we see (novice) handlers holding their end of the leash, smiling and watching the decoy's efforts to get a bite or a growl out of their dog. These people are not really "handlers", they are spectators: interested, indifferent, amazed and finally disappointed.

Dogs are pack animals. They play, work and hunt together, under the direction of a leader. By nature, they would not volunteer to fight a giant enemy (the decoy), they would instead try to avoid him. If the pack leader, however, decides to take up the fight, they will follow suit and do the job, together. Besides the pack instinct which causes the pack members to come to the assistance of their leader, the "Risk Shift Principle" plays a role here. It states that a group as a whole is willing to take more chances than each individual by himself.

You are the pack leader. If you don't commit yourself, if you just stand there and want to be entertained, your dog will do exactly the same: he will wait and watch.
Get involved. Act as if the situation were real. Don't smile, instead get angry at the "bad guy" who is harassing and threatening you. Alert the dog, shout at the decoy, hit his sleeve with the hand, push him, punch him in the shoulder. All these are appropriate actions to take.
As soon as the dog shows the slightest indication that he is willing to assist, give him lots of praise and encouragement. Let him know how much you appreciate that he comes to the rescue. Tell and reassure him with words and a pat on the flank that you approve of his action, of his initiative to ward off a threatening attack.
The physical reassurance, e.g. the pat on the flank, is very important at this point. Without it, the novice dog will take his attention off the decoy and look at you, just to make sure that you are still there to help, and that you still approve of the action.

The decoy should always give the dog a chance to win, by surrendering the sleeve, by running away, or by quitting the fight before the dog gets tired. This strengthens the dog's self-confidence. It also enables you to lavishly reward your dog with praise, laying a solid foundation for future protection work.

STAKE AGITATION

Stake agitation in its true sense refers to a kind of protection exercise where the tied-up dog is on his own, handler out of sight. It should not be confused with the all-or-nothing test in which the dog is cornered and pushed to the extreme, leaving him no choice but to defend himself or to face destruction. Stake agitation as we see it is a training approach to building confidence.

Since it requires some experience on the dog's part, novice dogs should be introduced to it in a slightly modified form, that is in the presence of the handler.
We need a sturdy collar for the dog (leather collar or choke chain on the dead ring) and a flexible spring chain. The spring softens the jolt on the dog's neck during agitation, yet there is a safety catch in case the spring should break.

Stand next to your dog and encourage him to fend off the would-be aggressor. The decoy uses sack, sleeve or stick to excite the dog until ready for a bite. While having stayed out of reach originally (Fig.32), the decoy now moves into the sphere controlled by the dog (Fig.33). He approaches at an angle and gives the dog a chance to bite while moving AWAY from him. Sack or sleeve must be held and moved ABOVE the waist line. This encourages the dog to reach for the prey with a firm bite. During the ensuing short fight the decoy must make sure that he remains well inside this circle so that the dog, while biting, never feels any pressure on the collar from the tightened chain.
The decoy then surrenders sack or sleeve and runs away, and you praise your dog without taking the prey away from him. As a matter of fact, you should encourage the dog to "kill" (shake) the prey, to reinforce this innate response.

This modified stake agitation is a very comfortable arrangement, well suited for novice dogs, novice handlers (as well as physically not so strong handlers) and novice decoys.

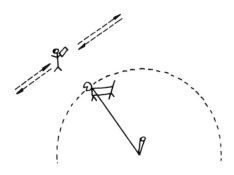

FIG. 32

FIG. 33

The handler does not have to worry about his dog getting out of control since a secure anchor, a good spring chain, and a sturdy collar take care of that. He can pay full attention to the reactions of his dog and give encouragement, reinforcement and praise at the proper time.

The dog acknowledges the undivided attention and the supportive involvement of his master and gains confidence quickly.

The decoy, lastly, is assured a safe operating arena as long as he stays outside of the circle controlled by the dog. He does not have to fear handler errors or unexpected reactions of the dog. He knows that after the fight he can just step back and be perfectly safe again.

Another modification of the stake agitation would be to stage an argument and a little fight between you and the decoy, just out of reach of the dog. By "coincidence" the decoy then happens to get into the circle, allowing the dog to bite the sleeve or the sack.

For the transition from here to the regular stake agitation you should move farther and farther away as the decoy works the dog just like above. This transition might take a few days or a few weeks, depending on the type of dog involved. It might also involve a regression where you have to go back to your dog to give him needed assurance.

In general, we suggest
- the angled rather than the frontal approach (Fig.37)

- short fights
- to let go of sleeve (sack) once in a
    while, while the dog is biting it.
Retreat and civil agitation just outside
the circle conclude the exercise.

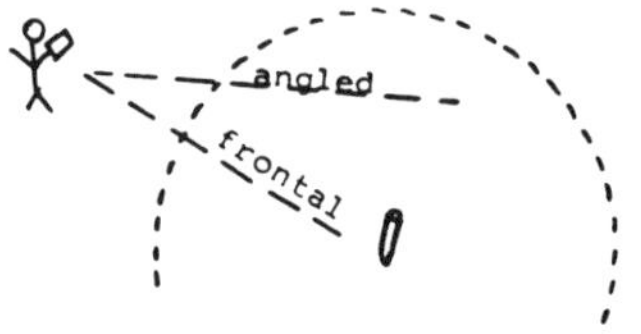

SLEEVE HAPPINESS
Sleeve-happiness is a term used to
describe a dog that is more interested in
the sleeve, the "prey", than in the person
carrying it. For young dogs, this may be
all right. Mature dogs, however, should
be taught that there is more to
protection work than just chasing a
piece of cloth.

FIGURE 34

Sleeve-happy dogs are usually
man-made, trained with the help of a stereotype. Any deviation from the normal pattern confuses
these dogs. It is, therefore, advisable
- to change decoys frequently
- to work with two decoys on the field, taking turns
- to change the protection gear frequently
- to use concealed body protection, and to wear street clothes over it
- to have the sleeve worn on the decoy's left arm, at other times on the right arm
- to agitate sideways, having the unprotected arm face the dog and to change sides only
    immediately before the bite
- to do civil agitation:
    After a regular fight the decoy surrenders the sleeve and runs away but comes back to
    re-agitate the dog. Without any equipment or protective gear, he shows hostile behavior, trying
    to get the dog's attention. The decoy might have to threaten or to lightly hit the dog with a stick,
    to make him let go of the sleeve. You should encourage your dog, but you must also hold him
    securely since the decoy is unprotected.
- to do muzzle agitation (with advanced, hard-biting dogs only; refer to that section).

LINE AND CIRCLE AGITATION
Line and circle agitation are two valuable methods available for the protection training of novice
and intermediate dogs. Advanced dogs, however, should rarely participate here. In these exercises
the dogs are exposed to high intensity stimuli for a rather long time before they get a chance to
bite. This is desirable for beginning dogs that need the time to "warm up". Advanced dogs, on the
other hand, would get conditioned to rely on an extensive amount of agitation before the actual
fight takes place. This is undesirable, even detrimental to our training purposes, since these dogs
should respond to the first sign of a threat.

For the decoy, the group agitation methods save considerable energy as well as time since several
dogs are watching the agitating movements simultaneously.
With more than 10 dogs, two decoys can work the same group.

For **LINE AGITATION** the handlers line up, leaving maybe 12 to 15 feet spaces between them. Each
handler is instructed to hold his dog securely, and to prevent close contacts with neighboring
handlers and dogs. Collars and leads are checked at this time to avoid possible problems. If a sturdy
fence or a row of trees is available, the handlers can grab it with one hand and hold the leash in
the other hand. This prevents a strong dog from dragging his handler forward.
It is also desirable to alternate dogs and bitches in the line, and to have a novice (or weak) dog
between two more experienced/sure dogs.

Then the action begins: The decoy agitates the first dog in line, waving his sack, the sleeve, the stick,
hitting the ground, hissing, retreating, advancing etc. At the same time, the handler encourages his
dog to fight off the bad guy.

The decoy stays out of reach of the dog, however, and advances to the next dog after a short while. This is repeated with dog #2, then dog #3 and so on.

The last dog in line gets a little more agitation and then he is finally allowed to follow the escaping decoy and to bite the sleeve or the sack. Note that while the whole line is in uproar, only the last dog gets the opportunity to bite.

At the completion of the fight the handler tells the decoy to "get lost" and moves with his dog to the start of the line. Then the game begins anew until all the dogs had a chance to take the sack or the sleeve.

CIRCLE AGITATION is very similar to line agitation. The handlers with their dogs form a ring, though, leaving again enough working space between themselves. The decoy operates in the hub of the wheel and for his safety, handlers are instructed to maintain their position. No-one is allowed to close in to the center. Instead, the decoy approaches the dog that he has selected to be worked.

Circle agitation allows for a little more flexibility. The decoy can more easily spot and relate to problems that individual dogs and handlers have. He can change equipment (sack, sleeve, stick) and methods (fearful or forceful approach) more readily, he can devote more time to problem dogs and handlers, he can agitate dogs out of sequence as needed etc.

During circle agitation the decoy must be "on his toes" constantly. At all times is he the absolute center of attraction, for all the dogs and all the handlers. The involvement of the dogs with the training is somewhat higher in circle agitation than in line agitation and, usually, more things can be accomplished more quickly.

FROM SACK TO SLEEVE
The use of sack and sleeve was recommended in the preceding exercises without further qualifications. While the choice is left pretty much to the discretion of the decoy, and maybe the training director and the handler, there are certain guidelines which should be observed (refer also to the equipment section):
- In initial protection training, a soft burlap or jute sack is used until the dog eagerly tries to get and to bite it.
- The bite roll (sausage) or the soft sleeve cover (all by itself, not on the arm!) are used next, both of which are operated just like the sack. A puppy sleeve is not necessary, but if available, it would be used in this phase.
- Transition to the (hard) sleeve with (soft) sleeve cover is often aided by draping the sack over the cover and pulling it away with the free hand at the last moment, when the dog is already committed to the bite. A soft, broken-in sleeve cover rather than a hard, new cuff should be used here, of course.
- For the transition it is especially important to get the dog angry and really excited before giving him the opportunity to bite. As soon as the dog has gotten a hold of the sleeve, the decoy should release it and run away without it, in obvious terror.

DEVELOPING THE BITE
Dogs that perform well in stake, circle and line agitation can be worked individually. The following is a list of points to consider which, by the way, also apply to the earlier described routines.

Preparation:
- The dog should be agitated long enough. He must be angry and almost frustrated before he gets a chance to bite.
- The decoy should play his part realistically and skillfully (hostile-afraid, but not overpowering).
- The decoy should agitate as long as the dog shows confidence and willingness to fight. He should immediately and quickly retreat when the dog becomes uneasy or fearful.
- The decoy should present his side view, not his frontal view to the dog (smaller, less intimidating profile).
- You, the handler, should support and encourage your dog, verbally and physically.

Initiating the bite:
- The decoy should run past the dog at an angle, not come in for a frontal collision, and he should give the dog a chance to hit the sleeve or the sack while passing.

- The decoy should not push his sleeve or the sack into the dog's face to initiate a bite.
- The decoy should offer the sack or the sleeve high (about the height of his chest, but no lower than his waist), to encourage a firm bite.
- After contact, the decoy should continue to move away from the dog for a step or two, before coming to a halt and to fight with the dog.

Maintaining the bite:
- The decoy should carry the sleeve about waist- to chest-high and hold it horizontally to get the dog's front feet off the ground. This usually discourages the dog from re-bites or grip changes, and it will also aid in the development of a firm, full bite. With a heavy dog, the decoy can lift up the far end of the sleeve with his free hand (watch out for the teeth!). If the sack was used, holding it with both hands, and lifting it up, serves the same purpose.
- A slow, gradual pull on sleeve or sack encourages the dog to maintain the bite. Hasty, sudden or ripping motions are painful and discourage the dog from biting.
- While the dog is on the sleeve, there must be a constant pull (slightly upwards and away from the dog, toward the decoy). The force of the pull should vary, like in a tug of war: sometimes the decoy claims the prey, sometimes the dog does. As long as the fight goes on, however, the decoy must not let his arm go limp.
- The decoy should move his sleeve arm slightly, maybe an inch back and forth in any direction, or he can twist his arm inside the sleeve. Moderate body movements accompany this.
- The decoy should use his free hand to gently touch the dog's head or shoulders during the fight (be careful!). This is done in preparation for the later introduction of the stick.
- The decoy must continue to display a hostile-fearful attitude. Friendly or casual talk with the handler should be avoided at this time.
- If the dog releases the sleeve prematurely, the decoy can
    a) use the prey/pursuit instinct (run away, encourage the dog to pursue and to bite the sleeve: "Escape")
    b) stimulate the competitive spirit and build up the frustration (work with another dog in full view, before paying attention again to the lacking animal)
    c) make the fight shorter (the dog may have gotten tired).
- After a firm bite, some (insecure) dogs "spin" the decoy to avoid frontal contact, to hide behind him. With your free hand, swing the sack or the stick behind your back (try for a hit). It will probably bring the dog forward. Keep him in front by bending your knees, pulling the sleeve closer to your chest, and working the dog between your legs. The pointed knees will prevent the dog from escaping sideways (leather pants and groin protectors are recommended).
- During the fight, some dogs "claw" the decoy's body with their front feet. Try moving the sleeve down and up, right and left, or hold the sleeve pressed against your chest and twist your body fairly rapidly to the right, left, up, down. If nothing helps, make it unpleasant for the dog to claw. Attach a 4-ft. section of tin roofing to the front of your suit (protect the sharp edges!), agitate after climbing into a top- and bottom-less oil barrel (steel or plastic), or just give in and work the sleeve closer to the ground than usual.

Finish:
        "The dog always wins."   He wins by:
a) carrying the sleeve off the field (prey instinct),
b) chasing the bad guy off the field (territorial instinct), or
c) having overpowered the bad guy and caused him to cease struggling (fighting drive).

Novice dogs benefit the most from the first two approaches.
The decoy should stimulate the dog to vigorously shake or yank the sleeve by rewarding him with the release of the "prey" (see "Delayed Victory", below). Initially the dog gets the sleeve as soon as he shakes or yanks it. Later on he has to fight a little longer, to shake it a little harder.

Releasing the bite after a fight (approach c)) should only be asked of dogs which have developed their fighting techniques. In that instance, the following suggestions apply:

- The decoy must come to an abrupt stop, standing motionless like a post. Proper protective gear, like suitable pants, as well as the handler's cooperation, will give the decoy the necessary confidence.
- If you have a beginning, soft dog, count to ten, get casually a hold of the dog's collar and praise and pet your pal. Usually this will cause the dog to release the bite.
- Tough dogs may require a correction, followed by praise, of course (see "Release").

THE CLEAN BITE

Schutzhund is a sport, requiring the contestants to obey certain rules. The dog should, for instance, bite the sleeve and not the throat, just like the boxer can not hit his opponent below the waist line. These rules do not apply for a confrontation with a criminal, of course. A dog shown in Schutzhund competition, however, can not be allowed to endanger the well-being of the decoy. If this happens, the dog must be removed from the field at once, and on leash. The owner will most likely disagree, he might even think of himself as a hero. The fact is, however, that the dog has publicly demonstrated very serious shortcomings of his handler, of the club trainer, and of the club decoy.

Since the dog should not be punished if he mixes up the anatomy, you must make sure that the dog just has no chance to bite anything else but the sleeve. It is a matter of conditioning, and the process is best started with the novice dog.
Initially, all exercises should be done with the dog tied to a stake. This way, you do not have to concern yourself with restraining the dog, the decoy knows exactly how far the dog can advance, and the dog has no choice but to bite what he gets. He gets either the sack or the sleeve.

Agitation for a sufficient length of time builds frustration, and as soon as the dog is really angry he is allowed to bite the sleeve (or the sack).
If this sequence of events is repeated for several weeks, and if the decoy performs sensibly otherwise, the dog will not even look for another place to bite.
The exercise can then be done on the six foot leash, with you controlling, and if necessary correcting, the dog's reaction.
Once the dog performs reliably on a *loose* leash in the course of several (maybe 10) training sessions, he can be allowed to work off lead. You should watch him closely, though, and initially you should stand nearby to fetch him in case of problems.

If the dog aims for anything else but the sleeve, he was pushed too fast. Stake and leash agitation must be resumed. Minor violations, however, can often be corrected with a timely command, or with a low-force karate chop: slice your hand between the decoy and your dog's mouth just before the bite occurs. Two other effective means are the skillfully used throw chain, or a snappy hit with the stick across the snout just before the dog actually bites (done by decoy or handler, depending on their skills), both followed immediately with re-agitation by the decoy.

Dogs that have developed the habit of biting the leg, the rear or any other part of the body except the sleeve arm must be retrained on the stake, just like the novice dog. With them, however, a very slow advance to the next stage - from stake to leash to off-lead - is even more important.
It is much more difficult to change a habit rather than to establish one.

IMPROVING THE BITE

The following suggestions are meant for the training of advanced dogs. They are based on the utilization of natural traits and instincts. Each one of the recommendations listed contributes in its own way to developing a firm bite which is defined as a forceful seizure of the sleeve with the full length of the jaws, in contrast to nibbling with just the canine teeth.

a) Equipment

In training, a suitable sleeve should be chosen, preferably one without a bite bar. If a dog wants to hold on to such a sleeve, he is forced to take a full bite with full jaw pressure. The habit will carry over into the trial where usually a bite bar sleeve is used, and it will result in superior performances. On the other hand, there are sleeves with a very thin bite bar and a guard rail to prevent slip-off. They will help some weak dogs but spoil the tough ones.

Sleeve covers should be sturdy yet giving, and they should provide some texture. The braided jute cover meets these requirements and helps beginning and advanced dogs in developing a firm bite. New, plain jute covers are hard, they tend to discourage novice dogs. For the same reason, advanced dogs are forced to bite harder in order not to slip off.

Burlap is a weak, fragile material. It has very limited applications for the conditioning of young dogs only.

Nylon covers or nylon-jute combinations should not be used since they can easily ruin a dog's teeth.

b) Frustration
The decoy should agitate the dog at close range, convincingly, and long enough, without giving the dog a chance to get a hold of the sleeve. As the tension builds up, but just before it declines again, the decoy must give the dog a chance to grab the sleeve - by planned coincidence. After a very short fight the dog should be allowed to obtain, "kill" (shake) and carry the sleeve (prey instinct), followed by some re-agitation (protective instinct). Repetition of this exercise in the same training session is not recommended.

c) Encouragement
While the dog is biting the sleeve, your encouragement may increase his holding power.

Physical contact with you, a pat on the rump, verbal encouragement serve this purpose. The dosage is important: the right amount does not take the dog's attention off the decoy, too much of it, however, will cause the dog to lose interest in the decoy.

d) Pride
Circle and line agitation may be helpful in toughening a dog's bite.

After enough frustration has build up, the one selected dog (who's turn it is) gets the chance to bite the sleeve - and all the others have to watch. Competing and showing off - surprisingly - is important to an animal also.

e) Restriction
While the dog is biting the sleeve, some tension on the leash attached to the dead ring on the chocke or leather collar will usually toughen the bite.

You must make sure that you do not yank the leash or increase the tension too much. In these instances the dog might release the bite in order to respond to your unintentional command.

f) Victory
Developing self-confidence in the dog automatically leads to a firmer bite. Specific instructions for mature dogs are:
- Kneel next to your dog, hold him by the collar. Alert him to the decoy who approaches slowly in a fearful-threatening manner. The decoy will hastily retreat as soon as your dog shows any signs of aggression. Your support and encouragement is needed.
  If the dog does not respond, the decoy will come closer, suddenly attacking you or your dog, maybe even stinging him with the switch. Jump up, assist your dog in chasing the decoy off the field. (The decoy must provoke the dog to bite, not intimidate him !)
- Tie your dog to a post and go out of sight. The decoy will approach the dog as before, being careful again not to be too overpowering. He will run away as soon as the dog barks or lunges forward. At that time, rush back and praise your buddy.
- If the previous exercises are mastered, then the decoy will walk toward the staked dog in a friendly manner (handler out of sight again). Once he reaches the critical distance of about 6 feet, he will suddenly become hostile and attack, maybe even sting the dog. The canine should respond in an aggressive way which will prompt the decoy to retreat hastily.
- Dogs that remain inactive need the support of their handler for a couple of times: rush out and kick and beat the bad guy off the field.

g) Delayed Victory
With the dog on leash, give him a chance for a bite. The decoy then lets his sleeve arm go limp and turns his back to the dog (the dog still "hangs" on the sleeve). Keep the leash reasonably taut. After a while start pulling on it a little harder (steady!). At that time, the decoy "revives" his sleeve arm,

trying to slowly pull the sleeve away from his adversary. Most dogs will respond by shaking or yanking the sleeve. This should be rewarded instantaneously in that the decoy surrenders/releases the sleeve. You can assist your dog by shouting at the decoy and chasing him off the field, and by lavishly praising your dog for the victory.

h) Suspension
The decoy should hold the sleeve clinched to his stomach or chest.
This not only gives him better physical control over sleeve and dog, it also forces most dogs to reach up and to lift their front feet off the ground. Holding the dog in this position, the decoy causes the dog to take a hard bite (otherwise he would fall off). It also prevents nibbling and bite repositioning.

i) Counter-Balance
With the leash, keep a steady tension on the collar (no tugs!) while the dog is biting. The dog probably will think you want to take him off the sleeve and holds on tight, as a result.

j) Teasing
A dog that barely hangs on to the sleeve will usually firm up his grip if the decoy blows into the dogs face, or if he slides his stick along the dog's feet, chest or belly. This makes most dogs angry and they will fight more vigorously now, usually shaking or yanking the "prey". The decoy should release the sleeve immediately or after some more struggling, depending on the prior training.

k) Surprise
Carry the sleeve under your arm and heel your dog on lead. Suddenly, an unarmed and unprotected decoy jumps out of his nearby hiding place, grabs the sleeve from you, puts it on his arm and runs away. Release your dog and encourage him to get the "thief".

l) Leap # 1
Hold on to a tree or another anchor with your left arm stretched out. Hold your dog by the end of the leash with an outstretched right arm.

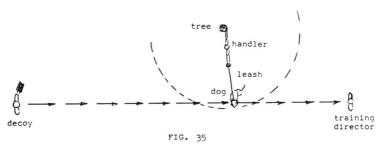

FIG. 35

The decoy then agitates in order to determine how far out the dog can go.
The training director observes and memorizes this spot. He then lines himself and the decoy up so that a straight line from the decoy to himself runs just within the dog's reach.
The decoy moves in great leaps at not too fast a pace, but at a rhythmic and constant speed, toward the training director, holding his bent sleeve arm sideways, outward, at shoulder height.
The bite bar, if the sleeve has one, should point at a slight angle downward (toward the ground, not up in the air). This may require some "arm-twisting".
The decoy wearing a right arm sleeve must have the dog/handler team on his right side. With a left arm sleeve, the approach should be from the opposite direction (dog/handler team is on the left side of the decoy now).
While leaping toward the training director (he may want to count "leap - and - leap - and - leap ....) the decoy advances at a constant speed and in a straight line. The dog can now mentally

prepare for the time of arrival and schedule his jump accordingly.
Upon contact, the decoy moves closer into the dog's circle and stages a short fight. The dog wins, captures the sleeve, chases the decoy away and gets his praise from you.

m) Leap #2 ("airplane")
The handler holds his dog by the collar for a modified version of the close-range escape.
The decoy runs away, holding the sleeve arm outstretched to the side like the wing of an airplane. Once the decoy is about 20 ft away, you release your dog. The decoy continues running away but takes smaller steps now to prepare for the impact. You encourage your dog to bite the sleeve. Follow him and try to catch up with him - mainly to encourage your dog, and to prevent the decoy from being bitten on other parts of the body.

As in the procedure described under l) above, this technique teaches the dog to take a hold of escaping prey. The dog will only be successful if he jumps to take a full, hard bite.

n) Leap #3 ("ball players")
Two assistants, about 20 feet apart, "play ball", using the bite roll or a sleeve cover instead of the ball. They throw it at a low angle, and at a slow pace first, faster and a little higher later on. You and your dog are stationed at the middle, and you feed your dog enough lead (and encouragement) so that he can catch the prey. If he gets it, praise him and allow, even encourage, him to "kill" (shake) it.

o) Leap #4 ("catch")
Tie a bite roll or a sleeve cover to a short line. Swing it above your head, then let it fly past the dog. He will jump for it and try to catch it.

p) Pause
Not doing any protection work with a dog for several weeks, or even months, may revitalize him. After being deprived of it for some time, he will give his best to enjoy the few precious moments he gets.

q) Changes
Boredom in dog training should be avoided under all circumstances.
A new training field, a new decoy, visits to another club, a change in the training routines, new exercises, games involving the protective or the prey instinct will often bring the spirit back into a dog which has become dull.
These changes will also make it more fun for you to work with your dog - in training and in competition.

RELEASING THE BITE
The clean release after a fight is of concern to most Schutzhund trainers, but it seems to be of even more concern to the "non-Schutzhund" people. This, unfortunately, has caused some trainers to place too much emphasis on the "out" at too early a time in training.
Sensibly approached, any normal dog can be taught to release quickly on command.
Locking jaws on a man's arm (padded or not) is not a natural response, the dog has to be taught to do it. Letting go of it, on the other hand, is the sensible and natural thing for a dog to do.
Therefore, the desired unnatural response (biting) should first be firmly established BEFORE the natural response (out) is forcibly impressed upon the dog. Otherwise, a mediocre performance in protection work will necessarily be the result.

A dog constantly worrying about "out" will pay more attention to his handler than to the decoy. His fighting spirit will be low, he will do the job half-heartedly only.
Excepting a few hard-headed dogs, it is, therefore, suggested not to bother with the "out" too much until the dog does spirited protection work. At that time the release can logically be dealt with, and quite effectively so.

To teach the "out" we suggest a gradual approach:
At first, ask the decoy to release the sleeve after the fight, then let the dog carry it off the field. You should stay close (use the leash, if necessary) and observe your dog. The moment he drops the sleeve voluntarily, say "out", hold him back a little and, with your foot, kick the sleeve out of reach.

After a couple of times, command "out" just before the dog will drop the sleeve anyway. If it works, use the "out" still sooner. Give him one second or two to obey. If he fails to release, step quickly on the sleeve with one foot and give a leash correction at the same time. Then praise him.
Ask the decoy to hang on to his gear after a fight once the dog releases the carried sleeve reliably. With the dog in tow, he should then move into the blind and "freeze". Wait for a few seconds to let the dog calm down. Then command "out", count quietly to ten, and enforce your command with threatening gestures, voice and a leash correction, as needed.

Consider the following:
a) Sensibly trained dogs do not develop the obsession for fighting which often leads to a refusal to release the bite. For them, praising and petting is enough of a diversion to shift the attention from decoy to handler, at least for a moment.

In these instances, you should casually approach the dog and reach for the collar. Calmly praising the dog with a steady stream of words, patting him on the shoulder, and very slowly lifting him up by the collar will get nearly all unspoiled dogs off the sleeve. The command "out" should be used in a relaxed (not threatening) tone here. Then send the decoy off, rather than taking the dog away.

b) After the release, the dog is supposed to guard the decoy without taking another bite. Giving the "down" command at this time will nicely serve both purposes (if the dog obeys it).

Since in a trial this additional command is not allowed, and since the dog does not really care which command is used for which exercise, clever handlers have taught their dog to lay down on the (obedience) command "out".
In order to lay down, the dog has to release the bite first; therefore, with sufficient practice, a nice trial performance can almost be guaranteed.

c) Excessive agitation and long fights, swinging the dog in a circle ("circus performance"), or use of the stick beyond reason cause the advanced dogs to get overly excited and angry at the decoy so that they will not release. Moderation in the decoy's performance will take care of the problem.

d) The decoy can assist the dog in a clean out by making the transition from fighting to quitting very abrupt, sudden (rather than gradual).

e) During initial training, the decoy can turn the sleeve abruptly from horizontal (fight) to vertical ("out"), pushing the far end of the sleeve onto the ground. The somewhat twisted head position will make the dog more responsive to the "out" command.

f) The decoy should stand motionless after the fight. If he moves, even if it is just to get more comfortable, then the dog will take it as a signal that the fight is still on.

g) Holding the sleeve horizontally in front of, and pressed against, the body, motionless, discourages the dog from hanging on, and from taking another bite. If necessary, the decoy can lift up the sleeve still higher with the free hand (possibly just below the chin), just before he stops fighting.

h) Giving the dog time to calm down insures better compliance with the "out" command. You should count at least to three (maybe up to ten), before giving the command.
Some trainers demand the "instant release". This can be taught by keeping the dog constantly in fear of punishment for disobeying an (unreasonable) "out" command. During the fight the dog will then pay more attention to you than to the "criminal", and he will lose much of his effectiveness. The "instant out" is a straight jacket for a dog's natural instincts. It does ruin his fighting spirit and should, therefore, not be used.

i) Startling the dog will momentarily divert his attention and get him off the sleeve. This may require:
- threatening sounds
- a bottle with carbonated water squirted into his face
- a few pebbles or the throw chain thrown at him
- the use of the sling shot
- the use of an electronic training collar or of a sleeve rigged up to an electric fence charger.
One should consider here that the dog learns faster and becomes more dependable when he can not quite determine who causes the disaster (who threw the chain etc.). The training director or an assistant on the field can be quite valuable; they are suspect to the dog even if they remained inactive, and even though the handler gave the correction.

j) If none of the above suggestions work by themselves, then force must be used in addition. The two-leash approach is suggested for these occasions: a chain fastened to a secure post in the ground, and a regular leash hooked to the live ring on the choke or prong collar (the secured leash will prevent the dog from coming back for a second bite).
Give your dog a chance to fight, both leashes loose. When the decoy stops fighting, reach for the buckle of the leash (close to the dog's neck), give a harsh "out" command and one quarter of a second later slam the end of the collar INTO the sleeve (not away from it!). This tightening of the collar, maybe in conjunction with a second command which should be a really mean scream "out" will always work if done right. Your behavior at that time must clearly indicate that a major disaster will happen if he should decide to ignore the command.
The decoy then steps back to prevent the dog from taking another bite.
A dog that has been abused (by people other than the handler) or made insensitive by constantly nagging him with half-hearted corrections will require a firm hand, but even here success is guaranteed
  - if a meaningful dog/handler relationship exists
  - if you are determined to correct the situation, leaving your dog no choice but to comply
  - if you give praise after the successful release.

FALSE ALARM
Forcing a dog to instantly release the bite (discussed above) causes as much psychological damage as sending him after an escaping decoy and then calling him back before a bite occurs. To avoid punishment, the dog will in both instances learn to be more concerned with the termination of the fight then with subduing the bad guy.

Such an association in the dog's mind is not well understood by many trainers, and the "dead run", also called "false alarm" or "protection recall", is quite popular with American Police K-9 handlers and other civilian trainers. They argue that the recall is necessary to prevent harm to a person who might turn out to be innocent. What they do not realize is that they trade in an effective weapon for a look-alike toy. The responsible Police Officer will decide if his interference is justified before he pulls the trigger, and before he sends his dog, not after bullet and canine are on their way already.

THE STICK
VDH Schutzhund Trial Regulations require that the dog's courage be tested, using a stick. This test is needed to find out if the dogs will stand their ground and protect their masters even when threatened or lightly hit. Without this test the Schutzhund title, a working dog title, has little value as a measure of the dog's worthiness for breeding purposes.

This requirement has caused considerable controversy and criticism, accusing Schutzhund trainers of a) cruelty and
    b) needlessly sacrificing the lives of their dogs by making them an easy target for the criminal. Neither is true. The use of the stick is more symbolic than painful.
There are some decoys who, with the approval of the judge, beat the dogs severely. We suggest that the handler calls his dog immediately and leaves the field, taking the (administrative) consequences that are sure to follow. If enough handlers have the courage to pull their dogs, these decoys and judges will be out of a job soon.
Such abuse, however, is neither the intention of Schutzhund training, nor is it common.

To comment on the second part of the critique: Schutzhund dogs are not trained for active duty with law enforcement agencies. Unless sold to and retrained by such groups, they will probably never face situations that are staged in a trial, so they will not needlessly sacrifice their lives. Furthermore, if a criminal really slaughters the dog hanging on his arm, then he must be very well prepared for it, he must be very skillful, very knowledgeable, and very determined. The sacrifice of the dog buying the handler a chance to survive is then justifiable.

In training it is important to properly introduce the stick to the beginner dog. A twig with leaves on it will do nicely here. Later on, however, we suggest to use a bamboo stick, about 2 ft. long and 3/8 inch in diameter (the dimensions are mainly a safeguard against abuse), or the whip (described in the equipment section). The decoy should raise, hold and shake it in a threatening manner above his head. After a firm bite, quick blows from above toward the ground are used to condition the dog to the sound and the motion of a hit. Without ever touching the dog, this phase is continued for several weeks or months, depending on the dog.

During Phase II, the handler still holds his dog on leash during the fight, encouraging and praising him as usual. The decoy will hit the taut leash, his upper sleeve and the ground in an erratic sequence. Phase II lasts until the dog is fully conditioned to the fake hits.
Occasionally the decoy should work without the stick during this phase, and he should touch the dog's head and shoulders with his free hand.

During Phase III the decoy holds the stick only between thumb and index finger, touching the dog's back (simulating a hit), the leash, the ground and the sleeve in an irregular pattern. There are two training modes, used alternately: the "blow" and the "wipe". The blow is the commonly known hit, coming from above and landing on the dog's back. In the "wipe" the stick comes from above again but it is stopped short of the dog's body. The stick with the portion that just emerges from the hand (not the far end) is gently laid on the dog's back and pulled across it, similar to the movement of a bow on a cello.

Phase IV is a repeat of Phase III but off lead, again with the stick held between two fingers.

In the final Phase V the stick is held normally and used at first gently, later with reasonable force on the dog, alternating fake hits and a few "blows" and "wipes" in an erratic sequence. "Reasonable force" means that the decoy should use no more power than he would be willing to take when hit on his own bare arm. Reasonable force can be practiced with an assistant who holds taut a page of a large newspaper. The decoy then hits the paper to make a loud popping sound, but without breaking or tearing it.
Even after successful completion of Phase V, one should never overdo the hitting part, and one should never attempt to find the limit to which a dog would be able to stand hard blows.
The decoy is not allowed to hit any sensitive

Fig. 36

parts of the dog's body, only back, withers and flanks may be touched (dashed in figure).

4. ADVANCED TRAINING

ROUND ROBIN
The round robin offers a very efficient way of protection training for a group of at least 3 handlers (HI,H2,H3) with their dogs, provided a reasonably large training area is available.
Start by laying out a course with several stations (SI, S2, etc.), each station concentrating on one particular exercise. Then ask each handler to take his turn, and to play his part.
For a group of three trainers, it might look like this:

```
                    (H = handler   ;   S = station)
CYCLE 1:            H1 ties his dog at S5 and decoys at S1
                    H2 ties his dog at S6 and decoys at S4
                    H3 takes his dog through the course. While he does obedience work at S2, H1
                        changes over to S3.
CYCLE 2:            H3 ties his dog at S7 and decoys at S4
                    H1 takes his dog through the course as above
                    H2 ties his dog at S6 and decoys at SI/S3.
CYCLE 3:            H2 takes his dog through the course as above
                    H3 ties his dog at S7 and decoys at S1/S3
                    HI ties his dog at S5 and decoys at S4.
```

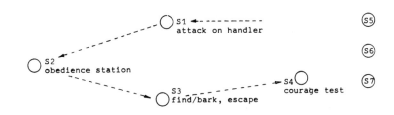

Following this sequence, each handler has a chance to work his dog with two different decoys, and to gain experience as a decoy for the other two dogs. Larger groups will, at any time, have most of their people working in obedience at station S2, until their turn comes. They could also lay out a more elaborate course with a greater variety of stations.

MUZZLE AGITATION

Muzzle agitation should be done only with advanced, hard-biting dogs, and only when a German-made police muzzle is available (imitations are likely to cause injury to dog and decoy). The dog must first be conditioned to the muzzle, which is done independently of protection training. During that time, regular protection work is conducted with the unmuzzled dog, including the "Leap #1", "Leap #2" (see "Improving the Bite") and the "straight-jacket" exercise. The last two routines are modified escapes, and all three teach the dog to jump up high for a bite.
Running away from the dog with the sleeve arm outstretched like the wing of an airplane forces the dog to speed up and to lunge with a powerful take-off (Leap #2).
Running away with the sleeve arm held across the back (like in a straight-jacket) again causes the dog to speed up and to jump for the bite. These exercises are later on done with the muzzled dog. The preceeding agitation and the excitement will let the dog forget momentarily that he is muzzled. Responding as he was taught, he will still jump up, bump the decoy in the back and cause him to fall. If the bump was not forceful enough, the decoy must still fall - that is part of the training - and then lay still. The handler rushes up to his dog and praises him, holds him and removes the muzzle while the decoy gets up. A little agitation and an escape attempt give the dog a chance to earn his reward: the bite (have the sleeve ready). Several training sessions later the decoy can run normally. He should maintain a rather fast speed, keeping both arms in front of the body. The muzzled dog has learned to bump into the back even when there is no sleeve as a target. The fall and the bite afterwards, however, are still important.

NIGHT EXERCISES

Night exercises provide an interesting change from the standard protection routines. They contribute greatly to building confidence, but only after a foundation has been laid already. Novice dogs, or those dogs who have not progressed satisfactorily in protection work, should not participate. Even advanced dogs should not be entered "cold" in a night trial.

Start by taking your dog along for a stroll around the neighborhood when it is really dark. On another night, surprise him with a trash can left in the middle of your driveway. Continue your nightly excursions to the park, in the field, in the woods, to the down-town section of your city. Keep your dog on leash, or at least close to you. Teach him to alert you to hidden strangers by barking or growling at them. If the dog ignores them, ask an assistant to hide and to sting your dog with a switch in passing.

Night trials will usually be sponsored by a club or an organization, since grounds, equipment and personnel must be secured. It has been proven advantageous to lay out a course with individual check points, spaced apart sufficiently. Each station provides a different attraction, which may be friendly or hostile, familiar or strange, startling or frightening.
The following suggestions are only starting points. They should be modified and expanded to suit the desires and the competence level of the participants.

a) Friendly Encounters
- a friend standing still, asking for the time
- a stranger with flashlight passing from the opposite direction, on foot or on bicycle
- a guard posted near a gate or a door, asking for identification
- a group of people, sitting, chatting and singing

b) Startling Encounters
- a stranger sleeping and snoring in a large cardboard box
- a parked car, suddenly turning on the headlights and blinding the team
- a couple of garbage cans, oil drums or other large objects placed on the road
- a hidden loudspeaker operated by remote control (voices, sounds, music)

c) Frightening Encounters
- a large white bed sheet suspended from a tree and agitated by an assistant via an attached string
- a scare crow dropped into the dog's path from above
- a bag of tin cans suddenly emptied on a nearby hard surface

d) Hostile Encounters
- a sudden and unexpected attack on the handler
- an escape of the decoy (illumination provided by the headlight beams of a parked car - move in and out of the light beam)
- a courage test, lighting as above.

5. ROUTINES

**** QUARTERING** ●●

GENERAL

Quartering is the first part of the protection work in a Schutzhund trial, common to all classes. Logically, however, this exercise belongs into the obedience category.
Natural hiding places (evergreens, dense shrubs) are seldom available on the training field. Artificial blinds can be constructed from a 4X8 sheet of plywood (Fig.37) for a permanent installation. A large tripod covered with heavy cloth or plastic and secured to the ground with tent stakes makes a useful portable blind (Fig.38).

OBJECTIVE

The dog is required to investigate a series of natural or artificial hiding places in a more or less systematic manner, on directions from the handler.

FIG. 37   FIG. 38

SUGGESTED COMMAND: "search"   or   "find it"

PSYCHOLOGY

Quartering can be taught via two different avenues, using either the hide-and-seek principle, or the systematic approach.

In the first case, the dog is told to find a hidden reward even though it may require to search some empty blinds first. To the dog, the essential part of the game is to locate the reward and to go to it as quickly as possible.
If the dog senses the location of the reward before having quartered all empty blinds, it would be an insult to his intelligence to prevent him from going directly to it.

The situation is quite different when the dog had learned in training that the object of the game is not so much finding WHERE the reward is, but HOW to get there. The dog then realizes that to get the reward in the last blind, he must go around all the empty hiding places first.

In a trial this second method insures reliable quartering. With the first approach, the handler has to pray that his dog does not detect the decoy prematurely.

On the surface, the systematic approach seems to defeat the intention of the trial regulations. Yet even a police officer searching an area for suspects is better off with a dog trained according to the systematic method. He can be sure that the area behind him is clean. A dog that detects a suspect and goes directly to him could miss an accomplice hiding behind the officer.

PREREQUISITES

It is helpful, although not necessary, when the dog already knows the go-out command.

TEACHING PROCEDURE

Select a field free of obstacles (no hurdles, scaling walls, bushes etc.). Set up the blinds fairly close together, maybe 50 ft. apart, and teach the quartering as follows:
- Sit your dog at (A) and proceed alone to (E).
- Excitedly call your dog and run toward (C).
- Once the dog passes you, give the command "search" or "find" or "check it out" and encourage him to continue toward (C) and to circle this blind. You may want to run with him toward (C), you may want to point to (C) with your outstretched arm, or you may want to give him a little push from behind to get the message across.
- When the dog reaches blind (C), run toward (E) on the connection line C-E, and call him from there.
- Then repeat the sequence: send the dog to circle the blind (E), advance to (F), call your dog and run toward (G) etc.

Praise your dog ("good boy") when he is behind a blind and while he is APPROACHING you, not when he is going away.
At the end of the exercise, praise and pet him lavishly, play his game (he played yours, remember!).

In the beginning, you might have to run with him all the way, even around the blinds. Later on it will be sufficient for you to approach the blind and to let him continue to circle it.

At a still later time the exercise could be described as follows:
    a) Send your dog from point (A) towards the blind (C). Make sure that he approaches and circles (C).
    b) At that time advance quickly to point (D). It is essential that you have reached location (D), the intersection of A-H and C-E, at the time the dog emerges from blind (C).
    c) Call your dog excitedly ("here").
    d) Without letting him slow down, send him on toward (E), running -if necessary- a few steps with him toward (E).
    e) Make sure that you arrive at point (F), the intersection A-H and E-G, when your dog is behind blind (E).
    f) Call him and send him on toward (G), just like above under d).

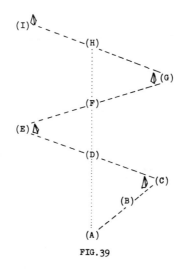

FIG. 39

Once your dog is fully trained you will not have to leave the centerline A-H. Locations (D) and (F), however, are still critical since they are the points from which you call and guide your dog in the search.

REFINING PROCEDURE
Move the blinds farther apart and practice quartering initially just as described above, without any further aids. However, once the dog understands the basic concept, enthusiasm can be developed by using material rewards. Basically three instincts can be utilized:
    the survival instinct (food)
    the hunting instinct (ball/stick)
    the fighting instinct (decoy).
The selection depends on what the dog responds best to.

Initially, hide the reward in the first blind, in the presence of the dog. He should know what the reward is and where it can be found.

If you use food or a ball, you can leave the dog in position (A) (you may have to tie him up there). Tease him with the reward without letting him have it and run toward blind (C). There you show him the reward once more before placing it on the ground. Then run back to your dog and send him to the blind as described above. Running is essential, to convey the message of speed to the dog. It also makes the game much more exciting.

If a decoy is used to teach quartering, he can, in the beginning, stand in front of the hiding place. You then send your dog to the blind, just as outlined above.

In all these variations you should follow your dog to praise him when he finds the reward: food can be eaten, ball or stick are being thrown and the decoy is asked to move so that the dog has a reason to bite.

After a few times of practice place the reward in the second blind, again with full knowledge of the dog. Here again, the decoy may initially just stand in front of the blind.

You must make sure that the dog goes around the first blind before proceeding to the second. Initially, this requires quite a bit of effort since EVERY attempt of a short-cut must be prevented. You can
- use sharp commands
- use a throw chain
- use a sling shot
- use a long leash
- use a physical barrier (like snow fencing) in the critical spots
- run with the dog around the blinds
- grab the collar and drag the dog around the first blind
- try to intercept when your dog runs directly to the wrong blind
- go back to the method described above, that is, standing at (B) and calling the dog
        from (A) toward (C).
Whatever you do, you must NOT let the dog go the direct route to the destination blind.

Move the reward to hiding place (G) once the dog reliably circles one empty blind, and so on.
In training it is desirable to work the field from the other end once in a while, or to start with blind (E) or (G). This teaches the dog to quarter on your directions, it also eliminates boredom from routine and it makes him more reliable on a strange training or trial field.

PROBLEMS
The dog skips blinds
- Practice the go-out first.
- Train without the decoy for several weeks (see systematic approach, above).
- Grab the dog and make him go around all the empty blinds first (maybe on leash with you running along).
- Quarter with the wind (air-scenting the decoy is more difficult then).
- Use several rewards in several blinds, at random.
- Use two decoys (#1 and #2) simultaneously (The success rate is low since many dogs tend to get confused, and most tire out too easily. They will still try to air-scent the decoy). Nevertheless, if you decide to use two decoys, proceed as follows:
    #1 steps out of blind C, agitates briefly and steps back again. The dog is sent after him, the decoy moves, engages the dog in a fight and then stands absolutely still. At that time #2 steps out of blind E, yells, agitates and steps back again. The handler now sends his dog to blind E and the dog is allowed to bite as above. While the dog is fighting with #2, the other decoy (#1) moves up to blind G and the whole cycle starts anew. Still later, two or three decoys are placed in the blinds at random. They are instructed not to reveal their where-about unless the dog wants to skip that particular blind.

The dog moves too slow
- Use only two or three blinds, for a while.
- Run along with your dog, get excited yourself.
- Run behind him, clap your hands.

- Get a different decoy.
- Ask the decoy to make the fight more realistic, more to the liking of your dog.
- Have the decoy do some close-range agitation before quartering, without letting the dog bite.
- Have an assistant in the blind who reels in the lure (burlap bag on a long string) just like in the dog races.

The dog leaves the field
- Build up enthusiasm (as above).
- Practice the down (it is better to take the penalty for an improper command than to fail the trial since the judge must excuse you if your dog leaves the field).

** FIND AND BARK ••

GENERAL
"Find & Bark" has useful applications in Police work, in Search and Rescue work, and also for the private dog owner.
The risk that an innocent person gets bitten accidentally is greatly reduced if the dog masters this exercise.

While it is not required, teaching the dog to sit while barking has certain advantages: the dog must get up first before he can break to bite, the dog is more likely to watch the decoy, and there is less of a chance that the dog will leave the decoy.

Some trainers attempt to teach their dog to lie down instead of to sit. It does not hurt to try it, but more often than not it will not work: it is difficult to teach the dog to go down in this situation, few dogs will bark in the down position, and if they do bark it will not be the aggressive staccato we want to hear (have you ever tried to intimidate someone while laying on your belly??).

OBJECTIVE
The dog alerts his master to a hiding or intruding person by constantly barking. He also guards the stranger until the handler arrives. Circling is undesirable but permissible if the dog continues to guard.

SUGGESTED COMMAND: none (for training only: "speak")
SUGGESTED RELEASE COMMAND: "OK"

PSYCHOLOGY
In Schutzhund training, the dog is not allowed to bite a person as long as that person stands still. Since this is a concept which can not easily be explained to the dog, a great deal of practice and of repetition is required.

The dog wants to bite, and he must learn that barking gets him what he wants. He must, therefore, always be rewarded with a fight after finding the decoy and barking at him - in training, that is.
The Find & Bark should be taught independently of the quartering, and the method used to teach it should be the one that best suits the dog's temperament.

PREREQUISITES
Speak on command
Protection work, SchH I level

TEACHING PROCEDURE
Various methods are available to teach the Find & Bark exercise. Most utilize the protective instinct, some are based on the prey instinct (see "Tease").
In general, dogs are more interested in the exercise if the decoy does some close-range agitation first and then runs away from the dog, to the blind.
It is also suggested to position the decoy in full view of the dog, initially. After you have sent the dog, follow him, sit him in front of the decoy, and give the command "sit, speak".

When teaching the exercise, the decoy should offer the reward (short fight, then surrender the sleeve) at the first sound/bark. With more advanced dogs, he will usually wait for a longer bark. The best performances are obtained when the conditions vary ("intermittent reinforcement"): sometimes he needs to bark just a little, sometimes he must bark longer before he can bite the sleeve. Some dogs need little encouragement, others need much stimulation from the decoy. Fearful/aggressive body expressions, brief, jerky movements, hissing and snarling usually do the trick. Watching a cornered cat that keeps a dog at distance will teach an observant decoy how to do it.

During advanced training, the decoy may sit, kneel or lay down in the blind before the dog arrives (use full protective gear). The dog must still indicate a "find" by barking.

a) Tease #1
The sleeve, or the sleeve cover, is propped up high in the blind, the decoy stands next to it. Some decoys put the sleeve on their head, some hold it behind their back. This is risky with new, or unknown, or "unclean" dogs.
Send your dog from 20 feet away and command "sit, speak".
The very moment the dog makes a sound he is rewarded with the prey: the sleeve is either just dropped to the ground and surrendered to the dog, or the decoy grabs it and runs away with it, giving the dog a chance to bite. Reassure your dog; this is essential.

b) Tease #2
Handlers with a fair control over their dog can use this approach:
The decoy engages in a fight and then drags the biting dog to the blind. A triangular, sturdy blind is preferred. Having secured back cover, the decoy freezes and observes the dog's behavior. When he senses that the dog intends to release the bite on his own, he signals the handler to give the "out" command. As soon as the dog disengages, the decoy quickly swings his protected arm behind his back and makes the sleeve inaccessible. This, of course, causes the dog to jump up and - to bark, since he can not get the sleeve.

After some barking, the decoy suddenly brings the arm out and tries to escape, giving the dog a chance to bite, and to claim the sleeve at the end. After several repetitions in subsequent training sessions, the successful dog can be worked away from the blind, just as described above.

c) Barriers
Some decoys prevent the dog from biting by standing on a table (running away, then jumping on the table - see above), sitting in a tree, or having a portable fence in front of the blind.
Unfortunately, many dogs forget that they are not supposed to bite as soon as the decoy stands unprotected in the blind.

d) Surprise
Somewhat better results are obtained by burying a mattress just in front of the blind (cover it with an inch or two of soil). The unusual footing teaches the dog to keep distance, and to bark.

e) Long Line
Use a sturdy, long line (20-30 ft.), one end of it fastened to a secure anchor, the other end attached to the dog's choke collar (for hard dogs, a pinch collar might be advisable).

Send the dog from the anchor to the decoy; the leash will stop him just short of his destination. Command "sit, speak" just before the correction occurs from the tightened leash. If the timing was right, then the dog will learn that obeying the command will save him from getting the leash correction the next time. You must, of course, run up to him, sit him and again tell him to speak. Make sure that there is some slack in the line, the dog can not bark with a compressed wind pipe. The decoy can help to stimulate barking by displaying suppressed aggression mixed with fear.

f) Shock Treatment
(Refer also to the equipment section)
An electronic shock collar or a rigged sleeve are used by some experienced trainers with success.

* The shock through the collar is given *after* the command "sit, speak", but only if it is clear that the will bite. Timing is important.
* The rigged sleeve incorporates a layer of metallized fabric as it is used to make suits for fencers (chicken wire or window screens may cause injuries to the dog), wrapped around the sleeve and covered with a layer of wet jute or burlap. Another piece of wire screen (chicken wire) is spread in front of (or around) the decoy, and covered with 1-2 inches of wet dirt. The two screens are wired to an electric fence charger, or to an induction-type generator (army telephone). The dog punishes himself by receiving a mild shock whenever he contacts the sleeve (closing the circuit).

After the dog has barked for a while - with enthusiastic support from you, of course - the electric circuit is disconnected, the decoy runs away, and the dog is encouraged to bite.

g) Sticks
An agile decoy can teach the Find & Bark with two sticks as his only tools. One stick is used to keep the dog at a distance. Most often it is pointed at the dog's chest, sometimes it even makes contact to push the dog away. The other stick is held inconspicuously at the side but ready for a quick, sharp hit across the dog's snout if he should decide to risk a bite. This hit comes from a flick of the wrist, with very little body or arm movement. It must be reserved for an emergency, to be given only after the dog is committed to bite (but before he actually bites!).

From a psychological standpoint it is preferable to have the handler dish out the correction, with stick, throw chain, sling-shot or electronic collar. Nevertheless, the decoy must be allowed to use his second stick if needed. Have a sleeve ready to give the dog a chance to bite, afterwards.

h) Chair
The following method is described in more detail since it has universal applications. It uses a methodical, gradual approach and is highly successful if done right.

Step 1: Hold your dog by the collar, about thirty feet away from the blind. The decoy briefly agitates the dog and then stands completely still. Release the dog.
Step 2: Most likely, the dog will charge and bite the sleeve even though the decoy stands still motionless. Do not say anything, just walk up and get your dog.
Step 3: Repeat steps 1) and 2).
Step 4: The decoy holds a light-weight aluminum lawn chair in his free hand and hides it behind his back.
Step 5: As in 1), lawn chair still hidden behind the decoy's back.
Step 6: When the dog has closed in to about six feet, the decoy suddenly brings the lawn chair up front and holds it between the dog and himself. He moves with the dog, always facing him, and he uses the blind to cover his back. The decoy may want to growl and shake the

chair lightly. Encourage your dog to speak.

Step 7: The decoy throws the chair aside (away from the dog) and tries to escape, giving the dog a chance to bite. Now rush to your dog's side and praise him.

Step 8: Repeat steps 4) through 7) as often as necessary.

Step 9: Similar to step 4), yet the decoy holds a shovel (blade down) instead of the lawn chair behind his back.

Step 10: As step 5), but using the shovel.

Step 11: As step 6), but using the shovel.

Step 12: As step 7), but using the shovel.

Step 13: Similar to steps 9-12, the decoy uses a shovel but this time with the handle down and the blade up.

Step 14: Similar to steps 9-12, the decoy uses a stick just as he used the shovel before.

Each one of these steps must be repeated as often as necessary. Usually the transition from chair to stick can be accomplished in 20-30 minutes total time. Some dogs, however, may need several of these sessions (for instance 1-8:day 1; 1-12:day 2; 1-14:day 3).

Cooperation between decoy and handler is important. While you encourage your dog to speak when prevented from biting, the decoy hisses, stamps the foot or makes other short, hasty movements to tease the dog. These minor movements must be distinctly different from the major

TOP WORKING DOGS

movements he makes after throwing the chair/shovel aside to let the dog bite the sleeve.
Since each section of this exercise ends with a fight, the dog eventually comes to realize that a motionless person is not to be touched but that angry, demanding, challenging barking gets the decoy to move and to fight.

PROBLEMS

a) No Bark
   - Practice "Speak on command" (obedience), often, and independently from protection work.
   - Agitate longer before allowing the dog to bite.
   - Let the dog watch when another dog close by does it right.
   - Hope that the dog will bark better when he has matured (quit baby-sitting him).
   - Some dogs will not bark after all. Often, they are marginal performers in protection work.

b) No Find or NO Guarding
Dogs who show no interest in finding or guarding may leave the decoy, investigate the surroundings, return to their handler etc. This is usually the result of improper training.
An escape or a fight should be the conclusion of every Search, Find and Bark exercise - in training - since it will keep the dog's interest focussed on the decoy.
It still can happen, though, that the dog is inattentive. Then the decoy can help by briefly moving a little, by growling or hissing. He can also escape in the direction opposite to where the dog is going. All this is not permitted in a trial, of course.
Some trainers teach their dog to automatically lay down in front of the decoy. While this usually cures the guarding problem (the dog can not leave) it may create another one: many dogs are less willing to bark in this position.

c) Biting instead of Barking
This is a basic training problem and you must go back to "Teaching Procedures" if it occurs.

For a Schutzhund I, however, you may want to tolerate this misbehavior. Discouraging the dog from biting in the blind often requires a harsh punishment which interferes with the development of the fighting drive. For a young SchH I dog, therefore, many handlers accept the penalty of three points lost in a trial for biting in the blind, in favor of having an outgoing, courageous dog. They postpone enforcing the bark until a later time.

d) Far Sit
A dog sitting too far away from the decoy while barking is more likely to prematurely finish the exercise on his own and to walk away.
A clever method to teach the close sit is to attach a 6 foot leash to the choke collar. The decoy engages the dog in a short fight and unobtrusively reaches for the leash, guiding it under the sleeve and holding it in his free hand. The dog will want to back off again after the fight, but a few tugs with the leash will prevent that.
It is important that the dog can not see where the corrections come from and that you assist in it by simultaneously giving the command "sit, speak".

TRIAL DECOY
The decoy stands well hidden in the blind for this exercise, and he remains motionless throughout. He looks straight ahead and avoids direct eye contact with the dog.
The sleeve on the right or left arm is held at an angle in front of the lower part of the body.
The other arm hangs down naturally. The stick in this hand is an extension of the arm and points to the ground. Arm and stick are held with slight pressure against the side of the body.

•• ESCAPE ••

GENERAL
The escape is one of the most basic, and also one of the most useful exercises in protection work. Some trainers even consider it a "cure all" for problems in manwork.

By nature, dogs would not normally seek a fight with a human who is taller, who is smarter, and who uses tools to increase his chances of winning. However, if the dog is shown in training that certain people - consistently - are weaker, give up, submit, run away, then an artificial response is established.

OBJECTIVE

Acting on his own, the dog will seize the sleeve of a suddenly escaping decoy, and he will try to stop him by resisting forward movement.

SUGGESTED COMMAND: none (in training: "get him")
SUGGESTED RELEASE COMMAND: none (in training: "out")

PSYCHOLOGY

Retreating from a confrontation is an obvious admission of weakness or defeat, and it tremendously boosts the ego of the opponent.
This psychological advantage is skillfully exploited in the manwork. We purposely deceive our dogs. We make them believe that they have an excellent chance to win over the "bad guy". Care must be taken, however, not to destroy this illusion - ever. One occasion where the dog is truly defeated, by an inconsiderate decoy, or by a real criminal, will require extensive retraining to at least partially repair the damage.

PREREQUISITES

While simplified versions of the escape can be practiced with beginning dogs, the complete, competition-style exercise requires a dog that will deliver a good fight and hold a firm bite after some close range agitation.

TEACHING PROCEDURE

Introduction:
Initial training is best done on a long leash.
The decoy agitates the dog with hostile/fearful movements towards you and the dog, staying just out of reach for a bite. Your encouragement helps the dog to gain confidence and to strengthen his desire for combat with the bad guy.

Contact:
The decoy will approach the dog from an angle (not frontal!) and arrange the situation so that the dog has to follow him for a few paces before the bite occurs, with you holding the leash.
At this time, give him enough freedom for the initial lunge onto the sleeve. Then pick up the slack in the leash and keep it taut (no pulls, no tugs, however).

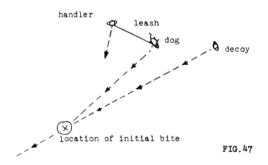

FIG. 47

Struggle:
The decoy tries to continue on his escape route even after the dog has gotten a hold of the sleeve.

He does not face or confront the dog, but he struggles to keep a steady pull on the sleeve, sort of playing a gentle tug of war. Jolts, or trying to rip the sleeve out of the dog's mouth, or any other sudden fighting movements are harmful.

If these instructions are followed closely, then the dog develops a technique to brace himself against the forward movement of the decoy, and to effectively slow down the decoy's escape. This is the purpose of the escape routine.

Termination:
During the initial training stage it is suggested that the decoy releases his grip on the sleeve, lets it slide off and continues his escape. Get a hold of your dog's collar and praise him lavishly.

Conclusion:
Depending on your training philosophy, the dog is now either
    allowed to carry the sleeve (prey instinct), or
    diverted away from it and alerted to the fleeing criminal (fighting drive).
Service dog oriented handlers prefer the second alternative, while (lately) the Schutzhund sport seems to favor the prey oriented training approach.
The exercise should not be repeated more than once during the same training session.

REFINING PROCEDURE
Once the dog masters the basics, the following training suggestions can be implemented, one at a time:
    - Surrender the sleeve less frequently.
    - Introduce the "out".
    - Introduce distractions (other dogs, other people, cats etc.).
    - Change training locations, decoys, clothing, equipment, routines frequently.
    - Increase the length of the pursuit.
    - Work off leash.
    - Practice the "out" from a distance.

PROBLEMS
a) No Pursuit
A dog might be reluctant to pursue the fleeing criminal
    - if the decoy comes on too strong and intimidates the dog
    - if the decoy does not sufficiently excite the dog
    - if you do not provide enough encouragement and support for him
    - if another major distraction is present (bitch in heat, urge to eliminate)
    - if he is exhausted
    - if he is ill.

These are temporary conditions which can be corrected by using common sense mixed with some patience.
However, when a working dog consistently refuses to pursue the bad guy under the given circumstances, then he is a poor candidate for the Schutzhund sport. Environmental problems (often originating with the owner/handler) or hereditary deficiencies (pet breeding) causing such behavior are very difficult or impossible to correct.

b) No Bite
The dog pursues well, but then he just runs along with the decoy and refuses to bite the sleeve. This is most likely the result of a very ambitious handler who pushed his dog too fast.
    - Go back and do several sessions of close range agitation.
    - Make the pursuit much shorter.
    - Check that the decoy is not too intimidating.
    - Make sure that the decoy agitates the dog well enough and long enough before he escapes
    - Eliminate any time gap between agitation and escape.
    - Give enough encouragement to your dog and run along.
    - Use the leash properly (do not tug on it).

- Drop the leash, let the dog drag it along.
- Work off leash.

c) Weak Bite / Premature Release / No Pull
The dog barely holds on to the sleeve, he does not pull back to slow down the decoy, or he releases the bite after a very short time.
The suggestions made above apply here as well. In addition, the actual fight/struggle should be made much shorter. Also, check the chapter on "Improving the Bite".

d) No Out
Advanced dogs should release the sleeve at the end of the escape routine. For training suggestions see the earlier chapter on "Releasing the Bite".

e) Afterbites (also called "nibbling" or "seconds")
Dogs that release but come back for a second or third bite must be watched very closely. You or a near-by assistant must instantaneously and firmly correct the dog the very moment he shows his intention to bite again. A harsh command, a slap with the hand, a "karate chop" between sleeve and snout just before the bite, a leash correction etc. are normally very effective. The correction should not come from the decoy, if possible at all.

The decoy can assist by holding the sleeve in front of his chest (not lower) and by standing absolutely still.

TRIAL DECOY

At the beginning, during guarding, and until the dog is biting, the decoy holds the sleeve steadily on his side, in a horizontal position. He is not allowed to hold the sleeve in front of his body nor may he swing his arm in an unduly fashion.

FIG. 48

The handler positions his dog to guard the decoy. The decoy stands so that he has no obstructions in front of him for at least 15 paces. He is required to run straight ahead in the direction he is facing, he is not allowed to take any other course.

birdseye view:

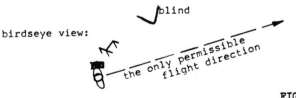

blind

the only permissible flight direction

FIG. 49

The exercise is done on instructions of the judge.

The decoy runs forward. Once the dog is on the sleeve, the decoy keeps going for another ten paces. Then he stops abruptly and remains motionless. There is no fighting in this exercise. Actually, the decoy pretends to not even concern himself with the dog.

** ATTACK ON HANDLER •••••••••••••••••••••••••••••••••••••••

GENERAL
A good performance in the "attack on the handler" is the true justification for training a personal protection dog. The exercise is also of great importance to handlers of police dogs and various other types of service dogs.

The exercise is part of all three levels of Schutzhund testing. The assault can come from a hidden person (SchH I) or from the decoy being back transported to the judge (SchH II and III).

OBJECTIVE
Acting on his own initiative, the dog will prevent a sudden attack on his handler by seizing the decoy's sleeve and biting hard. Upon command, he will release the bite.

SUGGESTED COMMAND: none (in training: "get him")
SUGGESTED RELEASE COMMAND: "Out"

PSYCHOLOGY
The attack is sudden, and the dog is surprised by it, ideally. This requires a considerate approach in teaching the exercise.

PREREQUISITES
The attack on the handler should not be practiced with a novice dog, prerequisite is that the dog delivers a good fight and holds a firm bite after some close agitation.

TEACHING PROCEDURE
Introduction:
Almost all of the training for the attack on the handler should be done on leash. This includes the actual fight.

Even the experienced dog is worked more often on than off lead.

In the beginning it is advisable to position the decoy in front of the hiding place, e.g. in full view of the dog. This helps to build confidence in the dog by eliminating the surprise effect.

Alert your dog while approaching the decoy: "watch that guy" (or the like). Speak with a low, subdued voice. Keep the leash short, bend down a little, point to the decoy, and pat the dog on the rump. The decoy can help by making himself noticed, moving and growling just a little.

Hostility:
Hostility starts once you have come within 15 feet of the decoy.

Both you and the decoy should start shouting, getting ready to beat each other up.

The decoy does not pay any attention to the dog, he just observes him out of the corner of his eye. The attack is directed toward you, not the dog!

Contact:
When teaching the exercise, the decoy takes ONE step forward, threatens you, and then retreats for several steps. This evokes the pursuit instinct in the dog and leads to a bite.

The novice dog is not quite sure if the bite was the right thing to do. He, therefore, will let go of the sleeve, look to you and ask for approval.

This, of course, is undesirable, and it should be avoided. Get involved, pursue the decoy, deal out a few punches. At the same time encourage and reassure your dog, both verbally ("good boy, get him") and physically, by patting your dog on the side. If done properly, this will prevent him from seeking further reassurance from you and from letting go of the sleeve.

(During this and the following segments you should hold on to the end of the six foot leash. Make sure that the dog can move freely and that he does not get entangled in the leash.)

Fight:
The fight should be realistic and noisy, but short.
The decoy must make sure that the dog does not experience any unpleasantness.
It is especially important that the arm is being moved all the time while the dog is biting. Twisting the arm inside the sleeve can be quite effective. Arm movements should be gradual, steady pulls away from the dog, not sudden, jerky jolts.
The sleeve should never be ripped out of the dog's mouth, nor should it be yanked into it.

Termination:
To terminate the fight, command the decoy to stand still. It is of great value in training when the decoy follows this command in a distinct manner.
His change from actively fighting to passively waiting for further directions must be sudden, abrupt, snappy; the transition should occur within a fraction of a second. The decoy should - for training purposes - stand absolutely still, that is: no adjustments of his position, no swinging arms, no body sway, no head movements - just perfect immobility.
Most dogs are sufficiently impressed by such a sudden change that they automatically let go of the hold. You can assist by giving the "out" command in a firm, if necessary threatening manner. Shouting is unnecessary and repulsive, here and anywhere else.

Conclusion:
During initial training, the decoy should always run away after the completed attack on the handler. The escape is one of the most suitable protection exercises to strengthen the self-confidence of the dog. It also relieves some of the tension that may have developed in the direct confrontation with the decoy.

REFINING PROCEDURE
Advanced dogs should practice the attack on the handler under varying conditions, on and off lead. Rigid routines or practicing the exercises always in the same order should be avoided.
The decoy should be hidden and stage an attack unexpectedly. If needed, he can use a stick to threaten and to lightly tap the dog during the fight, in training.
The retreat during and after the fight can be eliminated.
The attack should then be practiced in connection with the back and the side transport.

PROBLEMS

a) Forging
The attack on the handler in a Schutzhund trial is supposed to come as a surprise to the dog. Past experience, however, has often taught the dog the sequence of events, and hard dogs will forge in anticipation of the fight. That costs points, and in severe cases it may even interrupt trial proceedings.
  - Change routines so that heeling off leash (SchH I) or back transport (SchH II and III) not always end with an attack on the handler.
  - When practicing the attack on the handler, locations, hiding places, decoys, protective gear etc. should be changed as often as possible - the more the better.
  - Work with the leash (slip it through the collar for a quick release) more often than without it.
  - Practice heeling on and off leash, obedience style, while other dogs are performing protection exercises.
  - Use adequate leash correction (maybe aided by a prong collar) - followed with praise - while heeling the dog just before the attack on the handler.
  - Do a forceful about turn (leash correction !) whenever the dog forges even if it means to temporarily walk away from the decoy.
  - Avoid stimulating the dog's fighting drive while heeling.

The severity of a correction must be tailored to the responsiveness of each individual dog, of course. In addition, the last suggestion (g) does not apply to soft or insecure dogs. They need all the help they can get to build up their courage, and forging is not a severe problem with them anyway.

b) No Bite
Some dogs initially refuse to take a bite in the attack on the handler. In this case the decoy retreats right away, pursued by the dog for a few paces.

Support your dog with much encouragement as well as with much praise for pursuing the decoy so well.

It would be absolutely wrong trying to force the dog to take a bite, be it with special efforts of the decoy or by pushing the dog into the sleeve. A dog can not be forced to be protective.
Instead, practice close range agitation for a few more sessions, until the dog has gained enough confidence to protect you from the assailant.

c) Premature Release
Novice dogs may release the bite prematurely, even when the fight is very short.
The decoy does an escape if this happens and positions his sleeve conveniently for another bite. As soon as the dog has gotten hold of it he stops and stands still.
Moving the arm inside the sleeve, during the fight, might help.
(see also "Maintaining the Bite")

d) Release upon Hit
Some dogs release the sleeve when hit. The following suggestions can be tried:
    - Retrain your dog (see "Improving the Bite").
    - Give more encouragement and praise during the fight.
    - Ask the decoy to surrender the sleeve to the dog (to just let go of the handle) 1/4 of a second
      after the hit, and to run away.

TRIAL DECOY

SchH I:

The decoy hides behind a blind, a wall etc. and waits until the judge signals him to come out. At this time, dog and handler will be about five to ten paces away from him.

The decoy will move quickly, making threatening sounds and gestures in an effort to attack the handler. He holds the sleeve horizontally, chest high, a little away from his body, to soften the impact. The other hand with the stick he raises above his head. The stick points to the sky and is moved in a threatening manner back and forth in short strokes (shaking), all above the head.
    To invite the dog to take a bite, the decoy moves his body back just a little bit (back off).

FIG. 50

By now the dog should have a firm bite on the sleeve. The decoy, therefore, brings his sleeve back toward his body and presses it against his chest. This gives him better control over his arm and over the dog. With a little maneuvering the dog is now positioned for the hit as follows:

TOP WORKING DOGS

A decoy wearing a left-arm (right-arm) sleeve twists his body to the right (left) and walks forward in a side-stepping manner, left (right) foot out front. Decoys wearing a right-arm sleeve follow the instructions given above in parenthesis.

After one or two steps, the first hit is given. The decoy brings down the stick in one continuous motion with reasonable force, from above his head onto the back of the dog.

Then the stick is raised again above the head. This is followed by another (double) side-step and another hit, just like above.

FIG.51

FIG.52

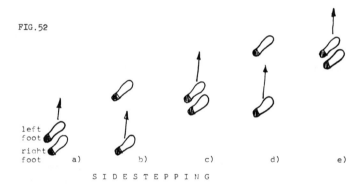

left foot
right foot
a)   b)   c)   d)   e)

S I D E S T E P P I N G

The time between the two hits should be about one second.

After the two hits, the decoy moves maybe another two or three steps and then he comes to an abrupt halt. The stick is lowered at this time and the decoy assumes

BASIC POSITION:
The decoy stands upright, facing the dog. The sleeve is held in front of, and pressed against the body, held in a horizontal position. The other arm hangs down naturally. The stick in this hand is an extension of the arm and points to the ground (see Fig.53).

The correct technique of hitting was discussed earlier (see "The Stick"). Only certain portions of the dog's body may be touched (back, withers, sides), and the force must be reasonable.

SchH II and III:

At some time during the back transport the judge will signal the decoy to attack the handler. The decoy will then suddenly turn around and proceed just as above. There are, however, no hits scheduled in this exercise.

FIG. 53

•• DEFENSE ••

GENERAL
The "Defense" (or "Re-attack") is practiced to teach the dog how to deal with a hostile person in the absence of his handler.
Service Dog agencies will benefit the most from this training.

OBJECTIVE
While guarding, the dog is suddenly attacked by the decoy. The dog must seize the sleeve firmly and fight, but he is also required to release the bite when the suspect gives up struggling. Then guarding continues.

SUGGESTED COMMAND: none (in training: "get him")
SUGGESTED RELEASE COMMAND: none (in training: "out")

PSYCHOLOGY
In contrast to the attack on the handler, the re-attack is directed toward the dog. During the exercise, the handler is either busy investigating the blind, or he is far away from his canine partner. The dog must, therefore, be taught to take action on his own.

PREREQUISITES
The dog must be able to perform acceptable protection work, especially "attack on the handler" and "courage test".

TEACHING PROCEDURE
Initial training should be done in your presence so that you can assist the dog in fighting the decoy. The procedures are identical to the ones described for "attack on the handler", except that the decoy pays no attention to you, he focuses his attention on the dog.
Most dogs understand quickly what is asked of them if they know the "attack on the handler".

REFINING PROCEDURE
Advanced dogs can be left guarding the decoy, with you standing a few yards to the side. Verbal encouragement during the sudden attack of the decoy is needed only initially.
Gradually, you can move farther and farther away, or hide in the blind.
You may give the "out" command for the release.

PROBLEMS
Difficulties that might arise here are discussed in the problem sections for the "escape", "attack on handler" and "courage test".

               TOP WORKING DOGS

TRIAL DECOY

In preparation for this exercise the decoy assumes BASIC POSITION (see "Defense; Trial Decoy").
He waits for the judge's signal to attack the dog and proceeds then just like it was described in
"Defense; Trial Decoy SchH I", including the hits, but excluding the initial hiding part, of course.

** COURAGE TEST •••

GENERAL

The courage test is a routine which benefits mainly the handlers of canines on duty with law
enforcement agencies.
A civilian is rarely justified to send his dog after a distant person. The exercise is, however, an
indicator of the dog's true talents in protection work, as the name implies, and Schutzhund fanciers
utilize it as such.

OBJECTIVE

The dog is sent after a fleeing, distant "criminal" who turns around just before contact, wielding a
stick and threatening the dog. The dog accepts the challenge, bites the sleeve and fights the
decoy. After a short fight the decoy stops struggling. The dog releases the bite and guards the
suspect until his handler arrives.

SUGGESTED COMMAND: "get him"
SUGGESTED RELEASE COMMAND: "out"

PSYCHOLOGY

In the courage test, the dog works independently, a great distance away from you. Without any
support or reassurance, he has to make several decisions (to bite, to fight, maybe to take a hit, to
release). It requires time, repetition and skill to prepare him for this task. Yet still, dogs not suited for
Schutzhund training will fail the test, even with the best preparation.

PREREQUISITES

The dog must be able to perform acceptable protection work, especially the "escape" and the
"attack on the handler".

TEACHING PROCEDURE

Kneel on your left knee, next to the dog, holding him with the right hand by the collar.

The decoy, about 20 feet away, agitates with threatening motions until the dog is ready for a bite,
then he runs away.
Having encouraged your pal all the time - the kneeling position makes it easy -, you now release
him and send him after the fleeing "criminal". The first few times you might even want to run with your
dog to catch the bad guy.
Once the dog has closed in to about 10 feet, the decoy turns around and comes back, lightly
threatening the dog with gestures and the stick raised above his head.
The dog, nevertheless, must charge him and bite the sleeve. After some struggling the decoy
suddenly "freezes", not moving at all. This is the signal for the dog to release his hold, which you can
enforce with an "out" command, if necessary.

REFINING PROCEDURE

Dogs that do well in the previously described exercise should be taught to
    - pursue over a longer distance (up to about 100 paces)
    - pursue with minimal prior agitation
    - fight in spite of more severe threatening
    - release the bite within one second after the decoy stops struggling
    - release without a command
    - guard well
    - do the "Defense" after the courage test.

PROBLEMS

a) No Pursuit

If the dog refuses to pursue the decoy, try
- shorter distances
- more initial agitation
- more encouragement from you
- running with the dog
- attacking the decoy yourself.

If none of the above help, then the dog is either ill, or not yet far enough advanced in protection work, or not suited for Schutzhund training.

b) Early Departure

The following suggestions can be tried if the dog has developed the habit of dashing out in pursuit of the decoy before the command was given:
- practice obedience while another dog does protection work
- use a slip leash (sliding the leash through the collar and holding on to both ends) to correct the dog; let one end of it go when sending the dog
- ask the decoy to walk up and down the narrow end of the field while you do the same at the other end of the field, heeling your dog. Exchange loud words with the decoy and make sure that the dog heels well. Send the dog after several passes, or walk up to the decoy, for variety.

c) No Bite / Weak Bite   See "Escape; Problems".

d) No Release   See "Training Techniques".

e) No Guarding

A dog leaving the decoy at the end of the courage test indicates that he considers the job done. This attitude can be changed by simply adding another exercise to the routine, in training. The "escape" or the "defense" are suitable.

In a trial the dog will expect this routine and guard nicely.

f) Afterbites

See "Escape".

TRIAL DECOY

More than any other routine, the courage test requires special knowledge and skill of the decoy. Anybody can play steamroller and chase a dog off the field, but few people can challenge and fight with the dog in a competitive, sportsman-like manner.

Since the impact in the courage test can easily break a dog's neck, the correct procedure will be described in detail.

We assume that the decoy wears the sleeve on the left arm (for right-arm sleeve handling, the directions have to be side-reversed).
- The decoy runs away, the dog is sent after him.
- Once the dog has closed in to about 10-15 paces, the decoy turns around and comes back, threatening the dog.

  The following steps, in sequence, last for a tiny fraction of a second only.
- The decoy holds the sleeve horizontally, chest-high but forward, away from his body by 10-12 inches (a).
- Just before impact, the decoy stops his forward movement, actually he even backs up just a little bit. He also bends his knees somewhat, and he turns slightly to the right (b).
- The impact of the dog's bite will initially bring the sleeve arm closer to the decoy's body. However, the decoy deflects the dog's movement upward and sideways, to his right. To do so, he backs off somewhat and straightens his knees - after the dog is on the sleeve already (c,d).

- At this time, the dog is airborne. The decoy continues to turn right. He bends his knees again slightly which will set the dog on the ground again (e, f). The dog is now facing the opposite direction.

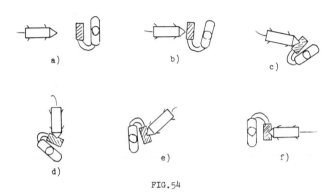

FIG. 54

- The continuation of the fight proceeds as described in "Defense; Decoy".

** TRANSPORT ••

GENERAL
With the "Back Transport", or with the "Side Transport", the apprehended suspect is brought to the training director, or to the judge in a trial.
This is a useful control exercise.

OBJECTIVE
The alert dog, remaining next to his handler in the heel position, assists in the transport of an apprehended suspect - mainly through his presence. He will not bother or bite the decoy.

SUGGESTED COMMAND:
SUGGESTED COMMAND: "heel "
SUGGESTED RELEASE COMMAND: "OK"

PSYCHOLOGY
Elements of obedience and of protection work are combined in the transport exercise.

Some dogs will not remain at heel since they are anxious to bite the decoy. Other dogs are disinterested, they trot along dutifully. You must stimulate the dog's interest in the decoy, but you must also control your dog to keep him at heel.

PREREQUISITES
Some prior obedience training, as well as some protection work is required.

TEACHING PROCEDURE
Initial training is best done on leash.
If you observe your dog constantly, you can give encouragement and corrections as soon as they are needed. Do not engage in any friendly conversation with the decoy during the transport.

The decoy should be instructed to do a few left and right turns and to round the corners, since the dog interprets sharp turns as an escape attempt. In practice, the decoy decides how far to walk and when to turn, regardless of what dog and handler do. This arrangement allows you to correct the dog for forging with an about turn (away from the decoy).

Inattentiveness requires the assistance of the decoy: he should give you a push (side transport) and/or run away (back transport).

In the side transport, the dog walks between you and the suspect, the decoy wearing the sleeve on the arm next to the dog (it is all right to wear a left arm sleeve on the right arm for the transport). In the back transport, you and your dog follow about five paces behind the decoy. The sleeve can be worn on either arm.

REFINING PROCEDURE

Advanced dogs should do the transport off lead.

For the transition, a short piece of rope can be slid through the ring on the collar. Hold on to both ends of the rope to be prepared for a correction, but later let go one end of it to quickly release your dog (a leash used in this fashion would get stuck on the release). The "slip lead" must be guided through the collar, not the ring.

PROBLEMS

a) Forging
- Work on leash.
- Do about turns.
- Practice heeling while another dog does protection work.
- Have a 30 ft. cord attached to the collar which is dragging behind, and which is handled by an assistant, if needed.

b) Biting, Nibbling
- Give a warning, and/or a quick, harsh correction (leash, nape grab).

c) No Guarding During Transport
- The decoy should suddenly attack you.
- The decoy should escape.

TRIAL DECOY

The decoy walks in a normal manner, swinging both arms naturally. He behaves indifferent, neither hostile nor friendly.

An optimist and a pessimist go hunting.
Mighty proud of his new dog, the optimist sends his dog to retrieve the duck he just shot. The dog walks on top of the water.
The pessimist is unmoved.
After the third performance, the optimist can't stand it any longer: "What do you say to that?"
"It looks like your dog can't swim".

E. TRAINING TIMETABLES

Training must follow a logical sequence, a logical progression. Superior results can not be accomplished without having first laid the proper foundation at a young age. This is symbolized in the pyramid below.

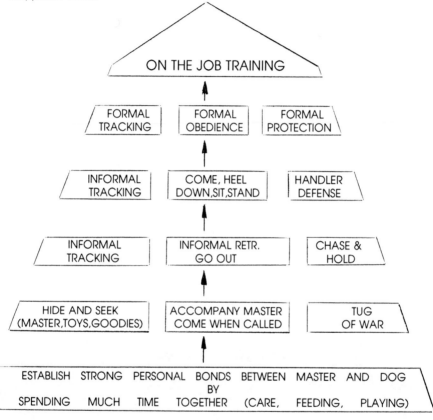

FIG. 55

The following timetables are guidelines only. Each handler must use his discretion and determine the rate of progression for his own dog.

PUPPY TRAINING - PROGRESSION CHART

age (months) / task	1	2	3	4	5	6
family contacts, handling	X					
sound conditioning	X					
contact w. strangers (dogs/people)	X					
come when called (inducive)		X				
simple straight tracks		X				
fetch, gentle tug-of-war (inducive)		X				
collar/leash conditioning		X				
house breaking		X				
follow on lead (inducive)		X				
watch the club training sessions		X				
sit and down (inducive)			X			
holding the dumbbell			X			
heeling (inducive)			X			
longer straight tracks			X			
stand for grooming				X		
speak on command (inducive)				X		
single, distant gun shots				X		
indicating a handler's article				X		
"out" (for stick, ball, bone)					X	
go-out (inducive)					X	
carrying dumbbell					X	
longer, older tracks w/ one turn					X	
long down (inducive)					X	
chasing and "killing" the rag					X	

TRACKING SCHEDULE - PROGRESSION CHART

age(months) / task	7	8	9	10	11	12	13	14
distractions	X							
obtuse/acute angles	X							
various ground cover		X						
multiple turns		X						
var. weather cond.			X					
var. geographic areas, if possible				X				
simple cross track						X		
SchH I Trial								X

OBEDIENCE SCHEDULE - PROGRESSION CHART

task \ age(months)	7	8	9	10	11	12	13	14
heel off lead (short)	X							
easy jumping	X							
quartering	X							
retrieve/flat	X							
long sit		X						
stand examination		X						
heel off lead		X						
sit out of motion		X						
down out of motion			X					
training in public places			X					
stand out of motion				X				
hurdle jumping				X				
obedience while another dog does protection work				X				
retrieve hurdle					X			
SchH I Trial								X
scale/descend wall								X

PROTECTION WORK SCHEDULE - PROGRESSION CHART

task \ age(months)	7	8	9	10	11	12	13	14
Leap # 3 (B)	X							
line/circle agit.(R,SP)	X							
barking (R,SP)	X							
"rabbit chase" (B)	X							
stake agitation (B,SP)		X						
escape, close range (B,SP)		X						
prot. work near blind (B,SP)		X						
attack on handler (P,SP)		X						
defense (P,SP)			X					
line/circle agit.(H,SP)			X					
cour.test,close range (P,SP)			X					
find,bark,escape,bite (H,SP)			X					
quartering,escape,bite (H,SP)			X					
Leap #1 (H,SP)			X					
Leap #2 (H,SP)			X					
reg.courage test (H,SP)				X				
agit.,bite,hit (H,SH)					X			
cour.test, defense (H,SP)						X		
"out" (H,SH)						X		
SchH I Trial								X

Explanation of codes:
- R = rag
- B = bite roll
- P = puppy sleeve or hard sleeve w/very soft cover
- H = hard sleeve
- C = civilian sleeve
- SP = stick present
- SH = stick hit

VI. THE RULES

A. VDH TRIAL REGULATIONS

More Schutzhund dogs are tested and certified according to the European VDH Trial Rules than on the basis of any other system. The following is a brief description of the requirements currently in effect.

The Schutzhund competitor is encouraged to obtain the Rule Book from the organization that sponsors the trial he wants to show at. Having trained a dog with "TOP WORKING DOGS", only minor and easily implemented adjustments will be needed to meet other specific requirements.

SCORING SYSTEM (POINTS)

SchH A	SchH I,II,III	FH	Rating
0-72	0-109	0-35	Unsatisfactory
73-149	110-219	36-69	Insufficient
150-159	220-239	70-79	Satisfactory
160-179	240-269	80-89	Good
180-190	270-285	90-95	Very Good
191-200	286-300	96-100	Excellent

Max.points: Track. 100, Obed. 100, Prot. 100, FH 100. Pass.Score: Track. 70, Obed. 70, Prot. 80, FH 70.

SCHUTZHUND A
This pre-Schutzhund degree is identical to SchH I without tracking.

SCHUTZHUND I

In **TRACKING**, the dog must follow an unmarked track of 300-400 yards laid by his own handler, while on a 30 ft. lead. Track age is 20 minutes minimum. There are two turns, and two articles are dropped which must be located by the dog.

In **OBEDIENCE**, heeling is done on and off lead at normal, fast and slow pace, including walking through a group of people. A gun will be fired when the dog is off leash. If the dog should shy, he would fail the trial. There is one exercise in which the dog sits, and one in which he downs while heeling, the handler continuing on. On the sit, the handler will return to the dog, and on the down the dog will be called to the handler. There is a retrieve on the flat and a retrieve over a 40 inch hurdle. Also, the dog must on command leave the handler going at least 25 paces ahead, and he must drop on command. The handler will return to the dog. A long down is done while another dog goes through his paces, the handler some distance away and his back turned to the dog.

In **PROTECTION**, the dog must first locate the hiding decoy and just bark, not bite. Then, while heeling off lead, the decoy will come out of hiding and attack the handler. The dog will be hit with a stick and must not show fear, he must also stop his attack on command. The decoy will then run, acting in a belligerent manner, and the handler will send the dog after the man to attack and hold. After releasing the bite on command, there is a side transport to the judge.

SCHUTZHUND II

In **TRACKING**, the dog is on a 30 ft. lead. He must find two lost articles on a stranger's trail, with two turns, 400-500 yards long, at least 30 minutes aged.

OBEDIENCE includes all the exercises from the SchH I test, except there are three retrieve exercises: on the flat (1000 g dumbbell), over a 40 inch hurdle (650 g), and over a 71 inch inclined scaling wall (handler's article). Also, the "go away" is for 30 paces minimum.

In **PROTECTION**, the dog must first search several hiding places on command and just bark, not bite. The dog then guards the suspect while the handler investigates the hiding place. To stop the escaping decoy, the dog must seize the arm (sleeve), and he must release the hold when the suspect stops struggling. Then the decoy threatens the dog with a stick. The dog has to bite the suspect's arm firmly, and he will be hit twice. During the following back transport the handler will be attacked which the dog is to prevent. In the courage test, the dog is sent after the suspect 50 paces away, and he is to firmly seize the arm until called off by his handler. A side transport to the judge concludes this part.

SCHUTZHUND III

In **TRACKING**, the dog must search for three lost articles on a strangers trail 800-1000 yards long, with three turns, at least 50 minutes aged. The dog may be worked off leash or on a 30 ft. lead.

OBEDIENCE includes all the exercises from the SchH II test, with the following exceptions: no on-lead heeling, 2000 g dumbbell in the retrieve on the flat, stand-stay out of normal pace (handler returns) and running pace (handler calls dog), "go away" for 40 paces minimum, and long down with the handler out of sight.

PROTECTION is identical to the SchH II exercises, except that there is another "defense" after the courage test where the dog gets hit again.

FH (Advanced Tracking Degree)

Only dogs with at least a SchH I degree can compete in this test. The strangers track is 1000-1400 yards long, at least three hours old, has six turns and four articles. It also intersects with a misleading cross-track in three places, it leads through different ground covers, and it crosses a road way.

GENERAL

To allow for fair competition, Schutzhund trial regulations are structured and regulated to a great degree.
Officials of the AZG meet at regular intervals to evaluate field experiences, implement changes as needed, and enforce uniform interpretation of the official trial rules.
Schutzhund competitors are thus assured to receive fair and uniform treatment from all judges, regardless of their affiliation with a particular dog sport organization.
The judge, however, expects that dog handlers who show under him are thoroughly familiar with the rules, and that they abide by them. It is in the best interest of the competitor to study the rules, the requirements, and their official interpretation.

In AKC obedience shows, an unexplained total score for each competitor is announced at the end of the trial. This is in contrast to Schutzhund competition where a feed-back is build into the system: once a competitor has completed a segment, the judge openly comments on how well the participant did in the individual exercises. The judge has to account for, and explain, his decisions (an incompetent judge would not last very long), and the handler can learn from mistakes and do better the next time.
Here are a some of the facts of Schutzhund competition that every contestant would *benefit* from knowing, and some requirements that every one is *expected* to know:

TEMPERAMENT TEST

The judge is required to conduct an informal temperament test before the dog starts tracking. Overly shy or aggressive dogs will not be permitted to continue.

TRACKING

- SchH I and SchH II tracks are either U-shaped or step-shaped, SchH III tracks are almost always R-shaped:

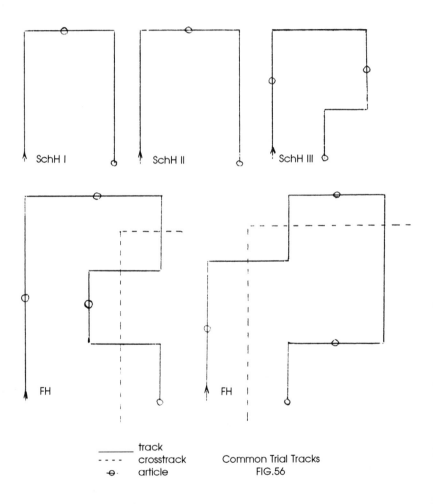

_____ track
- - - - crosstrack
-⊖· article

Common Trial Tracks
FIG.56

- The handler must inform the judge if his dog will "pick up" or "point out" the articles.

- The starting flag is always to the left of the starting scent pad, looking in the track direction.

- Articles are never placed close to a turn or close to a crosstrack.

- One article is always placed at the end of the track.

- Crosstracks will never be close to a turn or close to an article.

- The dog can take as long as needed, to start the track, and to work on the track (within reason).

- While tracking, the handler must stay 30 ft. behind his dog. If the dog comes closer or comes back, the handler should stand still and gather up the leash.

- When the dog has found an article, the handler must take it and hold it high over his head so that the judge can see it). The continuation of tracking is handled very much like the initial start (the handler follows when the end of the 30 ft. line comes up.

OBEDIENCE

- The judge is looking for a spirited, happy, pleasant-to-watch demonstration of obedience work.

- A heeling pattern, while not specifically required according to the rules, can help the handler to remember which exercises must be shown here.
  The judge may insist that the pattern be followed.

- Every exercise starts and ends with the basic position.

- Using the dog's name in connection with a command will be faulted as a double command.

- The handler should swing his arms normally. This is a requirement!

- The dog must not be praised/ rewarded during exercises; excessive praise between exercises is faulted also.

- Many clubs provide a set of dumbbells for the trial.
  If you insist on using your own, you can do so, but always bring your dog's favorite object for the retrieve over the wall.

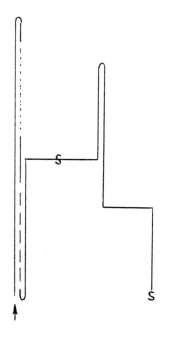

————	normal pace
. . . . .	fast pace
- - - - -	slow pace
⟹	about turn
S	sit

Common Heeling Pattern
FIG.57

- If the dumbbell has landed in an unfavorable location, the handler may ask the judge for permission to re-throw. There will be no penalty if he gives his permission.

PROTECTION

- SchH III dogs must come on the field off-lead.

- Commands in protection work do not have to be given instantaneously. Considerable leeway is given for timing the command (without penalty), and a slightly delayed command is often more effective.

- When quartering a dog, the handler should smoothly advance on the centerline of the field, adjusting his speed so that he can be at the proper location for calling and sending your dog. An erratic and discontinuous advance on the centerline indicates faulty training and costs points.

- If a handler must physically take his dog off the sleeve because he does not want to let go, the judge will fail that dog.

- A dog leaving the trial area while under test (be it tracking, obedience or protection) will fail.

B. SCHUTZHUND JUDGE'S CHECK LIST

During the trial, the conscientious Schutzhund judge will take notes to record the performance of a dog under test. He may use a list similar to the one presented here.
The aspiring or apprentice judge, as well as the dog handler in training, will benefit from such a check list also.

TEMPERAMENT TEST
aggressive
shy
self-confident

TRACKING
faulty / repetitive starts
short leash
excessive praise
handler assistance
circling / heavy circling
turns incorrect
nose high
incorrect finding of articles
running
hunting
eliminating

OBEDIENCE
Heeling
starting position
lagging
forging
going wide
crowding
faulty sits

	group problems
	sniffing
	incorrect response to gun shots
	handler assistance
	handler error
Sit/motion	slow response
	downs or stands
	follows / moves
	handler assistance
	handler error
Down/motion	slow response
and Recall	sits or stands
	follows / moves
	no/slow come
	poor finish
	handler assistance
	handler error
Stand/motion	slow response
(Recall)	sits or downs
	follows / moves
	no/slow come
	poor finish
	handler assistance
	handler error
Retrieve/flat	slow response
	no go-out
	no/slow return
	no retrieve
	no out
	drops / plays / chews
	poor finish
	handler assistance
	handler error
Retrieve/jump	slow response
	no jump (1) / (2)
	touches / steps on hurdle
	no retrieve
	no out
	drops / plays / chews
	poor finish
	handler assistance / error
Retrieve/wall	slow response
	no scaling (1) / (2)
	jumps from top
	no retrieve
	no out
	drops / plays / chews
	poor finish
	handler assistance
	handler error
Send away	slow response
	no go-out
	too short
	no straight go-out
	anticipates down
	gets up prematurely
	poor finish

	handler assistance
	handler error
Long down	slow response
	leaves position / creeps
	restless
	incorrect response to gun shots
	poor finish
	handler assistance
	handler error

PROTECTION

Search/Find	disinterested
	too few blinds
	one side only / predominantly
	eliminates
	handler assistance
	handler error
Bark	weak / no bark
	biting / nipping
	afterbite
	no guarding
	handler assistance
	handler error
Attack/Handler	uncontrollable
	no / weak bite
	premature release
	no / poor out
	afterbite
	no guarding
	handler assistance
	handler error
Escape	no pursuit
	no / weak bite
	premature release
	no / poor out
	afterbite
	no guarding
	handler assistance
	handler error
Defense	afraid
	stick shy
	no / weak bite
	premature release
	no / poor out
	afterbite
	no guarding
	handler assistance
	handler error
Transport	uncontrollable
	handler assistance
	handler error
Courage Test	no pursuit
	no / weak bite
	afraid / stick shy
	premature release

	no / poor out
	afterbite
	no guarding
	handler assistance
	handler error
Courage & Hardness	shies
	stick shy
	no / weak bite
	premature release
	no guarding
	returns to handler
	leaves field
	eliminates

C. HANDLER ERRORS

Small mistakes can add up to a big disappointment. In a Schutzhund trial, many handlers "give away" points, while they could easily have competed for top placement.
Listed here are some of the more common problems as well as some suggestions to earn higher scores:

GENERAL
- Know the rules by heart, abide by them.
- Practice in mock trials, fun matches, participate in AKC trials.
- Don't arrive at the last minute. Come early and relax.
- Give your dog a chance to explore and to sniff out the trial fields, if possible at all.
- Familiarize yourself with the grounds and the procedures.
- Don't be nervous, calm down. Your dog will be more relaxed that way too.
- Act normal, just like in training. Don't change your voice (pitch, loudness) or your behavior now.
- Listen to the judges' critique of earlier dogs, learn from it.
- Report to the judge before and after each trial section.

TRACKING
- Don't round the corners too much when laying the track.
- Don't drag your feet too much when laying the track.
- Untangle the long line before you start.
- Let the line run out to the full length before you follow your dog on the track.
- Avoid to jerk the line when starting on the track.
- Keep the line reasonably taut at all times.
- Maintain a reasonable speed.
- Let your dog do his job, don't try to steer him.
- Read your dog, and communicate with him. You are allowed to give calm reassurance/praise (when he is on the track), or low-key disapproval when he goofs.
- Keep your dog long enough at the article, to convincingly indicate a find.
- Hold the article up high for the judge to see.
- Don't make your dog come back if he over-runs an article but is still going strong on the track. If you call him back, you may ruin his performance for the rest of the track, and the points for the article are lost already anyway.
- Don't give up prematurely if your dog runs into problems. Think, take the most logical step to continue (re-start, cast your dog, praise or scold him, help him even if it costs a few points). Don't quit on your own, keep trying until the judge blows the whistle

- Carry on as usual, maintain your attitude, your posture, your voice. Consider the trial as another routine training session. If, for instance, you bellow your commands now, your dog gets confused.
- Have enough slack in the leash so that you do not inadvertently give a correction.
- Don't stop or make changes in pace too suddenly, your dog can not follow that quickly. The judge will not fault you, unless you overdo it.
- For off-lead work, get rid of the leash, hang it over your shoulder, or stash it away securely. Keep your hands free.
- Praise your dog only between exercises, unobtrusively.
- Avoid "body language".
- Don't use the dog's name (double command).
- With a SchH III dog, enter the field off leash.
- Heeling: Show all parts of the pattern. Go for the required distances.
- Sit/motion: Don't give the command too forcefully (or your dog will lay down). Don't turn your head to observe the dog.
- Down/motion: Don't turn your head to observe the dog. When you call your dog, wait until he pays attention to you.
- Stand/motion: Don't give the command too forcefully (or your dog will lay down). Don't turn your head to observe the dog.
- Retrieve: Throw the dumbbell so that it lands in the right place. Don't change your position, stay put. Don't send your dog from too close to, or too far away from, the obstacle.
- Send away: Lower your arm either right after the go-out command, or after the dog went down (otherwise it is a double command).
- Long down: Don't touch your dog when giving the "down" command. Get him to sit at heel before you leave the field with him.

PROTECTION
- Be authoritative when guiding your dog through the quartering routine.
- Be also authoritative when heeling your dog (transports, SchH I attack on the handler, etc.).
- Excite your dog, gear him up for the courage test. Talk to him, touch him, kneel next to him.
- Place your dog in an advantageous position for the defense exercise (see that chapter).
- Wait for the judge to tell you to give the "out" command.
- Give your "out" command loud and threatening (you only have one chance).

D. SIMPLE ARITHMETIC

Competing in a Schutzhund trial is, in a way, like gambling: you would be foolish to get into it without knowing the rules of the game.

Yet there is another common factor which many handlers ignore: you will, occasionally, have to take a temporary loss in order to increase your chances for a big gain in the end.

More specifically, you may want to give a second command - and take the penalty - if you can be reasonably sure that your dog's performance will improve as a result, for the rest of the trial. This has nothing to do with cheating or with dishonesty, it is just using simple arithmetic to increase the odds in your favor.

Another example: The protection work in Schutzhund I competition starts with the Search/Find/Bark exercise. The rules require that the dog does not bite at this time.

In training for this exercise, novice handlers often overemphasize the bark/no bite requirement. They argue: "I will lose points if my dog bites." Is that so? Let us look at the *whole* story.

Nearly all dogs going through this trial exercise react in one of the following three ways:

1. The dog rushes to the decoy, barks excitedly, challenges the decoy to move, guards him - but he does not touch the guy. This is a rare sight in SchH I, and dog, handler and trainer should be congratulated. In a trial, this performance will be rewarded with the full points.

2. Typical for the second group of dogs is the following behavior: After finding the decoy, the dog barks briefly and dutifully, or he does not bark at all. He will not bite, but he will not stay with the decoy either - no guarding.

Some dogs consider the job done at this point, others are just plain disinterested. Anyway, there is no incentive for them to stay with the decoy. These dogs also remember that fighting was not permitted at this time and that in the past they had been punished for biting. They want to stay out of trouble and to attend to more important matters, so they just wander off, or they return to their handlers, or - at least - they focus their attention on the handler.

This behavior pattern usually carries over into the other protection exercises as well.

The Schutzhund judge will dish out a heavy penalty for such a performance. Not only will he deduct many points in this exercise, he will also substantially lower his rating for the dog's courage and hardness. Together, these penalties will make a passing score highly unlikely.

3. A dog from the third group eagerly searches for the decoy. He may give one or two barks when he finds the guy, but without further hesitation he will hit the sleeve. He may or may not release the hold without handler interference, but if he does, he will focus all his attention on the bad guy. Afterbites here and in the following exercises are also quite common for this type of dog.

In a trial, the Schutzhund judge will deduct three points for biting instead of barking (SchH I). A few more points may be lost in the remaining protection exercises for possible afterbites. There will, however, be no loss in the rating of courage and hardness.

A summary of these conclusions is given in the following table.

SEARCH/FIND/BARK OPTIONS

	GROUP 1	GROUP 2	GROUP 3
overall behavior of dog	committed, dedicated, controlled	disinterested	committed, dedicated, uncontrolled
typical behavior during the find/ bark exercise	ideal (barks, guards)	weak bark, no guarding, leaves decoy	bites, guards
point deductions for this exercise	none	one or more	three
anticipated point deductions for other exercises because of behavior type	none	ten or more	four or more
negative effect on the rating of courage/hardness	none	severe	none
chances for a passing score	very high	slim	high

Given time and assistance, an experienced handler can train his dog to end up in either one of the three groups, at will.

A novice trainer with an unexperienced dog should always aim for group three. Usually he does not spend the necessary time and he does not have the knowledge and experience to make group one. His only alternative would be group two, the losers.

E. THE SCHUTZHUND TRIAL

A well planned and organized trial that runs smoothly can make or break the reputation of your club.
Start far ahead in time and:

1. Pick a trial date and an alternate date. Try to coordinate the event with other nearby clubs.
2. Appoint a Trial Chairman and a Trial Secretary.
3. Notify the Parent Organization of your club and obtain approval for the trial. Also request a copy of their Schutzhund Trial Regulations.
4. Contact the judge, either directly, or through your club's Parent Organization.
5. Secure grounds for the trial: a large tracking area, and fields for the obedience and protection work. Draw a rough map for the judge's approval.
6. Prepare for inclement weather: shades, heaters, a tent, hot coffee, umbrella for the judge, etc.
7. Consider buying/renting a public address system (loudspeakers, or a bullhorn)
8. Check the equipment:
   tracking - flags, articles, 2 tracklayers
   obedience - jump, wall, dumbbells, blank pistol, blanks (32 cal. preferred), 4-6 people for group
   protection - 8 blinds, sleeves and covers, leather pants, stick, first aid kit, 2 decoys.
9. Contact motels which will accept trained dogs.
10. Consider buying insurance for the trial.
11. Consider purchasing trophies for the winning entries.
12. Send out trial advertising at least 2 months before the trial (magazines, flyers, etc.).
13. Send out entry forms and give entry deadline. Include a list of motels, a map of the trial location, banquet information and entry forms. Request that prior score cards or judge's books, current rabies certificates, and signed injury waivers be submitted.
14. Contact the judge for detail arrangements on travel and accommodations.
15. Make banquet arrangements, reserve early. Consider also a Sunday lunch.
16. Decide on refreshments / food.
17. Contact a photographer for trial coverage.
18. Invite the local press as well as radio and TV reporters.
19. Secure adequate rest room facilities on the trial grounds.
20. Prepare a catalog, keep it simple. Include an explanation of the Schutzhund sport, what is required for each degree. List club officers, judge, agitators, entries.
21. Set up a practice trial about one month before the real event, to uncover potential problems and weak spots, and to give dogs and handlers a chance to prepare for the big day.
22. Send out final notices to all entrants, with information and instructions. Include day, date, time, and place to report. Also include starting numbers for entrants.
23. Make arrangements to meet the judge at the airport, and act as his chauffeur during the entire trial.
24. Make time for the judge to inspect the grounds, and to evaluate the decoys.
25. Assist the judge during the trial at all times, and eliminate delays by having handlers, dogs, helpers and equipment ready when needed.
26. Help the judge with all paperwork.
27. Consider a post-trial lunch on Sunday afternoon, for awarding the trophies.
28. Take the judge to the airport.
29. Write down what went well, what went wrong, suggest changes for the next trial.
30. Relax and write a short article about the trial for publication in your favorite newsletter/paper.

Some of these tasks should be assigned to responsible individuals or committees, but it is the trial chairman who will have to answer to the judge if any of these items are omitted. Early planning, good participation from all club members and thorough follow-through and check-up is the guarantee for a successful Schutzhund trial.

F. EASTERN EUROPEAN TRIAL REQUIREMENTS

Eastern European (Communist) countries used to generously support the training of working dogs by private citizens, in an effort to secure a large pool of suitable canines from which their military and law enforcement agencies could draw. As a result, the training, and the competition, was more rigorous and more praxis related than in Western countries. The former East German Trial Regulations are listed below as an example.

SCHUTZHUND I (SchH I)

Tracking	- owners track
(100 pts.)	- 600 yards
	- 30 minutes age
	- 2 ninety degree turns
	- 2 articles
Obedience	- heeling on/off lead with R,L,about turns in slow/normal/fast pace
	and through a group
(100 pts.)	- down / recall from 20 yards
	- retrieve/flat and over 1 m hurdle
	- long down/distractions (50 yards)
	- 2 gun shots
Protection	- search/find/bark
(100 pts.)	- guarding (20 sec.)
	- search and transport of decoy
	- courage test (60 yards)
	- guarding (20 sec.)
	- transport / attack on handler

SCHUTZHUND II (SchH II)

Tracking	- strangers track
(100 pts.)	- 1000 yards
	- 45 minutes age
	- 2 ninety degree turns, 1 acute angle
	- 2 articles
Obedience	- heeling off lead like SchH I
(100 pts.)	- down / recall from 50 yards
	- sit/down/stand from normal/fast pace handler remains with dog)
	- retrieve/flat and over 1 m hurdle
	- retrieve over 1.50 m upright scaling wall
	- walk over a suspended plank
	- long down/distractions (70 yards)
	- 2 gun shots
Protection	- search/find/bark
(100 pts.)	- guarding (40 sec.)
	- search and transport of decoy
	- courage test (75 yards)
	- guarding (40 sec.)
	- transport / attack on handler
	guarding (40 sec.)

SCHUTZHUND III (SchH III)

Tracking	- strangers track
(100 pts.)	- 1500 yards
	- 60 minutes age
	- 4 ninety degree turns, 1 acute angle
	- 1 cross track
	- 3 articles

Obedience (100 pts.)	- heeling off lead like SchH I - go-out (50 yards), handler out-of-sight for 60 sec., signal (only) for recall - sit/down/stand from normal/fast pace (handler continues for 10 more yards and returns to dog) - retrieve/flat and over 1 m hurdle - retrieve over 1.80 m upright scaling wall - crawling for 10 yards - long down/distractions (70 yards), handler out of sight - 3 gun shots
Protection (100 pts.)	- search/find/bark - guarding (60 sec.) - search and transport of decoy - pursuit (90 yards) of decoy who goes out of sight, courage test, guarding (60 sec) - transport - attack on handler, guarding (60 sec)

FAEHRTENHUND I (FH I)

Tracking (100 pts.)	- strangers track - 1500 yards - 90 minutes age - 6 ninety degree turns, 1 acute angle - 1 cross track - 4 articles
Obedience (100 pts.)	- heeling on and off lead like SchH I - down, recall from 20 yards - one-way jump over a 1 m hurdle - long down/distractions (50 yards), - 2 gun shots
Protection (100 pts.)	- attack on handler - escape - search and transport of decoy

FAEHRTENHUND II (FH II)

Tracking (100 pts.)	- strangers track - 2000 yards - 120 minutes age - 8 ninety degree turns, 2 acute angles - 4 cross tracks - 5 articles
Obedience (100 pts.)	- heeling on and off lead like SchH I - down, recall from 50 yards - one-way climb over a 1.50 m upright scaling wall - walk over a suspended plank - long down/distractions (70 yards), - 2 gun shots
Protection (100 pts.)	- attack on handler - escape - search and transport of decoy

FAEHRTENHUND III (FH III)

Tracking (100 pts.)	- strangers track - 3000 yards - 90 minutes age - 12 ninety degree turns, 4 acute angles - 8 cross tracks - 6 articles

Obedience	- heeling on and off lead like SchH I
(100 pts.)	- down out of motion
	- recall on signal only
	- one-way climb over a 1.80 m upright scaling wall
	- long down/distractions (50 yards),
	- 3 gun shots
Protection	- attack on handler
(100 pts.)	- escape
	- search and transport of decoy

People call their dog "Rover" or "Boy", I named mine "Sex".

Last night he ran off, again. I spent hours looking for him, and then this cop comes over and ask me "What are you doing in that street at three o'clock in the morning?" I told him I was looking for Sex.

My case comes up Friday.

VII. AUXILIARIES

A. DOG FIGHTS

There are many reasons for dog fights, yet all are related to a natural instinct: pack, territorial, protective, or survival instinct.
Find the cause and deal with it early. The problem compounds as the dog gains experience in fighting!

NOVICE FIGHTERS

During the original phase of a dog fight, it is fairly easy to separate the two combatants. It just requires that someone - not necessarily the handler - steps in fearlessly and energetically. Use the surprise effect: do something the dogs do not expect. For instance, jump with both feet (not barefoot!) between, or next to, the two dogs and scream as loud as you can. This impresses most dogs sufficiently so that they forget to fight - for a moment. However, the surprise maneuver works only during the preliminaries of a fight.

As soon as the warriors are separated you must try to find out which one of the two dogs is the most likely candidate to start the fight anew. He will be the more dominant animal, he will advance and assume a confident, aggressive, maybe even fearless, posture. Try to intimidate him with shouts and gestures, try to chase him away using any tools that are handy (stick, umbrella, briefcase, book, etc.).

In very rare instances the strange dog will then direct his aggression towards you. If this happens stand still and keep all your limbs close to your body. Avoid any continued movement, you want to be a statue in the eyes of the dog. Use your foot to kick him, or any available tool to hit him, with lightening speed if he gets too close, but don't hold your foot or your arm out like bait. Short, sharp shouts may help also.
Try to inch toward something that provides rear cover, like a wall, a car, a tree. Wait for the dog to move away or to be called off. Then leave the scene slowly - don't run.

SEASONED FIGHTERS

Real problems develop once the two dogs are locked unto each other at the height of a fight.
It is impossible to intimidate the two dogs sufficiently, or to command them to cease fighting so that both release their grip at the same moment. The first dog to comply with the request still feels the bite of the adversary, and out of self-preservation he must bite back.

Kicking or hitting the two fighting dogs will only intensify the battle, even if one could beat the two dogs at the same time so severely that they would release their grip for a moment.

It has been recommended to throw a blanket or a bucket full of water, sand or pebbles on the dogs. This impresses the dogs very little, as long as the fight is in full force. To shove sand in the dogs mouth holds very little promise either. Besides, the peacemaker risks losing a couple of fingers.

Reaching for the collar, even if it is a prong collar, will only aggravate the fighters. In addition, the hand comes in close proximity to the teeth while searching for the collar. Even your own dog may bite you in such an instance - not because he wants to, but because your hands were between his teeth when he closed his fangs.

Remote-controlled electronic collars accomplish the same as beating: the fight intensifies.
In professional dog fights, handlers use short wooden dowels to pry the fighters' fangs open. However, their dogs "work" according to certain rules (lock grip), which are unfamiliar to the occasional fighter. It is therefore very risky for non-professionals to use theses dowels, aside from the fact that they are usually not available when needed.

SEPARATING FIGHTERS

We have perfected the following procedure over the years. It carries the least risk, and we can safely recommend it to all those that might encounter a dog fight.

- One person is needed for each dog, preferably the two dog handlers. Each handler tries to get a hold of that part of his dog's body that is removed the farthest from the teeth: the tail (for docked dogs, one hind foot).
- As soon as the handler can securely hold the tail (do not pull!) he reaches with the other hand for one of the hind legs (more precisely: the metatarsus).
- As soon as the handler can securely hold one hind foot he lets go of the tail and transfers his grip to the other hind leg. Both handlers must securely hold both hind feet of their dog before they can proceed with the next step.
- Both handlers stand upright and lift - at the same time - the hind feet of their dogs off the ground (about one yard). This makes the dogs insecure and deprives them of their mobility and balance.
- Both handlers yell at their dogs and try to separate them by pulling on their hind legs at the same time. If necessary, they may bang on the fangs with their feet (shoes!).
- As soon as the dogs release the grip they must be separated, and kept separated!
- The dogs must be punished only when they try to resume the fight - one sharp hit with lightening speed for every attempt. Punishment must not be administered if the dog just stays alert!

CURING FIGHTERS

Seasoned fighters can only be cured by applying drastic measures. The forces however, must be goal oriented, and the dog must be able to connect it to the undesirable deed.

Many people still believe in "hanging" as an appropriate remedy. Even the editor of a well-known obedience training magazine supports it publicly in his periodical. We believe that hanging is despicable, senseless cruelty, nothing else. It could best be compared to the "expert" who wants to extinguish a small fire in the frying pan with the blast from a load of dynamite - the side effects are devastating in both cases.

We recommend that after a fight the two dogs be fitted with prong collars and short leads. The dog/handler teams then walk in opposite directions past each other, dog next to dog, but at this time the teams are separated by at least 20 feet. At the slightest sign of aggression, for instance raised hackles, snarling, curled lips, pulling toward the other dog, readiness to jump forward etc., the handler must interfere. Using the feedback principle, the handler should silently and quickly count to three and do the following on each count, to correct aggressive behavior:

1) Give a sharp, short command ("NO").
2) Observe the reaction of your dog.
3) a) If your dog did quit the hostilities on (2) and gives you his attention, then praise him ("good boy").
   b) If your dog continues to react with hostility, quickly correct him with the collar and give him ONE sharp blow across the snout with a short piece of rubber hose (Command: "NO").
Punish ONLY the offending dog, then praise him lightly.

Decrease the distance between teams and continue walking past each other until both dogs are under complete control when separated by only 12 inches. Practice on a loose lead, then on a long line, and finally off lead, under constant supervision by the two handlers.

B. BOARDING OR TRAVELLING

There are times when a dog owner must be away from home, leaving him the option to board the dog, get a dog sitter, or take the dog along.

Whatever your choice is, you must now -more than ever- make sure that your dog is in good health. A target list would include veterinary check-up; check for worms and treatment if necessary; rabies shots and other indicated vaccinations; cleaning the ears; clipping the toe nails; and grooming and bathing.

BOARDING

Boarding could be a traumatic experience in your dog's life, since you are unable to make him understand that he is not just abandoned at this strange place.

This holds true especially for the first time around. From a psychological viewpoint, therefore, it is desirable to make the first stay at a boarding kennel as brief as possible.

We suggest that you board your dog at first for a couple of hours only, then (a week later) for half a day, then for a day, then for a weekend, before you take off on that dream vacation.

This schedule requires long range planning, and the plan should be implemented even before you anticipate a need for it. One never knows when an emergency situation requires extended absence from home. Advanced planning also allows you to select the best boarding facility available, and to establish a friendly relationship with the operator.

When selecting a kennel, ask yourself:
1. Is the kennel escape-proof, showing solid construction, complete enclosure - including a roof panel, and with a second fence around the perimeter of the property?
2. Is it clean?
   Dirt, gravel and wooden floors can not usually be kept clean enough without excessive chemical treatment. Concrete floors, therefore, are important.
3. Does each dog have its own run?
   Is the separation between adjoining runs sufficient to prevent dog fights and spreading of diseases?
4. Are the runs large enough (at least 3 ft. by 10 ft. for a working dog)?
5. Does each dog have unrestricted access to a sheltered area inside the kennel building, or to a dog house?
6. Is there a shady, draft free, insulated resting spot provided in each run?
7. Is the operator friendly with the dogs, and competent enough to control them?
8. Does each dog have unrestricted access to clean, fresh drinking water?
9. What does the operator feed the dogs, how often, how much? Would he be willing to feed the food that you bring along for your dog?
10. How does the operator handle emergencies? Does he have a standing arrangement with a veterinarian, will he consult with your regular veterinarian if necessary?
11. Will kennel personnel exercise the dog (play, road work etc.), and will they take proper precautions to prevent an escape?
12. How much does the kennel charge, everything included?

Leaving the dog with a friend is not always a preferable alternative to a commercial boarding facility.

While a friend may give the dog more individual attention, he/she probably does not quite have the experience and the facilities of a commercial operator. Fights with your friend's dog and run-aways are a distinct possibility.

At any rate, a favored toy and a floor mat or a blanket from home left with the boarded dog will ease his anxiety somewhat.

DOG SITTING

An (expensive) alternative to boarding is keeping the dog at home and hiring a competent dog sitter. This usually means that you entrust your house to a total stranger (bonding is recommended), that your dog is alone at least 23 hours each day, that your dog may devise some kind of entertainment that will not find your approval, and that you may lose your dog if he manages to escape (he will be searching for you and is not likely to return to an empty house). If you decide to hire a sitter, have at least adequate facilities for confining the dog in the absence of supervision - preferably a well-built kennel. Also, require the sitter to spend with your dog at least 30 min. each on two separate visits each day.

The sitter must be thoroughly familiar with the dog and his daily rituals. He must, for instance, know the feeding, watering, exercising and sleeping routines. He should have handled, and taken care of, the dog in your presence. He must be familiar with the house, the property and the neighbors. He also must have been instructed what to do in case of emergencies. This includes leaving with him the phone numbers of one or two trusted dog trainers/owners, the veterinarian, the police and your vacation phone, if possible.

TRAVEL

Taking the dog along on a trip is a decision that should not be made lightly since it will restrict your freedom considerably. If this is understood and accepted, then proper preparations must be made. You must confirm that the dog is welcome at the destination, and at any intermediate stop. You should gather:

> food and water dishes
> sufficient food for at least a couple of days
> sufficient drinking water for the travel time
> leash
> metal tie-out chain and anchor
> muzzle (if needed)
> travel crate
> resting mat
> nail clipper
> brush, comb
> large towel (for a muddy or wet dog)
> flea powder, insect repellant
> medication (if needed)
> first aid kit
> a toy (ball, etc).

You should buy a wide leather collar for your dog which he can not slip off, to be kept on him until he returns home. Secure to this collar the dog's license tag, the rabies tag and a tag offering a reward (stating your address, area code and phone number).

CAR TRAVEL

In preparation for the trip, you can install in your car a wire screen barrier with the provided suction cups, to partition off part of the car. You can buy trunk lid extensions to enlarge the trunk space for transporting a dog. You can tow a small trailer, custom made for the transport of dogs. And finally, you can just admit your well-behaved dog to the passenger compartment in the rear without any physical restraint. It would be advisable, though, to fill the leg space of the rear seats with luggage, and to cover this enlarged platform with a heavy blanket or a throw rug. The dog should be kept in the back and out of the drivers seat. Use voice control, or an assistant, to teach him not to bother you at the wheel. It can make the difference between a safe trip and a serious car accident.

Also, the dog should not be allowed to stick his head out of the window. While the danger of a collision is remote, eye irritations or eye injuries happen very frequently.

Some dogs dislike automobile excursions, some may vomit, others may not want to get into the car in the first place, but all normal dogs can be conditioned to long car rides. While tranquilizers are often used for that purpose, they do not solve the problem, they just mask it. Besides, they can have undesirable side effects, and medication is not needed if you proceed sensibly.

Training Suggestions:

For stubborn or fearful dogs it is recommended to feed them their regular meal inside the (stationary) car for a few days. Do not use any force. Open the car door, set the food bowl down, and make yourself comfortable next to it. Patience is needed at that time.

If the dog does not eat within thirty minutes, discard the food and try the same procedure at the next regular meal time. Do not offer any other food in between. Eventually the dog will eat.
Once this step has been accomplished, take your dog for very short trips first (maybe just to the end of the driveway), and for longer trips later on. This conditioning process is greatly dependent on the destination of the rides. A dog that only gets to travel when it is time to see the veterinarian will most likely stay away from any automobile. On the other hand, a dog will jump into the car at every opportunity if he is usually taken to new and exciting places like parks, play grounds etc., and if you play with him there.

During the hot summer months, a couple of clean plastic milk jars can be filled with water and frozen just before departure.They will thaw in time and supply cool drinking water.
In general, reduce your dog's food and water rations somewhat while travelling.

Schedule rest stops frequently. Exercise your dog every hour or so, making sure that he can not escape. If he is off leash and suddenly decides to cross the road, his life, your life (trying to get him) and the lives of other travellers (trying to avoid a collision) are in jeopardy.
Even if no accident happens, the dog might chase an animal over great distances, too far to quickly find his way back to the car. In this case you should stay on the spot as long as possible. Your dog will undoubtedly be looking for you, but finding the way back will take time, sometimes days. If the escape happens close to home, however, there are equal chances that the dog will find his way back to the house.

If you have to leave your dog in a parked car for a while, without supervision, you must take certain precautions. Turn off the motor, remove the ignition key and set the brakes. There are recorded incidents where a restless (or smart?) dog has engaged the drive train and set the car into motion. Lock the doors, to prevent your dog from getting out on his own, or from being taken out by a thief. Roll up the windows, but do not close them completely, for the same reason.
Some ventilation is necessary to prevent suffocation. Park your car in the shade during the summer months, direct sunshine can turn an automobile quickly into a frying oven.

AIR TRAVEL
With the exception of Seeing Eye Dogs, airlines will not permit large dogs in the passenger cabin. Dogs must be confined to an airline-approved travel container which can either be rented from the carrier, or be provided by the passenger.
Even with this restriction, most airlines will allow no more than two dogs on any one flight. You should, therefore, make your reservations, and those for your dog, far in advance.

In preparation for the journey, accustom your dog to the crate in which he actually will be travelling. Some dogs do not mind this at all. Other dogs have to be coaxed into the cage and be persuaded to stay in there for a short time. Make sure that you do not close the door on such a dog right away. Instead leave the door open and talk the dog into remaining inside the crate for a while.
During the next few days or weeks, extend this time until your dog enters the crate willingly and remains in there calmly for a couple of hours.

We suggest to securely fasten a large sign to the top and to at least one side of the crate. The sign should read   **LIVE ANIMAL**   in large letters. It should also show the dogs name, your name, address and phone, your destination address and phone, the departure airport, the destination airport, and the flight number. For the return trip you must update the sign, of course.

Cargo compartments in commercial aircraft certified for the transport of animals are heated and pressurized just like the passenger cabins although to somewhat less stringent standards. Yet, sudden changes in air pressure, the confinement, and the separation from you will make the trip anything but a pleasurable experience for your dog.

Give your pet a chance to exercise, to eliminate, to drink some water just before departure, as late as practically feasible. Do not feed him before the flight, however, or leave any food with him.

Some airports allow the traveller to take his dog - in the crate - up to the gate. This decreases the total time of isolated confinement often significantly. Normally, however, the dog must be dropped off as just another piece of luggage. As such he may go through the same kind of ordeal that a suitcase - sometimes - does, including getting lost.

*** YOU SHOULD MAKE EVERY EFFORT TO ***
 *** ACTUALLY OBSERVE THE LOADING AND UNLOADING ***
 *** OF YOUR DOG AT BOTH ENDS OF THE TRIP. ***

If anything unusual happens, insist to see the airport manager and report to him incidents or problems without delay.

INTERNATIONAL TRAVEL
Travelling with a dog to Canada or Mexico is a fairly simple matter, if a recent health certificate and a rabies vaccination document can be presented to the border guard. Regulations change, however, and we suggest to check with a customs office well in advance.

When travel to other countries is involved, a letter written in advance to their Government Department of Health, or to the Department of Agriculture in that particular country will often be the only way to obtain reliable information. This correspondence should be taken along on the trip, it might come in handy in case of a dispute.
Travel agencies can be contacted more easily for information. Their files, however, may not always show the latest regulations. Even a minor oversight can spell serious trouble at the border.

Some countries require a quarantine which is longer than the average vacation.
Other countries require special vaccinations and/or special documents to prove that the dog does not carry communicable diseases.
Upon re-entry, US authorities also insist on certain formalities for bringing the dog back home (vaccinations, proof of ownership etc.).

All these conditions can usually be met for a well-kept dog, at some expense, and at some inconvenience.

As a conscious dog owner, however, you will find that it is often best for all parties involved to leave the dog at home, all considered.

C. SCHUTZHUND SPORT IN NORTH AMERICA

EUROPE

The Schutzhund concept evolved in Europe at around 1900. Concerned dog fanciers embarked on a training and testing program for privately owned canines of the working group. The intention was to give the dogs a chance to develop and to demonstrate their full capabilities. In return, the handlers gained an immediate benefit from the utilization of the many talents working dogs have. They also received valuable clues for selecting the best breeding specimen.

Early training programs were highly individualistic. Exchange of ideas and competitive spirit, however, soon required that standards be established. Today, dog/handler teams throughout the world compete according to the "VDH Trial Regulations" (or slight modifications of it) which offer the SchH A, SchH I, SchH II, SchH III titles, the international Schutzhund titles INT I, INT II, INT III, an advanced tracking degree (FH), a watchdog degree (WH), a traffic-steady companion dog degree (VB) and others.

NORTH AMERICA

In North America, Schutzhund had a late start, for various reasons:
- Traditionally, dog sport meant conformation and obedience only. Tracking gained support only in the last few decades, and protection training still faces rejection by many.

- Unfavorable publicity and distorted press reports have branded the Schutzhund as a killer dog. Clever but unqualified "attack dog trainers" contributed to the molding of such a false image.

- Pending, or enacted, legislation in many states classifies the Schutzhund as an attack dog.

- Some breeders of Working Dogs resist the rigors of this type of test fearing perhaps they have lost the true "working dog" character in their quest for conformation titles.

- The AKC's negative attitude towards Schutzhund training is transferred to the many loyal AKC exhibitors.

Sporadic attempts to promote Schutzhund training in North America during the fifties and sixties failed. At that time small, usually two or three man groups worked their dogs individually, independently and often unnoticed by the rest of the world.

One such group was the Peninsula Police Canine Corps (PPCC) with Gernot Riedel in the San Francisco area, another one Henry Friehs' group near Los Angeles. Both groups were German Shepherd Dog oriented and supported German SV (Shepherd Club) trial regulations and breed standards.

NSA
The first real effort in the U.S. to start an organized national Schutzhund movement was the foundation of the "National Schutzhund Association (NSA)" on January 1, 1969 under the leadership of Dr. Herbert Preiser. 1970, at a meeting in Northbrook, IL with other, mainly Westcoast and Canada based groups, NSA became NASA, the "North American Schutzhund Association". Its founding members agreed on basic issues and on an organizational scheme, and they decided to train and test their dogs according to the German Dog Sport Model. Unfortunately, this organization collapsed in less than a year because of personality conflicts. While many of the founding members got disillusioned and avoided getting involved in organizational matters again, three of them continued: Dr. H. Preiser, Mr. A. Ertelt and Mr. K. Marti.

ASCA

Following the direction its founders had determined, Dr. H. Preiser reorganized the club and named it "Affiliated Schutzhund Clubs of America (ASCA) ". Under his guidance, and together with a team of advisers, ASCA pioneered the idea of non-commercial Schutzhund Trainer Schools with European staff members, and of a national periodical devoted exclusively to Schutzhund training and Breed Survey ("The Schutzhunder").

ASCA was the first national Schutzhund organization to hold a combined SchH Trial and Breed Survey (Jun.70), the first to conduct an American SchH Judges Apprentice Training Program (1974) and the first to establish contacts with the AKC through personal visits at their office in New York City (Oct.1972).

NASA

The other two men (Ertelt/Marti) assumed leading roles in the "North American Working Dog Association (NASA)", founded in 1971. NASA decided to become self-sufficient (in an effort to win the approval of the AKC - which did not pay off), in contrast to most of the other American Schutzhund groups who were seeking support and guidance from their European counterparts.
NASA judges awarded Schutzhund degrees that were recognized within the organization only. It was NASA's goal to become a member of the FCI and thereby to validate its Schutzhund degrees. The mere existence of the AKC, however, was preventing NASA from being considered as an FCI Member Club.

WDA

Working Dogs of America, Inc. (WDA) was formally established on April 2, 1975 through efforts of Dr. Dietmar Schellenberg, the first licensed, FCI accredited German Schutzhund Judge to reside in North America. It was set up from the very beginning not to be accountable to, and not to be controlled by, professional breeders, professional trainers, professional dog importers, dog businesses or even breed clubs.

To offer international, FCI recognized Schutzhund titles to its members, WDA pursued the idea of affiliating with an already established all-breed Schutzhund organization.
After long bargaining, the German DVG established an American Division in October 1975. Dr. Schellenberg was appointed its Managing Director. In May 1976 the Division was officially accepted as a DVG Landesgruppe, named "Working Dogs of America, DVG Division USA, Canada, Mexico, Member VDH, Member FCI".
This acceptance was a milestone in the history of the American Schutzhund sport since competitors and their dogs could earn an FCI recognized Schutzhund title for the first time right here in America. All ASCA affiliated Member Clubs responded with the unanimous decision to join WDA, other groups and individuals did likewise.

WDA incorporated in the State of New York as a not-for-profit organization, and it obtained recognition from the US Government as an educational institution with tax-exempt status. WDA's quarterly publication "WDA TRAINER" gained the reputation of the best Schutzhund periodical anywhere in the world.

Lack of organizational, financial and ideological support, repeated breaches of the affiliation contract by the DVG, and finally the DVG's attempt to force new, crippling rules upon WDA, led to an emergency meeting of the seven-member WDA Board of Directors in Detroit. There, in April of 1979, it was decided to sever all ties to the DVG and to seek affiliation with another FCI organization. During the subsequent one year interim period, WDA lost many individual members and clubs to other organizations.

In March 1980, WDA affiliated with the BHV/VLDG and thereby became a member of the largest all-breed German Dog Sport Organization.

USA

During the summer of 1975, the American Kennel Club announced that all Schutzhund activities are in violation of its rules and regulations. Member clubs were threatened with expulsion in case of continued involvement in this sport.

In response, the German Shepherd Dog Club of America (GSDCA) terminated all its Schutzhund activities in August of 1975 and abandoned in the process several formerly sanctioned Schutzhund clubs (GSDCA changed their mind later on and established in January 1983 the "GSDCA Working Dog Association").

The Peninsula Police Canine Corps (PPCC), a very active local club in the San Francisco area, was the best known of them. This club had gained in the past considerable support from the GSDCA and from its Schutzhund Chairman Mr. G. Riedel. In that position the club had been able to extend its influence and to gain a high reputation among its peers.

Facing the AKC challenge, Mr. G. Riedel on behalf of the PPCC invited interested parties to a meeting. Ten delegates (Flawson, Hansen, Liedtke, McArdle, McFarland, Memming, Schellenberg, Strasser, Stuermer and Tackett) representing 15 Schutzhund clubs and organizations, and many guests, met on November 21, 1975 in Palo Alto, CA. The delegates declined an invitation to join the recently established DVG/FCI Division North America and voted instead to form an independent Schutzhund and Breed Association for German Shepherd Dogs under SV guidance and VDH Trial Regulations. The organization was named "United Schutzhund Clubs of America (USA)", and Mr. L. McFarland was elected its first chairman.

The organization went through a very turbulent growing stage, and its controversial issues were given widespread publicity. Nevertheless, USA has expanded to become the largest Schutzhund organization in the United States with about 200 local clubs (as of 1994).

Dogs of many breeds can participate in USA Schutzhund trials, however, participation in international (WUSV) competitions and breed surveys are open to German Shepherd Dogs only.

While close contacts to the SV (Shepherd Club of Germany) do exist, USA is independent and not affiliated with it or with any other national or international organization.

The USA operate their own judges' program and license the successful graduates. A loose arrangement exists with the SV for recognition of USA-Judges and of titles awarded by them, yet USA Schutzhund titles are not SV degrees, and their international recognition is still a matter of debate.

GSDCA

Regretting earlier decisions (see USA, above), the GSDCA re-established Schutzhund activities in 1983. The GSDCA/Working Dog Association now has several clubs throughout the United States who operate under the guidance of, and with assistance from, the German SV.

DVG America

Having lost a prime position in the Schutzhund sport in North America through disputes with WDA (see above), the DVG re-entered the scene in 1979. At that time, personality conflicts within the leadership of the United Schutzhund Clubs (see USA, above) led to an expulsion of several key members. They were immediately recruited by the struggling DVG and operate now several local Schutzhund Clubs, mainly in the South-Eastern US.

NSC

Because of common interests in the sport, the various Schutzhund organizations in North America would benefit from a coordination of their activities.

Early documented efforts date back to 1974, when Dr. Schellenberg suggested to form a council ("North American Schutzhund Council (NSC)"). With support from the WDA Board of Directors, the proposal was renewed in 1978, inviting the presidents of NASA, USA and WDA to an organizational meeting in New York City. USA refused to participate, and both NASA and WDA agreed to postpone a decision of jointly forming the NSC for the benefit of the movement in general.

The need for such a body is still apparent, to present an undistorted image of the Schutzhund dog to the public, to coordinate publicity for the Schutzhund sport via the News media (press, radio, TV), and to deal intelligently and successfully with detrimental Schutzhund legislation.

D. FEDERATION CYNOLOGICQUE INTERNATIONALE (FCI)

The FCI, the World Dog Federation, is an umbrella organization for national dog club associations throughout the world. It was founded in 1911 by representatives from five countries (Germany, Austria, Belgium, France, Netherlands). Today it has 40 full member countries (Argentina, Austria, Belgium, Brazil, Chile, Columbia, Czechoslovakia, Denmark, Dominican Republic, Ecuador, England, Finland, France, Germany, Hongkong, Hungary, Israel, Italy, Japan, Luxembourg, Madagaskar, Morocco, Mexico, Monaco, Nepal, Netherland, Norway, Panama, Paraguay, Peru, Poland, Portugal, Rumania, South Africa, Spain, Sweden, Switzerland, Uruguay, Venezuela and Yugoslavia) and 29 associate members (non-voting). Organizationally, it is divided into five regions (Europe, Latin and South America, Asia, Africa, Oceania, Australia).
The largest national canine organization represented in the FCI is the VDH of West Germany with more than 350 000 individual members.

Neither Canada nor the USA are FCI affiliated. If they wanted to be represented, it would have to be through their national canine organizations CKC and AKC, respectively. Since the FCI is concerned with all phases of the dog sport of which Schutzhund, for instance, is just a small part, no other American organization would qualify for direct membership in the FCI, now or in the foreseeable future.

Each FCI member country nominates one representative from its largest, approved parent organization for the dog sport. For Germany this is a delegate from the VDH, for the USA it would be a representative from the AKC - if the US were a member. Together, these delegates constitute the FCI Assembly, meeting bi-annually to discuss and to decide upon breed standards, international conformation shows, membership affairs etc.
Each (full) member country has one vote, regardless of the number of represented dog fanciers. The VDH delegate speaking for 350 000 members, for instance, has no more rights than the delegate from Monaco, representing a little over 100 members.

Important issues are decided by the FCI Assembly, while general business is entrusted to a nine-member Board of Directors, chaired by a President. These officers are elected for four-year terms.
Special committees, including a scientific committee, advance the work in particular areas. One of them, and a rather minor one, is the Commission for Working Dogs, staffed predominantly by Swiss representatives. They see to it, for instance, that Schutzhund degrees from an organization affiliated with the FCI are recognized by all other clubs and judges associated with the FCI.

The FCI World Championship for Purebred Dogs (conformation) is an annual event sponsored by the FCI. It is held in a different country each year, and CACIB titles are awarded at these (and other) shows.

The FCI offers three titles:
CACIB (conformation)
CACIT (performance)
INT SchH DEGREE I,II,III.

The titles are awarded by local judges and recorded with the national organizations. For the first two, however, permission from the FCI is needed to hold the trial.

Requirements for the International Schutzhund Degrees I, II, III are very much like those for the corresponding VDH degrees, and, of course, they are the same for all FCI member countries.

The FCI has neither a registry for performance nor one for conformation. The FCI has no breed registry or stud book, it does not have judges as such or even member clubs (it does, however, register kennel names). The FCI is an umbrella organization for the all-encompassing dog sport associations (parent clubs) of individual countries.

E. SCHUTZHUND ORGANIZATIONS

North American Schutzhund Association, Inc. (NASA)
7318 Brennans Drive
Dallas, TX 75214

United Schutzhund Clubs of America (USA)
729 Lemay Ferry Rd.
St. Louis, MO 63125

Working Dogs of America, Inc. (WDA)
3910 Wesley Chapel Rd NE
Marietta, GA 30062

German Shepherd Dog Club of America /
Working Dog Association
17 West Ivy Lane
Englewood, NJ 07631

F. SCHUTZHUND ABBREVIATIONS

Many abbreviations used in connection with Schutzhund training are of German origin since this is the country where the sport originated. Here is a compilation in alphabetical order, together with a brief description.

A St.	"A Stempel"	= OFA Certification normal
AD	"Ausdauer Test"	= Endurance Degree
ADRK	"Allgemeiner Deutscher Rottweiler Klub"	= General German Rottweiler Club.
AZG	"Arbeitsgemeinschaft der Zucht- und Gebrauchshundverbaende"	= Affiliation of Breed and Working Dog Organizations. Oversees VDH Trial Rules and their changes, for instance.
BVH	"Berliner Verband Hundesportvereine,e.V."	= Berlin Assoc. for Dog Sport Clubs, Inc.
BC	"Boxer Klub"	= Boxer Club.
BLH	"Blindenhund"	= Seeing Eye Dog
BpDH	"Bahnpolizei Diensthund"	= Railroad Police Dog
CACIB	"Certificat d'aptitude au championat international de beaute"	= Certificate of championship achievement in conformation, intern. FCI governed conformation championship trials/titles.
CACIT	"Certificat d'aptitude au championat international de travail"	= Certif. of achievement of championship in performance, intern. FCI governed working dog championship trials/titles.
DBC	"Deutscher Bouvier Club v. 1911, e.V."	= German Bouvier Club.
DH	"Diensthund"	= Service Dog. Refers to dogs in active service with the police, railroad police or customs agencies.

DHV	"Deutscher Hundesportverband"	= German Dogsport Association. Association of 7 German Working Dog Clubs with equal rights. The BHV is one of them, VLDG and DVG are two others. Founded 5-21, 1977. Represents over 70,000 members.
DV	"Dobermann Verein"	= Doberman Club.
DVG	"Deutscher Verband der Gebrauchshundsportvereine"	= German Association for Working Dog Sport Clubs. Parent Club for Schutzhund and Police Dog Clubs, mainly in northern Germany. Founded 1902.
FCI	"Federation Cynologique Internationale"	= Association for Cynology International. Umbrella organization for national dog club associations throughout the world. Founded 1911, 40+ member countries.
FH	"Faehrtenhund"	= Tracking Dog. Advanced training degree according to the VDH Trial Rules.
G	"Gut"	= good (Show / Performance Rating)
GHK	"Gebrauchshundklasse"	= Utility Dog Class
HGH	"Herdengebrauchshund"	= Herding Dog
IPO	"Internationale Pruefungsordnung"	= International Trial Regulations (SchH)
KFT	"Klub fuer Terrier"	= Club for Terriers. Airedales are served by this club.
KK 1	"Koerklasse 1"	= Breed Survey Degree 1 (excellent)
LH	"Lawinenhund"	= Avalanche Dog
M	"mangelhaft"	= lacking (Show / Performance Rating)
PH	"Polizeihund "	= Police Dog
PSK	"Pinscher-Schnauzer Klub"	= Pinscher-Schnauzer Club. Giant Schnauzers are served by this club.
RGH	"Rauschgifthund"	= Narcotics Detection Dog
RH	"Rettungshund"	= Disaster Dog
RZVHH	"Rassezuchtverein fuer Hovawart-Hunde"	= Breed Club for Hovawart dogs.
SchH	"Schutzhund"	= protection dog.
SG	"Sehr Gut"	= very good (Show / Performance Rating)
SV	"Schaeferhund Verein", official name: "Verein fuer Deutsche Schaeferhunde (SV) e.V."	= Club for German Shepherd Dogs. Founded 1899 by von Stephanitz.
U	"ungenuegend"	= insufficient (Show / Performance Rating)
V	"vorzueglich"	= excellent (Show / Performance Rating)
VB	"Verkehrssicherer Begleithund"	= Traffic-Steady Companion Dog
VDH	"Verband fuer das Deutsche Hundewesen"	= Association for German Dog Affairs. Parent organization for German Dog Clubs, equivalent to the AKC or CKC. Founded 1949, heir to similar organizations that date back to 1878.
VLDG	"Vereinigung der Landesverbaende fuer das Deutsche Gebrauchshundewesen"	= Association of regional clubs for the German Working Dog movement. Parent Club for Schutzhund and Police Dog Clubs, mainly in Southern Germany.
WH	"Wachhund"	= Watch Dog (degree)
ZB	"Zuchtbuch"	= Stud Book
ZB	"Zuchtbewertung"	= Conformation Show Rating
ZH	"Zollhund"	= Customs Dog

G. RELEASE FORM

To minimize potential problems it is suggested that Schutzhund Clubs and training groups incorporate, that they buy insurance coverage, and that they have all members, participants and guests sign a release form.
The form suggested below may require some modification for your group, it may not provide all the legal protection you are seeking, it may not even be recognized by some courts of law. It will prove, however, that a person who signed it understood, and accepted, the risks involved in this sport.

WAIVER, ASSUMPTION OF RISK AND AGREEMENT TO HOLD HARMLESS

I understand that attendance of a dog training program is not without risk to myself, members of my family or guests who may attend, or my dog, because some of the dogs to which I will be exposed, as well as my own dog, may be difficult to control and may be the cause of injury even when handled with the greatest amount of care.

In consideration of, and as inducement to, the acceptance of my application for training, I hereby waive and release
                    XXXXXXXXX YYYYYYY (X. Y.),
its employees, officers, members and agents from any and all liability of any nature, for injury or damage which I or my dog may suffer, including specifically, but without limitation, any injury or damage resulting from the action of any dog, and I expressly assume the risk of such damage or injury while attending any training session, or any other function, of X.Y., or while on the training grounds or the surrounding area thereto.

I also agree to indemnify and to hold harmless X.Y., its employees, officers, members and agents from any and all claims, or claims by any member of my family, or any other person accompanying me to any training session or function of X.Y., or while on the grounds or the surrounding area thereto, as a result of any action by any dog, including my own. I shall personally assume all responsibilities and liabilities for any loss or injury which may be alleged to have been caused directly or indirectly to any person or thing by the act of my dog while participating in an X.Y. dog training program or while on the training grounds or the surrounding area thereto.

(My dog in the above statements means any dog in my custody upon approaching the training grounds or adjacent areas)

SIGNATURE   DATE

STREET

CITY   ZIP

H. ILLNESS

We all have seen our club's most consistent worker fail in one way or another on a certain day in Schutzhund training or in a trial performance. The dog's basic temperament has not changed from one day to the next, but what about his physical make-up? Was he ill?

TRACKING can be influenced by respiratory infections, sinus problems, allergies, increased body temperature and certain medications.

OBEDIENCE can be influenced by soft tissue injuries (sprains and bruises), bone injuries, arthritis, ocular defects, ear infections, parasites (internal and external), shoulder, elbow and hip dysplasia, diarrhea, and many other medical problems.

PROTECTION work can be influenced by mouth, gum, and teeth problems, fractures of the small bones in the throat where the collar presses, neck injury, ocular defects, ear infections and structural defects.

Dogs can not easily tell us where it hurts. YOU must make sure that he is in good health before you give him a harder correction.

I. FIRST AID

If at your next club function, one of the people faced a medical emergency, what would you do? To be properly prepared consider the following:

1. Prepare a list of emergency phone numbers and keep it with the First Aid kit. Know where the nearest phone is and have change handy.
2. Have a First Aid kit available at all club functions. A list of items it should contain is given below.
3. Invite a Red Cross team or a physician to your next club meeting. Ask questions, learn from them.
4. Know the basic First Aid procedures. However, do not do more than necessary until professional help arrives, and call a physician as soon as possible.

POISON IVY
Repeatedly wash exposed area with soap and water.
STINGS/BITES
from snakes, scorpions, black widow spider, brown recluse spider, bees: make victim lie down, tourniquet on limb between wound and heart but don't stop blood stream completely.
FOREIGN MATERIAL IN EYE
Immediately hold eye lid open and wash for at least 15 minutes in a gentle stream of water.
BRUISES
Apply cold compresses.
BITES, CUTS, ABRASIONS
Prevent infections. Cleanse with soap and warm water, then stop bleeding with sterile pad.
HEAVY BLEEDING
Immediately try to stop bleeding by pressing a pad against the wound. Offer (don't force) plenty of liquids, like water, coffee, tea.
SPINE, NECK, HEAD INJURIES
Don't move the victim. Call physician immediately.
FRACTURES
Prevent further injuries by applying splints. Stop bleeding.
DISLOCATIONS
Treat like fractures.

SPRAINS & STRAINS
   If necessary treat like fractures. Apply cold compresses.
SHOCK
   Has many causes. Make victim lie down, head lower than feet. Keep air passages open.
UNCONSCIOUSNESS
   If uncertain, treat like head injuries.
BREATHING STOPPED
   Start artificial respiration immediately (manual or mouth-to-mouth), keep air passages open.

CAUTION:
If a tourniquet should be required, use only a strong, wide piece of cloth, never any narrow material. Mark the letters "TK" and the time on the victims forehead with crayon, pencil, soot, etc. Do not cover the tourniquet.
Apply the tourniquet just tight enough to stop bleeding. If there is delay in getting to a doctor, cautiously loosen the tourniquet after 20 to 30 minutes.
If no bleeding recurs, leave tourniquet loosely in place and keep it under continuous observation.

FIRST AID KIT (suggestions)
   band aids (various sizes)
   sterile dressing in sealed envelopes
   roller, triangular and adhesive bandages
   alcohol preparation pads
   large bath towel
   adhesive tape, safety pins
   scissors with blunt tips
   tweezers
   eye cup, eye pad
   ammonia inhalant
   burn ointment
   Anacin tablets
   splints
   tongue blades
   tourniquet and short stick
   flashlight
   First Aid instructions
   coins for emergency phone calls

EMERGENCY TELEPHONE NUMBERS

   Physician - day

   Physician - night

   Police Department

   Fire Department

   Ambulance

   Hospital

   Pharmacist

K. LIST OF ILLUSTRATIONS

L. BIBLIOGRAPHY

Anderson,B.; Cognitive Psychology; Academic Press 1975
Barbaresi,S.; German Shepherd; TFH 1957
Barnett,S.A.; Modern Ethology; Oxford Univ. Press 1981
Bartlett,M; Puppy Aptitude Testing/AKC Gazette 3/1979
Barwig/Hilliard; Schutzhund Theory/Methods; Howell 1991
Bechthold,W.; Ausbildung zum Schutzhund; 1982
Beckman,E.; Praise and Reward; Putnam 1979
Benjamin,C.; Dog Problems; Doubleday 1981
Benjamin,C.; Mother Knows Best; Doubleday 1985
Bennett,J.; Command-train your Dog; Spec. 1979
Bergmann,G.; Why does your dog do that; Howell 1971
Bodingbauer,J.; Wesensanalyse; 1973
Bosshard,M.; In Freiheit erzogen; 1979
Braund,K.; Obedience Training Manual; Denlingers 1982
Brehm,P.; Schaeferhunde;
Brown; Bring Your Nose over here; 1982
Brunner,F.; Der unverstandene Hund; 1961
Bryson, S.; Search Dog Training; Boxwood 1983
Burke,L.; Dog Training; TFH 1976
Burnham,P.G.; Play Training; St.Martin 1980
Burtzik,P.; Dienst- and Gebrauchshunde; Meissner 1967
Burtzik,P.; Erziehung/Ausbildung d.Hundes; Meissner 1965
Busack,W.; Der Deutsche Schaeferhund; Falken
Busack,W.; Hundebuch; Falken 1970
Button,L.; Practical Scent; Alpine Publ. 1990
Buytendijk,F.J.; The Mind of the Dog; Aver 1936
Campbell,W.E.; Behavior Problems in Dogs; Am.Vet.
Campbell,W.E.; Owner's Guide to Better Behavior in Dogs; 1989
Cleveland,R.; Your German Shepherd: Hawthorn 1966
Cree,J.; Training the Alsatian; Merrimack 1978
Cross/Saunders; Dog Care and Training; Greystone 1962
Daniels,J.; Enjoying Dog Agility; Doral Publ. 1991
Davis,H.; New Dog Encyclopedia; Galahad 1970
Davis,W.; Go Find; Howell 1974
Denlinger,M.; German Shepherd; Howell 1961
Dilder; Schutzhund Obedience/Training and Drive; 1992
Dobson,J.A.; 14 Day Method; Winchester 1981
Dunbar,I.; Dog Rehavior; THF 1979
Eden,R.S.; Dog Training for Law Enforcement; Detselig Ent. 1985
Eisenmann,C.; Stop,Sit,Think; 1968
Elton,C.; Animal Ecology; Methuen & Co.; 1966
Fatio,A.; Prakt. Handb. Erziehung/Ausbildung des Hundes
Fischel,W.; Seele des Hundes; Parey 1961
Fischer,W.; Koennen Tiere denken?; Leipzig, 1970
Foerster,U.; Der Deutsche Schaeferhund; 1980
Fox,M.; Understanding Your Dog; Coward,McCann 1972
Fryer/Henry/Sparks; General Psychology; Barnes & Noble 1954
Fuller,W.; Strength/Aggressiveness Factors in Dobermann Temperament
Gibbs,M.; Leader Dogs for the Blind; Denlingers 1982
Goldbecker/Hart; German Shepherd; TFH 1967

Granderath,F.; Hundeabrichtung; 1981
Grewe,J.; Schutzhund Training; Quality Press 1981
Haberhauffe/Albrecht; Schutz/Diensthunde; Neumann 1980
Hacker,A.; Deutscher Schaeferhund; Falken 1969
Haggerty/Benjamin; Dog Tricks; Howell 1982
Harmar,H.; Train/Show; David & Charles 1983
Hart, E.; Train your Dog; TFH
Hartmann,W.; Uebungsleiter; W-B Dressurverband 1960
Hegendorf/Reetz; Gebrauchshund; Parey 1980
Hilgard/Atkinson; Psychology; Harcourt 1975
Hillgemann,M.; Private Conversations
Hillmann,W.; Train Retrievers; Seattle Pub. 1979
Hirschhorn,H.; Guard Dogs; TFH 1976
Hollinghaas/Capps; Trained Dog; Barnes 1979
Holmes,J.; Training and Care; ARCO 1981
Holmes,J.; The Obedient Dog; David/Charles Publ. 1985
Hulse/Egeth/Deese; Psychology of Learning; McGraw-Hill 1980
Humpal,N.; Rassehunde; Landwirtschaftsverlag 1982
Humphrey/Warner; Working Dogs; John Hopkins 1934
Johnson,G.; Tracking Dog; Arner 1975
Johnson,G.; Tracking Trainers Handbook; Arner 1975
Jones,R.; Guard Dog Training; David/Charles Publ.
Kasco,N, Dog Owners Guide; Toledo 1950
Kee,R.; Obedience Champion; Condor 1981
Kenworthy,J.; Dog Training Guide; Pet Library 1969
Kerr,D.; Training your Dog; David & Charles 1978
Kessopulos,G.; Dog Obedience Training; Wilshire 1975
Klever,U.; Dein Hund, das unverstandene Wesen
Klinkenberg,T.; Hundeerziehung ohne Zwang
Knorr/Seupel; Aufzucht von Hunden; Landwirtschaftsverlag 1973
Koch-Kostersitz; 400 Ratschlaege; Neumann 1973
Koehler,W.; Dog Training; Howell 1962
Koehler,W.; Guard Dog Training; Howell 1973
Koehler,W.; Tracking Dog Training; Howell
Kramer,C.L.; Agility Dog Training; Cascade Press
Krech/Crutchfield/Livson; Psychology; Knopf 1969
Lamprecht,J.; Verhalten; Herder 1972
Lembke,B.; Der Polizeihund; Lehrmeister 1972
Levorsen,B.; Mush; Arner 1976
Loeb,J.; Supertraining; PH 1980
Loeb,J.; Complete Dog Training; PB 1977
Lorenz,K.; Vergleichende Verhaltensforschung; 1978
Lorenz,K.; Man Meets Dog; Penguin 1953
Loring,M.; Your Dog and the Law; Alpine Publ.
Luce,G.G.; Biological Rhythms; Dover 1971
Lucky,M.; Trick Training; Denlingers 1981
Luedicke, H.; Polizei/Schutzhunde; Stern 1957
MacInnes/Badyk; Schutzhund Annotated; 1988
MacInnes/Badyk; Through the Judges Eyes (Schutzhund); 1988
Maller/Feinman; 21 Days; S&S 1979
McMains,J.M.; Dog Logic, Companion Obedience; Howell 1992
Mech,D.; The Wolf; NHP 1967
Meiners,J; Zucht, Haltung, Ausbildung des SchH; Reutlingen 1976

Menzel,R.; Hundeausbildung; Falken 1974
Messent,P.; Hunde - Verhalten/Sprache; Piper 1980
Miller,F.; World of Dogs; Chronicle 1972
Mooney,H.J.; How to train your own dog; B&B 1908
Morsell,C.; Win Obedience Titles; Howell 1976
Most,K.; Training Dogs; Popular Dogs 1972
Mueller,M.; Spezialausbildung des Schutzhundes; Reutlingen 1980
Mueller,M.; Vom Welpen zum idealen Schutzhund; Reutlingen 1961
Mueller,M.; Der erfolgreiche Hundefuehrer, Reutlingen 1979
Mueller,M.; Leistungsstarker Faehrtenhund; Reutlingen 1982
Mulvany,M.; Obedience Training; Merrimack 1983
Mundis,J.; Guard Dog; McKay 1970
National Geographic; Man's Best Friend; NGS 1971
New Skete; Dogs Best Friend; Little/Brown 1978
Nicholas,A.; Dog Judging; Howell 1970
Oberlaender,G.; Dressur/Fuehrung d. Gebrauchshundes; 1983
Ochsenbein,U.; Hundeausbildung Dienst-/Rettungshund; 1979
Patterson,G.; Schutzhund Protection Training; Sirius 1989
Patterson,G.; Tracking, From the Beginning; Sirius 1992
Pearsall/Leedham; Dog Obedience Tr.; Scribner 1956
Pearsall/Verbruggen; Scent; Alpine Publ. 1982
Pfaffenberger,C.; Dog Behavior; Howell 1974
Philipp,W.; Das Alpha Tier; Safari
Pickup,M.; German Shepherd Guide; Pet Library 1969
Pinkwater,J/M; Superpuppy; Seabury
Pryor,K.; Don't Shoot the Dog; 1984
Radakovic,R.; Psyche of the Dog
Raiser,H.; Der Schutzhund; Parey Verlag 1979
Rapp,J.; Rappid Obedience/Watchdog Training; Denlingers
Reiter,F.; So erzieht man seinen Hund zum Hausgenossen
Research Machines; Psychology Today; Delmar 1970
Rheenen,J.; Hundefreunde Lexikon; Safari 1969
Restle,F.; Learning; McGraw-Hill 1975
Rolfs,K.; Abrichten des Jagdhundes; Landwirtschaftsv. 1982
Rose/Patterson; Training Competitive Working Dog; Giblaut 1985
Rossi,B.; About Dogs; Banner 1973
Saunders,B.; Obedience Training Courses; Howell 1976
Schnabel,E.: Unser Hund wird gut erzogen; 1981
Schnabel,E.; Hundekindheit; SV-Zeitung 1977-1979
Schneider,E.; Train your dog; Pet Library 1975
Schoenherr; Erziehung and Ausbildung
Scott/Fuller; Dog Dehavior; U of Chicago Press 1965
Scott,T.; Obedience/Security Training for Dogs; Traf.Sq. 1987
Seiferle,E.; Grundlagen/Wesenspruefung
Sessions,B.; Watchdog; TAB 1975
Seupel,I.; Hunde; Landwirtschaftsverlag 1974
Seupel,I.; Rassehunde; Landwirtschaftsverlag 1976
Sir,J.; Wie richte ich meinen Hund ab; Bauernverlag 1953
Skinner,B.F.; Technology of Teaching; Appleton 1968
v.Stephanitz,H.; Der Deutsche Schaeferhund; Lehrmeister
v.Stephanitz/Foerster; Zuechten, Aufzucht, Haltung des Deutschen Schaeferhundes
Stern,H.; Bemerkungen ueber Hunde
Strickland,W.; Expert Obedience Training; Macmillan 1970

Strickland,W.; Obedience Class Instruction; Macmillan 1972
Sundberg,N.; Assessment; Prentice Hall 1972
Syrotuck,W.; Scent & Scenting Dog; Arner 1972
Tembrock,G.; Grundr. Verhaltenswissenschaften; Jena 1968
Tembrock,C.; Grundl. Tierpsychologie; Berlin 1971
Thomas; Dogs for Police Service; 1963
Thorne,M.; Handling your dog; Doubleday 1979
Tortora,D.; Schwieriger Hand, was tun? 1979
Trayford/Hall; Puppy and Dog Care; McCall 1970
Trumler,E.; Ratgeber fuer den Hundefreund; Piper 1980
Trumler,E.; Hunde ernst genommen
Trumler,E.; Mit dem Hund auf Du
Trumler,E.; Hunde kennen and lieben; 1980
Trumler,E.; Your Dog and You; Seabury 1973
Tuerk,F.; Der Deutsche Schaeferhund; Cosmos 1978
Ullrich,W.; Tiere - recht verstanden; Leipzig 1969
Verband Deutsches Hundewesen; Pruefungsordnung
Vine,L.; Total Dog Book; CBS Publications 1977
Vine,L.; Behavior and Training; ARCO 1977
Volhard/Fisher; Step by Step; Howell 1983
Watson,M.; Basic Dog Training; TFH 1979
Weiss/Rose; Protection Dogs for You/Family; Denlingers 1992
Whitney,L.; Dog Psychology; Howell 1975
Working Dogs of America, Inc.; WDA TRAINER, 1976-1981

ABOUT THE AUTHOR

Dietmar Schellenberg, the author of "Top Working Dogs", is one of those few people who through a life-long association with domestic animals have come to really understand and truly communicate with pets, and dogs in particular.

As a practicing Animal Behavior Specialist he saw the plight of the working breeds who's owners kept and treated them as overgrown lap dogs. He knew that *Schutzhund* training was the cure.

Few Americans had heard of it. Still fewer had seen it. And there was no literature, no book available to teach it.

"Top Working Dogs, A Training Manual"
was an idea who's time had come.

That Dr. Schellenberg would write it is no coincidence: very few people are equally well qualified to do it, judging by his credentials and by the success the past two editions of the book have achieved.

Dr. Schellenberg gathered a wealth of knowledge and experience in canine matters, from various breed and training clubs as well as such prestigious institutions as the German Police Dog Academy and the German Railroad Police Dog School, and through his many associations with cynological authorities.

He personally trained and supervised the training of more than eleven thousand dog/handler teams. He is an acclaimed Animal Behavior Specialist and operates a dog training and boarding facility in Georgia ("AA PET RESORT, Inc."). He is well known as an internationally licensed Police Dog/Schutzhund Judge, author of a book on dog training, editor of a dog training magazine, writer, lecturer, consultant, Canine Specialist for the Technical Advisory Service for Attorneys (US/CANADA), President of Working Dogs of America, Inc., Founding Member and Officer of the North American Schutzhund Association, Inc., and Honorary Member of many Schutzhund Clubs. He has appeared on a variety of radio and TV shows.

Dr. Schellenberg is a native German, and he holds two Ph.D's (Nature Science, and Psychology/Education).

NORTH AMERICAN SCHUTZHUND COUNCIL
3910 Wesley Chapel Rd, Marietta GA 30062